PRAISE FOR Quick and Easy Vegan Bake Sale

"Grab this book and have a bake sale! From can't-miss standards like Lemon Bars and Peanut Butter Cookies to imaginative creations like Rhubarb Squares, Chai Chocolate Mini Loaves, and Parsnip and Orange Muffins, the recipes in *Quick and Easy Vegan Bake Sale* are sure to be a hit at your bake sale, with your friends and coworkers, and with you! Carla Kelly fills this fantastic cookbook with super-useful, simple-to-read sections on how to follow recipes flawlessly, match baked goods to the seasons, plan a vegan bake sale, and more. *Quick and Easy Vegan Bake Sale* is a valuable ingredient in creating delicious, memorable baked desserts and savory dishes for all occasions."

—**GARY LOEWENTHAL**, founder of Worldwide Vegan Bake Sale

"*Quick and Easy Vegan Bake Sale* is full of creative, quick, fun recipes that will delight vegans and meat eaters alike. Carla takes all the guesswork out of baking with simple how-tos that will turn even the most novice baker into a pro in no time. I love the way Carla infuses both sweet and savory treats with fruits and vegetables—my taste buds have never been so happy and my kitchen has never smelled so good!"

—**ALICIA C. SIMPSON**, author of *Quick and Easy Vegan Comfort Food* and *Quick and Easy Vegan Celebrations*

"*Quick and Easy Vegan Bake Sale* gives everyone a very good reason to bake—*because they can*! Carla draws on years of baking experience, crafting goodies to satisfy both sweet and savory inclinations. Offering extensive tips, advice, and recipe variations throughout, Carla steps in as your very own baking tutor. Strap on that apron, it's time to release your inner baker!"

—**DREENA BURTON**, author of *Eat, Drink and Be Vegan*

"Whether you are raising money for your sixth grader to go to camp, looking to help out a local animal sanctuary, or simply trying to spread the vegan word with delicious cookies and cupcakes, you'll find that *Quick and Easy Vegan Bake Sale* is not only chock-full of delicious recipes (specifically designed for bake sales) but also contains a whole chapter of helpful information on holding the perfect vegan bake sale."

—**JONI MARIE NEWMAN**, coauthor of *500 Vegan Recipes* and *The Complete Guide to Vegan Food Substitutions*

"As soon as I bit into one of Carla's Green Tea Latte Cookies and after that, her Ginger Crunch, I was officially hooked. This is a must-have cookbook for anyone who loves baking, and for everyone else who doesn't even know they love baking yet."

—**CELINE STEEN**, coauthor of *500 Vegan Recipes* and *The Complete Guide to Vegan Food Substitutions*

"Everybody wants their creations to steal the show at a bake sale. Especially vegans. That just got easier, thanks ... ory and sweet goodies, *Quick and Easy Vegan* ... y ... sure that your bake sale is ... ight."

—TAMASIN N... Vegan Kitchen

D0004291

More Than 150 Delicious
SWEET and SAVORY Vegan Treats
Perfect for Sharing

QUICK AND EASY

DATE DUE

SEP 27 2011	
JUL 26 2012	
NOV 2 1 2013	
MAR 0 5 2014	
JUN 1 4 2017	

THE EXPERIMENT
NEW YORK

QUICK AND EASY VEGAN BAKE SALE:
More Than 150 Delicious Sweet and Savory Vegan Treats Perfect for Sharing

The Experiment, LLC
260 Fifth Avenue
New York, NY 10001-6408
www.theexperimentpublishing.com

This book contains the opinions and ideas of its author. It is intended to provide helpful and informative material on the subjects addressed in the book. It is sold with the understanding that the author and the publisher are not engaged in rendering medical, health, or any other kind of personal professional services in the book. The author and publisher specifically disclaim all responsibility for any liability, loss, or risk—personal or otherwise—which is incurred as a consequence, directly or indirectly, of the use and application of any of the contents of this book.

The Experiment's books are available at special discounts when purchased in bulk for premiums and sales promotions as well as for fundraising or educational use. For details, contact us at info@theexperimentpublishing.com.

Library of Congress Control Number: 2010934225
ISBN 978-1-61519-026-3
Ebook ISBN 978-1-61519-129-1

Cover design by Susi Oberhelman
Cover photograph copyright © StockFood|Eising
Author photograph by Karen Jackson
Text design by Pauline Neuwirth, Neuwirth & Associates, Inc.

Manufactured in the United States of America
Distributed by Workman Publishing Company, Inc.
Distributed simultaneously in Canada by Thomas Allen & Son Limited
First published April 2011

10   9   8   7   6   5   4   3   2   1

To my family, for their patience, understanding, and only occasional complaining while I did nothing but bake and work on the computer for months, my unending love and gratitude. Mike, Mhairi, and Rhian, I would be nothing without you.

. . . .

You Cook For Us.
A POAM BY MHAIRI KELLY, AGE 8

It's dilishish
It's newtrishish
and it's good to eat
'cause it's not meat.
If it's not made by Mum
it's just dum.
    (Spelling and composition by the author.)

. . . .

Contents

Note: 📷 indicates that the recipe is pictured in the photo insert.

Welcome!

WELCOME TO THE *Quick and Easy Vegan Bake Sale* book! Glad to have you holding this in your hot little hands. Are you ready to do some baking and delight your taste buds? Then you've come to the right place!

First, would you like to know a little about me?

You know my name is Carla; you know I'm obviously mad about baking; but what else is there?

I'm a happy stay-at-home mum, married with two wonderful children, one of whom loves baking, too—and both of whom love eating it! I'm originally from New Zealand, and now reside in beautiful British Columbia, Canada. I came here after periods of living in Queensland, Australia, and Edinburgh, Scotland. How very Commonwealth of me! I'm also vegan.

I came to veganism slowly—no overnight conversion for me. I gradually stopped eating meat from childhood. I didn't like the taste of it, or didn't like the way it felt in my mouth. Mum is a great cook, but she had seven people to cook for, so she couldn't cater to everyone's tastes, and usually made what she wanted to make. The rule was that if you didn't like what she made for dinner, you made your own. We all learned to cook pretty early on, and developed preferences and tastes from early experimenting. My brother even became a chef! For

a long time, I still ate dairy products and eggs. After my second child was born with lactose intolerance (when I consumed dairy, it upset her stomach after she nursed), I did a great deal of investigating my diet and health and finally made the switch.

I have completed a Hospitality diploma, which included a basic chef-training component. That, along with a couple of stints working in commercial restaurant kitchens, taught me how to place ingredients and flavors together creatively, enhanced my basic cooking and baking skills, and supported my love of being in the kitchen.

I draw inspiration from my background, the food I grew up with and loved, as well as the other cuisines that I became acquainted with along the way (often in a "fusion" manner). These flavors from my past have molded and fused with those foods I've experimented with as I have grown surer of my skills and tastes. As such, my baking has mainly a strong British Commonwealth slant that will be familiar to anyone with an English, Scottish, Australian, Canadian, or, in my case, New Zealand, background and upbringing (or Anglophiles!).

Don't recoil with horror. My baking is not "traditional" but more a take on the traditional, updated for a more modern palate and fused with cuisine styles and spices from all over the world. So perhaps calling it "global" would be more appropriate than "British Commonwealth"—drawing from all the corners of the world yet remaining familiar and comforting.

I tend to cook in a random, what-is-in-the-fridge-and-how-can-I-turn-it-into-deliciousness manner, and to some extent I bake in the same way, rarely following the recipes in the many cookbooks I own. To be honest, I rarely use such books as more than reference, or to get ideas I can adapt. In baking, this leads to wonderfully delicious accidents incorporating perhaps unexpected ingredients. The food itself is my inspiration and continues to be so, the more types and styles of food I try.

I'm not a dietician, a nutritionist, or a professional chef, nor do I run a vegan business of any sort. So why would I think I could write a cookbook?

Why?

Because I can.

Because I want to.

Because I love to cook, love to bake, love to experiment in the kitchen, love to share what I discover, and love to feed people tasty food that I know is good for them!

I believe food tastes best when it's shared—with friends and family, with laughter and love. Whether it's for everyday or for a celebration, food brings us together.

But sometimes, when we choose to eat differently, it can be a factor in keeping us apart.

Think of all the days or occasions that, to a greater or lesser extent, revolve around food—you know them. You also know that if you . . .

* are vegan or vegetarian
* are seriously watching your weight
* have allergies
* follow a low-cholesterol (or even cholesterol-free) diet
* are diabetic
* or have any other reason to need to eat differently in some way

. . . you dread these days and occasions for what you end up *not* eating, more than for what you *do*. It's no fun having to be the one who cooks all the time, or having to bring along something you are able to eat, because the main cook or caterer doesn't know how (or thinks he or she doesn't know how) to make something suitable. Or to *not* bring something, and then not be able to find anything on offer that is safe for you to eat! It's even less fun to be hungry!

It doesn't have to be that way.

In putting together this book, I wanted to gather a selection of vegan recipes that will provide ideas for both the special times through the year and for everyday baking . . . keeping in mind also when things are in season. I wanted to write a cookbook that can be shared with and given to loved ones, so they can make delightful vegan dishes to share with you, for nonoccasions as well as holidays.

I also wanted to provide a tool to assist anyone interested in hosting a bake sale, for any reason. I have participated in bake sales both as part of an organizing team, and as a baker providing items for sale, and have found that what separates the good sales from the not-so-good sales is organization and variety. My hope is that this book will aid in a smoother operation, and provide ideas for a greater variety of goods to sell. (See pages 1–4 for more information.)

I've included recipes that fit the standard food holidays where I live and grew up. There are also foods that just celebrate the seasons, and all that they offer. Most ingredients are not difficult to find (even for nonvegans or readers who may not yet know where to look) and I often suggest substitutions and variations.

Speaking of which—I want you to feel free to change things a little, to adapt my recipes to your tastes and preferences. It may take time for you to feel comfortable with this, especially if you are a new baker, but it's not a big deal, seriously. If you don't like raspberries but like the look of the recipe, change the berry! I also encourage you to scribble notes throughout the book, to help you with a recipe next time—there are "Remember" spaces available for this very purpose.

Please visit me at http://veganyear.blogspot.com, or at Vegan Bake Sale on Facebook, for other vegan meal ideas, not just for baking, or to leave a comment, ask a question, or give me some feedback. I'm always happy to hear from you, and I'll help if I can. Armed with this book, and with the recipes on my Web site, you'll always have something to share and something to celebrate with those you love!

Friends and family, laughter and love—brought together by good food, all year long.

QUICK AND EASY

Vegan Bake Sale

Bake Sales and Baking for Sharing

THERE IS NO better way, I think, to spread the vegan message than to have people eat vegan food. By doing so, everyone will know you don't live off alfalfa sprouts and tofu, but have access to delicious and delectable recipes for everything, from varied and interesting main courses to cakes and cookies. You can share the edible message in so many ways, from taking a dish to a potluck (or hosting one yourself) or to the school playground, serving it at a party, or by selling it at a bake sale (which has the bonus of raising money for a good cause).

Baking lends itself to sharing so much more easily than does cooking, because many items come preportioned from being baked that way—cupcakes, muffins, scones, and cookies immediately spring to mind. But that is not to say cakes, pies, and other larger baked goods aren't perfect for sharing—you just have to slice them. That itself forms a nice part of the sharing ritual.

Now, don't be fooled by the title of this book. These recipes are not just for bake sales. These items are for all occasions, the sorts of situations you find yourself in every day, as well as for special times, too. They can be shared at a potluck, a picnic, an afternoon tea, a baby or bridal shower, a family gathering, a holiday meal, a birthday, a brunch or breakfast gathering; can be given as a gift; or can be baked just to eat yourself!

Unfortunately, I can't recommend living off only the food in this book, as the recipes are mainly treats and meant to be a little decadent—not for every meal, every day. Balanced diets, please, with lots of fresh fruits and vegetables, preferably local and organic if you are able to obtain these! However, you can remind everyone that these goodies are all cholesterol free, are a lot lower in fat than standard baked goods, and many contain heart-healthy whole grains. I mean, if some of the children's breakfast cereals on the market can advertise themselves as a source of dietary fiber, then most of these recipes certainly can, too!

HOLDING A BAKE SALE

If you are looking to have a bake sale, and have picked up this book hoping for ideas and suggestions, great, welcome, read on! Whether it's for a school, sports team, church group, preschool or day care, charity organization; or a response to a disaster, such as the 2010 Haitian and Chilean earthquakes; or just for an individual fund-raising event, a bake sale is a great way to generate money, as well as to spread the edible message of veganism.

In New York City on Election Day, I'm told, there are bake sales everywhere! As most of the polling stations are schools, stalls are cleverly set up on the way into the polling station, selling voters their breakfast, morning snack, lunchtime treat, or on-the-way-home "hunger staller"! What a good idea.

For a bake sale, there's so much to think about and organize. If you'd like to run a bake sale from scratch, here are some things to consider:

Why are you having it? To publicize the event, get people involved, and to generate as many sales as possible, you need a clear idea of why the funds are being raised and what they will be used for.

Who is going to be involved? Is it going to be a one-person show, with you doing all the baking and selling, or do you need to organize volunteers? If volunteers are needed, how many people do you need, where will you find them, and how will the duties be divided? Who (if there are more organizers than you) will be the point person(s) to handle any questions or problems that crop up? Setup, baking, creating the display, selling, and cleanup can each be the responsibility of a different person or team. If the sale is for a group—a church fund-raiser, for example—members of that group are the logical place to start looking for help.

Where will you hold the sale? Location, location, location! Is there a venue that springs immediately to mind? You need to determine what permissions are needed to hold the sale there, whether there is going to be a fee for the space or table (and if there is, can you afford it? Remember to factor in how much you may be spending on supplies), and what competition may be nearby. Decide if it is to be inside or outside (a wet weather backup venue may be needed), how much foot traffic the area generates, and what sort of foot traffic it is. For example, setting up outside a butcher's shop may not produce the most vegan-friendly clientele!

When is the best time and day for the sale? Timing is everything, after all. Consider your chosen venue, weekend or weekday, morning or afternoon, as well as volunteer availability and your own available time, before making your decision on when to hold your sale.

How will you publicize your sale? You'll need to ensure the best possible attendance. Are you able to put fliers or leaflets in stores and offices in the area where your sale will take place? Hand them out to people days in advance, or on the day? Are you allowed to post them in public places, such as on power poles? Is there a community radio station, Web site, or even television station that will allow you free publicity spots in a "What's going on in the community" segment? Will local newspapers allow you to post a free listing, or perhaps include your sale in a columnist's discussion of things to do? Remember, also, you can post notes on blogs, on Facebook profiles, and on Web sites such as www.veganbakesale. org to broadcast the message to a broader audience.

What will you sell and where will it come from? If you are doing all the baking yourself, what you will sell is what you bake. But if relying on donations, you'll need to set guidelines as to what kind and size of items is preferred; for example, does everything have to be sweet? You'll need to think about how you're going to serve the items—plates or not? Also consider your target market (kids like cookies!), and make sure everyone knows that everything should be vegan, and homemade, of course! Is there a special theme, such as a particular occasion or setting, which should be echoed in the foods? Do you want to include allergy-free options such as items that are gluten free or nut free (and labeled as such)? Have available a selection of recipe suggestions (from this book, perhaps) for those who may feel stumped for an idea, or for nonvegan friends wanting to help out.

How will the prices be set? Are the prices going to be set in advance, made up just before the sale begins, or decided as you go along when you see which things are popular? How are you going to communicate those prices— do you need labels or signs? How will all the volunteers know what the prices are—are items priced clearly by kind or portion? Or are you going to go with a "by donation" bake sale where people pay what they think the item is worth (and what they can afford!)?

How will you look after the money? There are lots of housekeeping things to think about in advance, so that everyone involved is clear about them, with no ambiguity. Things like: Where will the "float" (your starting cash) come from, and how much will it be? Will there be a designated "money person" during the sale, or will everyone who is volunteering have access to the kitty? Who will count the money afterward? Who can be a designated runner to get more change, and where will that change come from? Also, how will you ensure that your profits reach the intended recipient(s)? Do you already know which contact person or office should receive the money, and what kinds of documentation may be necessary?

How will you display the items for sale? Will the goods be on platters, in baskets, displayed on tiered platforms? Will they be wrapped up all fancy, or displayed as they are? Will you offer or have an area set up with free sample tidbits? Will everything be out at once, or just a few items that are replenished as sold? This will depend on the space you have, the display materials available (where is the table coming from, by the way?), and how much you have to sell. Will you have a coordinated look, with matched napkins, tablecloths, and so on—perhaps one tying in to an occasion or a school's colors? (See page 43 for presentation ideas.)

How will you serve, and keep things clean? Your sale has to be sanitary! You'll have to provide tongs, pie slicers, or individual pieces of parchment paper to pick up the items, and paper napkins (look for those from recycled paper); you'll also need bags (preferably paper) or containers for your customers to take purchases away, unless they bring their own (which you can request they do). You'll also need to keep "dirty" money away from your "clean" items for sale. The venue will need a hand-washing facility, or you'll need to bring water-free sanitizer

for the sellers. Some communities require that all food handlers wear plastic gloves; be sure latex-free gloves (in case of allergies) are available to your volunteers if this is the case. If you use disposable plates or forks, are you able to provide those made from recycled/recyclable materials? How can you keep track of whose serving pieces, trays, and plates are whose, to be able to return them to the correct parties after the sale?

Cleanup time! If you want, even potentially, to use the venue again, make sure you do the right thing!

For more information about running a vegan bake sale, please see this Post Punk Kitchen blog post from January 2010: http://www.theppk.com/2010/01/how-to-put-together-a-bake-sale-fast. Also, there is a fantastic resource online at www.veganbakesale.org, which gives so much quality information that I really must refer you there if you are interested in learning more. I am not formally affiliated with either site, and they have nothing to do with this book or the recipes in it, but I do think they are wonderful resources.

That's the sale part looked at; what about the actual baking?

A Brief History of Baking

THIS IS NOT meant to be an extensive investigation into how baking has evolved from the dawn of time. This overview will give you a little information about baking and some types of baked goods you will find in this book.

First, a definition—my own, blended together from various online sources: Quick breads are anything baked in a pan from a batter, using chemical raising agents that require no kneading or rising.

This term therefore incorporates muffins, scones, biscuits, cakes, cupcakes, and so on—pretty much everything except yeasted breads (which have their own chapter, starting on page 191). The thickness of the batter for each type of baking varies, but is usually in a 1:1 to 2:1 ratio of dry to wet ingredients. Leavening with a chemical agent (more about that in a minute) gives uniform, reliable, and quick results, as opposed to yeast that requires a long rising time and is more affected by changes in humidity and temperature.

Most nonyeasted baked items use one of three basic methods to combine their ingredients: blending, creaming, and rubbing in. Let's look at each of these methods in turn, so you know what I'm talking about.

The Blending Method

This is the most common method used for muffins and loaves. Blending is also known as the "quick bread method" and is perfect for quick and easy baking. Using this method, you mix the dry and wet ingredients separately, then quickly mix them together gently, so as not to stimulate the gluten in the flour, which would make the resultant item tough and gummy.

The Creaming Method

Creaming is used more frequently for cakes. A solid fat (such as margarine) and the sweetener (usually granulated sugar) are creamed, or beaten together, until smooth and fluffy. The liquids are then mixed in, followed by the dry ingredients, with any extra additions added last. The creaming method combines the rising gained from air pockets created during the creaming step, with the rising from the chemical leaveners. When creaming by hand, I find it easier to start mixing with a wooden spoon, then I switch to a whisk once the fat and sweetener are combined, to incorporate the dry ingredients as lightly as possible, and then I switch back to a wooden spoon for stirring in the remaining ingredients. This allows lots of air into the creamed mixture (this is what whisks are designed for, after all), and the wooden spoon gives you a firm yet gentle touch, which you need for the rest of the mixing. The creamed solid fat also provides structure to the baking, and when used in cookies, allows them to spread into the expected cookie shape.

The Rubbing-In Method

This method adds a solid fat to sifted dry ingredients. The fat is "rubbed in," or cut in with a pastry cutter, to form a dough with a pebble- or crumblike texture. This creates little pockets of fat within the dough that, when baked at high temperature, melt to create a light and flaky product. This method is more commonly used for scones, biscuits, and pie crusts, where that flaky texture is especially welcome.

Baking using these three methods didn't come into being until after the discovery of chemical leavening, obviously, in the form of baking soda, which was quickly transformed into the more usable, stable, and storage friendly baking powder. Until then, to bake anything leavened you needed to use yeast, or a sourdough starter, or something similar, all of which took time. Hence the use, all over the world, of unleavened breads such as lavash, chapati, tortilla, pita, roti, and matzo.

These chemical agents work by releasing carbon dioxide gas into the quick bread batter, which expands and causes it to rise, but they work slightly differently. Baking soda (sodium bicarbonate), when combined with a liquid and an acidic ingredient, produces these bubbles at baking temperatures. Not generally used by itself for baking, except in cookies, baking soda is used in recipes in this book with lots of acidic ingredients in conjunction with baking powder to assist in the rising. Baking powder combines baking soda with an acid, cream of tartar, and also a starch, such as cornstarch, to increase its shelf life and make for a more stable chemical reaction. Baking powder is available as single-acting or as double-acting, and doesn't need to have acidic ingredients in the mixture, as its raising action comes "built in." Single-acting powders are similar to baking soda, reacting only when they are heated. Double-acting powders react in two ways; first, some gas is released at room temperature when liquid is added, and then the rest (and most) of the gas is released after the temperature increases in the oven. The standard proportion for raising baked goods is to use 1 teaspoon of baking powder per cup of flour, moistened with a cup of liquid.

In their earliest forms, many baked goods were quite plain, only lightly sweetened, with maybe some dried fruit added. They were baked on the day for consumption during that day, as they still are, by home bakers everywhere. There were not the food preservatives then that you'll find in commercially made goods today. Baking has taken on different shapes, too, as time has progressed, with a wide variety of pans and pan sizes. The new nonstick technology has made it possible to bake goods with less fat than used to be necessary.

The basic nature of baking has not changed much over time, however. You take flour and chemical raising agents, mix those with liquids, often add sweeteners and some extras, then shape or pour into a mold of some sort and bake until firm, and there you have it.

Equipment for Baking

ONE OF THE beauties of basic baking is that most of the equipment you need may be found in the standard kitchen. The few specialty items you need are widely, and relatively inexpensively, available.

First, if you're contemplating making muffins or cupcakes, you'll need to make sure you have a set of **muffin pans**, also known as cupcake cups, which commonly come in standard-size twelve- and six-cup options. The recipes for this book are for the standard-size twelve-cup muffin pan. The recipes all halve well, so you may find a six-cup pan handy for when you don't want to make a full batch. Muffin pans also come in a twenty-four-cup mini size and a six-cup maxi size, both of which are used in some of my recipes.

I also use **mini-loaf pans** in some recipes, and there was a little confusion about this terminology with my testers at the start. I am referring to a large pan, similar to a muffin pan, which has eight rectangular indentations in it as opposed to twelve round ones, and not to the 4½-inch long petite loaf pans to make individual, small loaves.

You'll find a rimmed **baking sheet**, also known as a cookie sheet, super handy—for toasting nuts; for putting under pie plates to catch drips; as well as for baking cookies, scones, and biscuits.

It gets lots of use. Even if it's nonstick, if you line it with parchment paper before you use it, cleanup is a breeze.

If you plan on making your own pie crusts, you'll need a **pie plate**. If you prefer to fill store-bought crusts with homemade filling (which is fine!), they come with their own disposable foil plate, which just needs to be placed on a baking sheet prior to baking the pie. As long as it is unpunctured, that kind of pan can be washed well and reused. I have a 9-inch nonstick metal pie plate. I know lots of people swear by glass, so use what you have and/or can afford. (Remember to lower the oven temperature by 25°F, or slightly shorten the baking time, if using glass.) I also have an 11-inch loose-bottomed **tart pan**, for making tarts (and quiches) in. The loose bottom makes it easy to remove and serve your tart. Handily, this size pan uses the same amount of pastry as a standard 9-inch pie plate.

I have two **brownie pans**, one of which is a 7 by 11-inch rectangle, and the other an 8-inch square. These pans are also great for baking squares (bar cookies or slices), as they have nice high sides. I also use these pans for cakes and breads, on occasion.

For making cakes, I have a selection of **cake pans** for layer cakes, and **springform pans** for deeper, larger ones. I also have a 10-inch **Bundt pan**, which is great for creating beautifully shaped cakes. I've made sure to include Bundt cake recipes to get some use out of this lovely pan!

You'll find the standard-size pans, and often the larger/smaller sizes, in the baking equipment section of supermarkets, department stores, and specialty kitchen stores. They come in a variety of materials, nonstick as well as uncoated, and lately in brightly colored silicone. I like a nonstick pan myself, as it makes removing the finished product so much easier and gives more consistent results than does silicone.

You may choose to use **cupcake liners** to bake your cupcakes and muffins. These are round sheets of paper or sometimes tinfoil, with fluted edges, which go inside the muffin pan to line the cups. They are used to facilitate removal and cleanup. To be honest, I only really use them for cupcakes and prefer nonstick muffin pans and a quick spray of cooking oil for muffins. I find that muffins with loads of add-ins stick to the liners far too well, and there is nothing worse than a mouthful of paper from an improperly peeled muffin. Use them if you want to.

You'll also need an assortment of **bowls**, little ones for holding ingredients while they "wait their turn" and big ones for mixing the ingredients together. I have a set of three glass bowls and a larger set of plastic bowls, which nest inside each other, and I find these more than adequate. I use soup or cereal bowls if smaller bowls are required. You can use whatever you have: ceramic, metal, glass, or plastic. If some of the ingredients are going to be heated, however, don't use plastic—you don't want any plastic residue in your baking. Also, be careful when using metal bowls. Not only do they *not* microwave, but if they are made of anything but stainless steel, you don't want to have anything too acidic sitting in them (such as mixtures left to curdle) for any length of time.

To get the ingredients into the bowls and ready to be mixed, you'll need a few things. **Measuring cups and spoons** are necessities; see the table at the end of this section for the standard sizes of measuring cups and spoons. I have two sets of each; it's easier to have a backup than to realize halfway through a recipe that you need your ¼-cup measure for a dry ingredient but it's been used for a wet one. Having two sets is not essential, one set each of cups and spoons is fine, but it saves on the mad rush to wash when you're in the swing of the recipe. And yes, I use dry measuring cups to measure out exact liquid ingredients, as I prefer the control over the amount—there's no going over the line.

For the dry ingredients, you'll need a **sieve**, or a sifter as it is sometimes called, to prevent clumping and to add air. If using whole-grain flour to make muffins or quick breads, after sifting, I return any bran left in the sifter to the bowl—you want that goodness in your tummy!

You'll also need a **set of knives** and a **chopping board** for cutting up everything from fruit and vegetables to dried fruit and chocolate, especially a large chef's knife and a smaller paring knife. A **potato peeler** is handy, too, for taking skins off all sorts of things and for shaving chocolate.

You'll need a **box grater**, with sides for both larger and smaller grating. A **Microplane grater** is a super device for zesting (removing the top layer of peel from) citrus fruits and grating ginger and garlic; but if you don't have one, don't worry, your box grater will do the trick.

Your standard kitchen **saucepans** and **skillets** (also known as frying pans) get used, too! Sometimes you need to make a sauce from fruit to go in the mixture, or melt some chocolate, or even sauté the odd vegetable. You don't need a double boiler, but if you've got one, great! Otherwise, just take a heatproof bowl and set in atop a saucepan—presto, double boiler.

Your good old **kitchen kettle** is valuable for boiling water in a hurry. Not only for a cup of tea for the cook!

At times, I'll call for you to use a **food processor** or **blender** for getting ingredients super smooth. I often use an **immersion blender**, and the cup that comes with it, as I find this very convenient and less time consuming than bringing out the food processor or big blender. As long as you have a device that will get things super smooth, I'm not fussy

about which you use. And to be honest, in many instances, if you don't have one, as long as you have a whisk and are willing to use a bit of elbow grease, you'll do just fine.

And while I'm on the topic of electric kitchen gadgetry, I find a **spice or coffee grinder** really helpful for grinding small amounts of nuts and seeds, as well as making small amounts of whole grains into flour. You can use your food processor or blender if it is powerful enough, but for small amounts, it tends to do a poor job.

For mixing the ingredients together in the bowls once they've been chopped and peeled and grated and sifted and toasted and sautéed, you'll need a **wire balloon whisk** (often made out of silicone), a couple of **wooden spoons**, and a **silicone or rubber spatula**. I find the latter tool very handy for getting the last of the batter out of bowls and into pans. A silicone spatula is also great for mixing hot ingredients, as the silicone can withstand very high temperatures without melting into, or tainting, the food (don't try it with a rubber spatula, though). I prefer to use a wooden spoon for mixing and folding, but you can use a fork, if you prefer. Sometimes I find a **potato masher** helpful for squashing things, when a fork isn't enough and a whisk gets clogged up.

I don't have an electric hand mixer, or a stand mixer, as I prefer the greater feel you get when mixing by hand, and you mostly need a gentle touch anyway. However, when I'm in the middle of a double batch of buttercream, I sometimes think it would be handy! If you have a **stand mixer with a dough hook**, that's a huge time and hand saver when kneading bread dough!

For spooning the batter into the pans once it's mixed, I just use a large metal **serving spoon**. If you have a perfectly sized **ice-cream scoop**, spray it lightly with cooking spray and use that. As long as the batter gets in the pans, pretty much evenly, it doesn't matter what you use.

My **pastry brush** gets a workout when I'm making pies and breads, as I like to brush a little soy milk to really bring out the gold in the crust, and it's also useful for applying glazes.

One piece of equipment you may not have, which I really would recommend buying if you don't own one, is an **oven thermometer**. Many ovens (even new ones) are inaccurate by up to 50°F. That's an awful lot when you're baking! The thermometer lets you see what the temperature is in your oven while you're preheating and mixing, and gives you the option of holding off putting the wet and dry ingredients together until the oven is at the required temperature. You may find it also gives you an indication of the amount of time your oven needs to preheat. Mine takes ages, but once there it holds true.

Once the baked item is made, you're going to need a "high-tech testing device"—a **toothpick** works well—and **ovenproof gloves**. You think I'm joking? Try grabbing a batch of muffins out of the oven with a damp tea towel!

Then you'll need a **wire cooling rack**. You want your baked item to cool evenly and completely, and if it stays in or on the pan for too long it will not do that. These are available in supermarkets and even dollar stores, everywhere. Buy several, if you will be baking in quantity or making layer cakes.

For decoration purposes, you'll need a **palette knife** (also called a **metal spatula**) for spreading buttercream on cakes and cupcakes. I find a **piping bag and nozzle set** handy for cake decorating, and I even use it on occasion in recipes, too.

Then there are the kitchen disposables, **parchment paper**, **tinfoil**, and **plastic wrap**. Every kitchen needs all three for so many uses during baking and for storage.

Like I said, many of these items may already be in your kitchen, and if they aren't maybe you can work around that for now. Start by choosing a recipe you know you have the equipment for, and put other equipment you don't have on a birthday or Christmas wish list. You could post this list on the fridge door so there is no doubt what you want!

Once you've assembled the equipment, you need to proceed to your pantry to see what ingredients you're going to need!

And, before I forget, here's that table I promised you.

MEASURE	VOLUME CONVERSION	TABLESPOON/TEASPOON CONVERSION	FLUID OUNCE CONVERSION
1 cup	250 ml	16 tablespoons	8 fl ounces
½ cup	125 ml	8 tablespoons	4 fl ounces
⅓ cup	75 ml	5 tablespoons + 1 teaspoon or 16 teaspoons	2½ fl ounces
¼ cup	60 ml	4 tablespoons or 12 teaspoons	2 fl ounces
1 tablespoon	15 ml	3 teaspoons	½ fl ounce
½ tablespoon	7.5 ml	1½ teaspoons	
1 teaspoon	5 ml		
½ teaspoon	2.5 ml		
¼ teaspoon	1.25 ml		

Ingredients for Baking

THIS IS A pretty comprehensive run-through of the standard and not-so-standard ingredients called for in this book. While it doesn't list all of them, as some of the ingredients may be used in just one recipe, the list does give you a rough idea of what you may be in for.

I have stipulated in the recipes that all ingredients need to be specifically vegan—but you'd know that anyway, right? I've included the designation in the recipes as reminders, just in case someone may be proceeding without first reading this chapter or ingredient labels.

Many of these ingredients you'll already have in your kitchen, especially if you are a long-term vegan, a foodie, or just like to keep a well-stocked pantry. However, you may need to go to the grocery store for some, or even to the health food store. Most ingredients are pretty easy to find, and hopefully nothing should be so obscure that you can't find it somewhere in a decent-size town, especially if you live in North America. There is also a selection of online stores selling vegan specialty items (see page 23). Most of my testers from elsewhere in the world had no issues with locating ingredients or making substitutions (see page 37).

FLOURS AND MEALS

Flour is the main ingredient of most baking, so it makes sense to start here. I've included some nonflour things in this section because I use them like flour.

All-Purpose Flour

All-purpose flour is used in at least half of the recipes, often in combination with other types of flour so some nutritional value, or flavor, is added. It is made from only the endosperm (starch) of the wheat seed. All the goodness in the bran and the germ has been removed, so this flour is usually enriched. I use unbleached all-purpose flour, which isn't as pretty as the ones that have been bleached, but I am not keen about putting bleaches into my food and my family. Anyway, you can't see the color of the flour when you're through with it!

I don't use self-rising flour. If it's all you have, you can substitute it (one for one) for all-purpose flour—but, if you use it, leave out any baking powder or baking soda in the recipe, as the self-rising flour already contains all the leavening you need. Don't use flour that is labeled specifically for bread unless you are baking bread (where it is specified).

Bread Flour

Bread flour is made from a harder winter wheat that contains a higher level of gluten than does all-purpose flour. This gives yeasted goods their elasticity once kneaded, as the kneading activates the gluten and makes it stretch. This is great for bread but would make other types of baking tough and dense.

Whole-Wheat Pastry Flour

In a lot of recipes you'll find I use whole-wheat pastry flour half and half with all-purpose flour. This is made from the whole

grain of soft spring wheat, leaving the germ and bran intact, and is processed so it is very fine. You get all the goodness of the whole grain but not the heaviness. My local grocery store carries this in small (expensive) packages, and my health food store has it in big bags—guess where I buy it from? Please don't mistake this flour for . . .

Whole-Wheat Flour

Whole-Wheat flour is heavier than the above, being less finely milled. Made from a blend of wheat types, this flour contains more gluten than does whole-wheat pastry flour. It contains the bran and germ as well as the endosperm, so is nutritionally a good choice. I use this (mainly) in muffins where I want a more obviously healthy taste and texture, but please don't use it in recipes where whole-wheat pastry flour is called for.

(Wheat) Germ and Bran

Germ and bran are the bits left over when the grains are refined to make all-purpose flour. I add them back to some of the recipes to both increase the nutritional content and to make the taste healthier. You can use oat (or rice) bran or germ instead of wheat bran or germ in the recipes that call for it.

Vital Wheat Gluten

Vital wheat gluten is the protein part of wheat that has been removed, and comes in powdered form. It's the basis for making seitan (wheat meat), a meat substitute, and is what gives the stretchiness to bread dough. It is available in many supermarkets or health food stores in the baking aisle and even in bulk bins.

Spelt Flour

Spelt is my favorite nonwheat flour and, as such, you'll find it in a bunch of recipes. Spelt contains less gluten than wheat, but is still a gluten-containing grain and is therefore not suitable for those with a gluten intolerance or allergy. However, even if you don't have a problem with wheat, it is good to give your body a rest from it now and then, and the recipes using spelt flour are perfect for that. Spelt flour is made from the whole grain, so it is nutritionally superior to all-purpose flour.

Other Flours

I use small amounts of other types of flour in specific recipes, and have found all of them at my local health food store or supermarket. They may be available in the bulk bins if your store has them. In a pinch when I've needed only a small amount and had none in the cupboard, I've had good results using my coffee grinder to grind up uncooked grains of millet, quinoa, or oatmeal to make flour.

Examples of the types of flour that I use include oat, quinoa, yellow corn (made from the whole grain, as opposed to cornstarch, which is made from the endosperm only and is white), chickpea, and rice. All have subtle, yet different, flavors. These flours complement the other ingredients where they are used. Some of them contain gluten and some do not, so check if you are baking for a wheat- or gluten-intolerant friend. I often use these flours in conjunction with wheat or spelt.

I must make a note here about chickpea flour. It adds a wonderful savory, almost "eggy" taste when baked, but in raw dough tastes *really awful*! Please don't be tempted to taste any raw batter containing chickpea flour; it may put you off a delicious end product!

Let me take a minute to touch again on gluten-free flour. I am the first to admit I am not an expert in gluten-free baking. When I need to make something gluten free, I tend to use a commercial gluten-free mix, one of those ones you replace in a 1:1 ratio for all-purpose flour

(or as the package specifies), because it's easier and that way I'm sure it is gluten free.

All flours and meals may be stored in your pantry, if you wish. However, if you want to avoid the possibility of bugs in your flour or you have flour made from a number of different whole grains, and you have space, store them in either your fridge or your freezer, if at all possible. Flour from whole grains tends to spoil quicker than processed flour does because of the presence of the germ, hence the need for cool storage. Flours may be used straight from cold storage, but for best results I recommend bringing them back to room temperature first.

Nut and Seed Meals

Nut and seed meals are definitely not flour, but in a number of recipes I use them as a dry ingredient in place of some of the flour. As you'd expect, they are just finely ground nuts (or seeds) which I have made myself or have bought ready ground. The most commonly used, and easiest to find ready ground, is almond, followed by pecan and hazelnut. In your local store, the former may be known as almond meal, almond flour, or ground almonds, and is most economical to purchase from a bulk bin if your supermarket or health food store stocks it this way. The little bags can be wildly expensive, so check your bulk bins first.

GRINDING NUTS INTO MEAL

If you can't find a nut meal ready ground, the easiest way I have found to make this at home is to take a quantity of nuts or seeds equal to the quantity of meal required (toasted or untoasted). Chop roughly and place in your trusty spice grinder, high-powered blender, or food processor. Pulse in short bursts until the desired flourlike consistency is achieved. Keep a close eye on the process and only do a few pulses at a time—the nuts can quickly become nut butter! A spice grinder works best for small amounts, a powerful blender or food processor for larger quantities. If you use ground nuts and seeds often, it is a good idea to dedicate a spice grinder to that purpose, and not use it for coffee, or to grind a large batch and store the ground nuts or seeds in the freezer until required.

· ·

Adding a nut or seed meal to the dry ingredients adds texture to the finished product and also adds the flavor of the nut, especially good in some recipes where you want a layered taste.

Store these nut meals in your fridge or freezer, as you would whole nuts, seeds, and wholegrain flour to avoid premature spoiling.

Cornmeal

Cornmeal isn't flour, either, and is different from both corn flour, mentioned earlier, and cornstarch. Cornmeal adds texture to the recipes I've used it in, and a pleasant, subtle crunch, which makes the results interesting. It is commonly used in Southern cooking; you may be familiar with it as an ingredient in corn bread. It is also the main ingredient in polenta.

Cornmeal comes in a range of sizes, from fine ground to quite coarse, but it is not powdery like flour. In recipes where this has been used, please use the size you have easiest access to, or prefer. I like a quite finely ground cornmeal. My testers each had an individual preference for the grind of cornmeal to use, which is why I have referred each recipe to here to say, "Use what you prefer"! If you don't have an opinion, all recipes were developed with finely ground cornmeal (my preference), so use that.

RAISING AGENTS

Baking powder and baking soda have been discussed more fully in A History of Baking (page 5) and yeast will be looked at further in Yeasted Treats (page 191). I'm not going to go into detail again, but if a recipe calls for only baking powder, this should be a double-action type.

Make sure your baking powder, baking soda, or yeast is fresh, as all have a limited shelf life. If yours is old, your baked item won't rise the way you're expecting and you'll be disappointed. If you are concerned about your baking powder, test it by adding 1 teaspoon to ¼ cup of warm water; it should bubble nicely. A similar test works for baking soda: Add a ¼ teaspoon to 1 tablespoon of vinegar. Yeast needs to be "proofed" before each use; please refer to Yeasted Treats (page 191), as this process is described there.

If any of these tests don't work, your baking powder, baking soda, or yeast is old and inactive, and will be ineffective as a raising agent. Throw out the package and buy a new one. A handy hint: Unless you bake very frequently, buy these items only in small quantity.

BINDING AND THICKENING AGENTS

Binders and thickeners are the ingredients you use to make things thicker or stick together. They are very helpful when baking without eggs, as they can replicate binding properties eggs bring to nonvegan baking.

Cornstarch, Arrowroot, and Tapioca Starch

Although they look like flour, cornstarch, arrowroot, and tapioca are not flours. They are just the ground-up endosperm (the bran- and germ-stripped starchy part) of a grain (in the case of cornstarch), or a tropical root (tapioca and arrowroot). In cooking, they are often used for thickening sauces. In baking, the addition of these to a batter, in small amounts, helps hold the flour together to form a nice crumb/texture. I use these more often when using nonwheat flour.

These thickeners are pretty much interchangeable for baking purposes, so if you do not have my preferred and specified thickener, use the one you do have. When making sauces, arrowroot is the best option for clear, thick results. It will be specified in the recipe if that is the case.

Agar Powder

From a Japanese sea vegetable, and also referred to as simply "agar," or agar agar. Agar is available in powdered, flake, and strand form. I use agar powder exclusively in this book. If you can find only flakes or sticks, just grind these to a fine powder in your spice grinder, blender, or food processor prior to using.

Agar is used to set liquids to a gel or mousse-like state, depending on how much you use per cup of liquid. For a gel, use 1 teaspoon of powdered agar to a cup of liquid, and for a more mousselike texture, ½ teaspoon of agar to a cup of liquid. Agar will set firmly at room temperature but does so much faster if refrigerated.

Ground Flax and Chia Seeds

Flax and chia seeds form a "gloopy" mess when soaked in water, which is handy to bind and thicken dough. The whole seeds do it much better than the ground seeds, but they are a lot less pleasant to find in your baked goods, which is why I use the ground form.

I use flax more often, as it is more widely available, but in some recipes where I don't want visible flakes of flax I have used ground chia seeds, most commonly sold under the brand name Salba and available from health food stores.

If you can't find these seeds preground, then, using a spice grinder, grind your own. You need to grind them to quite a fine powder, but larger bits of seed are okay, too, if that's how it comes out.

MILK

The most commonly used milks in this book are plain soy, almond, or rice milk, as these are the ones I've found most easily! On occasion, I also use soy creamer, flavored soy milk, and coconut milk (from a can as opposed to packaged for drinking; this is specified where I have used it). There's no reason you can't use oat or hemp milk, if that's what you have. The recipes were tested with store-bought milk. If you make your own, I don't see why that would be a problem.

Speaking of soy creamer: If you don't have any, or it isn't available where you live, you can make a substitute, using your blender.

* * *

HOMEMADE SOY CREAMER
MAKES 1¼ CUPS CREAMER

Place ¼ cup of plain soy milk and ¼ cup of canola oil in your blender, and on high speed, blend until really smooth and creamy.

Add another ¾ cup of soy milk, 1 to 2 teaspoons of agave nectar, and, if desired, ½ teaspoon of vanilla extract, and blend until super smooth and frothy.

How much sweetener you'll need will depend on how sweet you like creamer, and how sweet your soy milk was to start with!

Use as you would commercial soy creamer and store in a tightly covered container in the fridge. I use leftover agave nectar bottles for this!

. . . .

In some recipes, I use a different liquid to replace some or all of the milk you'd be expecting to use in such a recipe. Don't be alarmed—it is okay and is often done for reasons of flavor.

If you want information on substituting one type of milk for another, see Substitution Suggestions (page 37).

Note: If you are in transition to becoming vegan, or are vegetarian, please be advised that some of my recipe testers were not vegan, and they had acceptable results by substituting dairy products for the nondairy milk and other nondairy products. Not that I, as a vegan, am recommending this; just pointing it out.

VINEGAR

As you may know already, a little bit of an acidic ingredient is a good thing in baking. Vinegar reacts with baking soda, giving more rise, a better crumb, and softer texture, even if the batter is loaded with add-ins. It's like using buttermilk in nonvegan baking, and, as such, vinegar is usually added to the milk to curdle it, and then used in the recipe.

The most commonly used vinegar is apple cider vinegar, as it is very mild and doesn't add a specific taste to the end result. Occasionally a different vinegar, most notably white balsamic or regular balsamic vinegar, is used, because I want the specific gourmet taste of those to come through in the finished product. At times, I use another acidic liquid, such as lemon or lime juice, to take the place of the vinegar. It does the same job.

FATS

Fats, in baking, act as flavor carriers so that the decadent ingredients you are using are easily tasted in every bite; they also act as binders, to hold everything together. They give a rich mouthfeel to your baking, which, along with the sweeteners (more about those soon), make these items very more-ish.

Oil

Although I have specified canola oil in most recipes, it's because I just want you to use neutral, mildly flavored oil. If you prefer another oil for a neutral taste, then use what you prefer. I tend to use an organic, first-press canola oil, but sunflower or a mild vegetable oil (most commonly made from soy) would work, too. I have specified, at times, another particular oil, when I want the oil to add its flavor to the recipe. If you don't have the oil specified, it's okay to use your neutral oil instead.

Margarine

For those recipes that are margarine based, I choose a nonhydrogenated, vegan margarine such as Earth Balance. Margarine adds structure and support to cakes and cupcakes; in cookies, it enables them to spread.

Shortening

Shortening is just a vegetable oil that is solid at room temperature. It is great for creaming and rubbing in while adding a neutral flavor. It functions much like margarine and often gets used in conjunction with that. Again, nonhydrogenated is the name of the game, if you can get it. Make sure you buy an "all-vegetable" shortening, and check the ingredients.

Depending on where you live, your shortening may be more or less firm than mine at room temperature, so you may need to soften it a little for creaming purposes, or place in the fridge for a short while if rubbing in. Use your discretion.

Coconut Oil

Coconut oil, derived from coconuts, is solid at room temperature (unless the room is very hot) and goes completely hard in the fridge. It spreads and melts very well, and I even freeze and grate it to get flakes for adding to some recipes. Unrefined coconut oil does, however, have a slight but distinct coconut aroma and flavor, some brands more than others; if this is an issue, choose refined coconut oil, which is more neutral. This oil is also touted for its health benefits, not my main consideration in using it but nice to know, and it is available in some supermarkets, and most health food stores. It can be quite pricey so I usually use it in conjunction with a neutral (and cheaper), fat such as all-vegetable shortening.

FREEZING COCONUT OIL

To get frozen coconut oil flakes, I place a layer of coconut oil in a plastic container in the freezer for a few hours to freeze solid. The coconut oil may need to be warmed to make sure it is easily transferred. Once it is solid, I remove the block of oil from the container, and holding the block with a paper towel (so not to get the melting oil on my hands), I quickly grate it over a sheet of tinfoil, using the side of my box grater with the largest blades. It will look like flakes. I wrap the flakes in the tinfoil and return them to the freezer until required. The oil remains as flakes and doesn't refreeze as a lump.

In a number of recipes, you'll find that some or all of the oil has been replaced. I have used at times, alone or in combination, applesauce, fruit puree, vegan yogurt, or blended tofu as a partial or complete fat or oil replacer. You won't miss it.

SWEETENERS

Obviously, sweeteners are used to make your treats taste sweet! Nutritionally, not all sweeteners are created equal. I have tried to give a range of options, using more natural, less refined sweeteners than using only processed granulated sugar, which is, of course, the least nutritionally sound. (Check the list of sugar-free options on page 257 for more details.)

Dry

Dry sweetener really means sugar. You knew that. If I haven't specified which kind, then I've used a plain, white, non-bone-char-processed, granulated sugar. Some recipes call for light brown, dark brown, confectioners' (also known as powdered or icing), or turbinado (raw) sugar, so please use what has been specified if there is a specification. If you prefer, you may use the dry sweetener you usually use whatever that may be, instead of the granulated sugar, but be aware that the texture of the finished product may be affected.

Light or dark brown sugar should be packed into its measuring cup, for the correct volume.

I don't bake with artificial sweeteners, but if you're used to using them, you'll know how to add them to a recipe in place of sugar.

Liquid

The main liquid sweeteners I have used are maple syrup, agave nectar, brown rice syrup, and blackstrap molasses, all of which are commonly available in North America. Both agave nectar and brown rice syrup are said to be lower on the glycemic index than other sweeteners are, apparently causing a slower rise in blood sugar levels. Avoid maple-flavored "pancake syrup," which is primarily corn syrup.

In some recipes, I've used fruit and/or dried fruit puree, including pureed dates or apricots, as a natural sweetener. These items are less sweet than those made with sugar, so bear that in mind as you make them. If you don't have access to the liquid sweetener specified, see Substitution Suggestions (page 37) for ideas of what to use instead.

A handy tip: When measuring liquid sweeteners and other sticky substances, spray your measuring cup or spoon with nonstick spray prior to measuring, to help the sweetener slip out!

VANILLA AND OTHER EXTRACTS

When it comes to extracts, you get what you pay for. Isn't that always the way? But, in all seriousness, I find it is better to pay a little extra to get a natural, quality extract and not the artificial essence. You get the flavor you've paid for. If nothing else, buy a good-quality vanilla extract, as this is the one that is used most often, and that may be used in place of any other you don't have access to.

Besides vanilla, other extracts used in this book include orange, lemon, mint, almond, chocolate, and rose. Wow, that is quite a list! I found most of these in the local supermarket; my mum and dad sent me some; and some of the more obscure ones, I found in a little Indian food store. Flavored extracts may be available where you least expect them.

HERBS AND SPICES, SALT, AND PEPPER

The most commonly used herbs and spices include cinnamon, ginger, allspice, cloves, nutmeg, cardamom, thyme, rosemary, and paprika. There are more, but if you have these basics you'll do fine. When you are buying herbs and spices, please resist buying a huge package of something, unless you're going to use it frequently, as these have only a limited shelf life. If your dried herbs and spices are old they may be musty, and could make your baked goods the same. Not nice.

I have specified in the recipe if herbs and spices are to be fresh. If at all possible, please try to get the fresh if I've recommended that. If I have not specified this, the herbs are dried and the spices preground.

I refer to "pie spice" in some recipes. This is either pumpkin pie spice or apple pie spice, whichever you have, or prefer, if you're buying it premixed from a store, that is. I also know it as "mixed spice," so you may see it as that for sale, too, depending on where you live. If you'd like to make your own, try my mix of spices.

PIE SPICE
MAKES ABOUT 5 TEASPOONS PIE SPICE

2 teaspoons ground cinnamon
1 teaspoon ground ginger
1 teaspoon ground nutmeg
½ teaspoon ground allspice
¼ teaspoon ground cloves

In a small bowl, combine all the ingredients and mix well. Store in an airtight container.

Where I have used salt, I've used sea salt, not the superexpensive stuff but a good-quality natural sea salt all the same. If all you have is iodized table salt, then that's what you should use.

If I've used black pepper, I've used it freshly ground. If you don't have a pepper grinder, ask Santa for one; they're not expensive and the freshly ground pepper does taste better, though it is harder to measure. What I do is put down a small square of parchment, grind the pepper onto that, then scoop up what I have ground and measure it. Naturally, preground is fine if that is all you have.

FRUITS

I've used lots of fruit in the recipes: fresh, raw, and cooked, as well as frozen and dried. I'll specify in each ingredients list whether you need to do anything other than a rinse and trim to make the fruit ready for use. If I call for fresh or frozen fruit, without any further specification, then it's perfectly fine, even preferable, to use the fruit in its frozen state. Obviously, use fresh fruit if it is in season, frozen if not. Frozen berries shouldn't make the batter too soggy unless they are old frozen berries and have lots of ice crystals clinging to them. In that case, I tend to jiggle the berries about a bit in a sieve and loosen that ice off, then pat dry before adding to the batter.

If you have loads of bananas in your fruit bowl, going brown faster than you can use them, peel, break into 1-inch pieces, and pop into a resealable plastic bag or wrap in plastic wrap, then freeze. They can be used from frozen for some of the recipes in this book, as well as in smoothies, or thawed and used as you would fresh bananas in baking. Please remember to peel first, as frozen bananas are not easy to peel!

Many recipes call for the zest of citrus fruit; this is the very thin outer layer of the skin. Please be careful when grating the zest not to get the white pith layer, too—the white part is bitter and you don't want bitter. I find remov-ing the zest from the fruit is quickest and easiest with a handheld Microplane grater.

Some fruit juices have been used instead of milk, as mentioned earlier—mainly citrus and apple, but also pomegranate, cranberry, or others. Freshly squeezed is great, but store-bought, shelf-stable juices are fine, too.

Sometimes I have soaked dried fruits to soften them prior to adding to the batter, sometimes not. It was just how I felt the recipe would be best served. If you have a preference, by all means soak or not soak, as you like, if there is no other apparent reason for the fruit being used in the manner specified. Sometimes dried fruits have been cooked, or soaked, and pureed, as mentioned earlier, to replace the fat or the sugar in the recipe; the results of this are super yummy.

VEGETABLES

The vegetables I've used in the recipes are mainly fresh and cooked. A few are frozen or canned, and sun-dried tomatoes are used here and there. All are fairly easy to find when they are in season.

I do use roasted garlic a few times, and although I give instructions at the pages concerned, I thought you'd like to have it here to for ease of reference.

TO ROAST GARLIC
Preheat the oven to 400°F. Remove the loose papery skin from the outside of the garlic head, and slice ¼ inch off the top of the head, removing the tops of most of the cloves. Place the trimmed garlic on a square of tinfoil and drizzle a little olive oil over it. Wrap the garlic in the foil and roast for 20 to 25 minutes, until soft

to touch. Let cool to make handling easier, then peel.

. . . .

GRAINS

With the exception of rolled oats, all the grains added to the recipes are in the form of flour, and have been touched on already. Where rolled oats are used, it is up to you whether you prefer to use old-fashioned or quick-cooking, or a combination. Do not use instant oats.

NUTS AND SEEDS

I mentioned nuts and seeds in the flour section, where they are ground and used as a flour replacer, but I also use these (or their butter) in many recipes to provide flavor, texture, and a pleasant crunch.

Buy only small amounts at a time, as nuts and seeds may go rancid quite quickly if stored incorrectly. Buy from a store that has a high turnover of stock, especially if purchasing from a bulk bin, and store in your fridge or freezer (especially if you don't use nuts or seeds that often).

Unless specified in the recipe, the nuts and seeds should be bought raw, then toasted as needed. To toast nuts or seeds (and other things such as shredded coconut), two methods are commonly used, one in the oven and the other on the stove top. For my recipes, you really only need small amounts toasted at a time, so I use the stove-top method as follows:

. . . .

TO TOAST NUTS, SEEDS, OR COCONUT

Place nuts (or seeds, or shredded coconut) into a small skillet over medium-low heat.

Stir frequently to move the nuts in the skillet as they heat, and keep a close eye on them, as they can go from bland to burned very quickly.

After about 5 minutes, the nuts should start to color and you should get a lovely toasty aroma filling your kitchen.

Remove from the heat as they become a golden color but continue moving them around in the hot skillet for a few more minutes. Then remove from the skillet, and you're done.

. . . .

I often ask for the nuts to be chopped, either roughly or finely. To chop the nuts roughly, I just use my large chef's knife on my chopping board. For fine pieces, I find it easier to place the quantity of nuts in a re-sealable plastic bag and roll a rolling pin over them a few times, giving any stubborn nuts a good bang if they need it. A spice grinder also works well for small quantities, but be sure to grind in short bursts or else you will end up with nut butter!

Commonly used nuts include almonds, pecans, walnuts, pine nuts, peanuts, hazelnuts, and pistachios. And then there are the seeds: sunflower, pumpkin, poppy, hemp, and sesame. There are others, of course, all of which are commonly available at a good grocery and health food stores, as are their butters.

CHOCOLATE

I've used good-quality (again, you pay for what you get) semisweet vegan chocolate or chocolate chips. Check the label: The ingredients should be only sugar, chocolate liquor, cocoa butter, and soy lecithin. If you prefer dark chocolate, by all means use it, though the result will end up less sweet than if you use semi-sweet chocolate.

I've also used both plain and Dutch-processed cocoa powder. Unless I have specified Dutch-processed, use a plain cocoa powder. "Dutched" cocoa powder has been specially processed so it is alkaline and not acidic. Whichever kind of cocoa you use, be sure it is unsweetened.

Vegan white chocolate (which is not really chocolate at all, as it contains no cocoa butter) is becoming more and more commonly available, though at health food stores, not in mainstream supermarkets, so I have included recipes that call for it. Read the labels carefully as many brands do contain dairy products or hydrogenated fats.

Some recipes use carob instead of chocolate; they've been tested with carob and chocolate chips, and carob and cocoa powder. Use what you prefer. My children love both! Again, read the fine print, as some carob products are not vegan.

SOY-BASED PRODUCTS

I'm including in this section nondairy replacers for sour cream, cream cheese, yogurt, and cheese; also marshmallows and tofu. Many mainstream supermarkets carry soy dairy replacers these days, and, if not, health food and vegan specialty stores (online and storefront) will have what you're looking for. Take care when buying cheese alternatives, as many soy cheeses, even those that are labeled "lactose free," still contain casein (a milk protein). Likewise, not all soy yogurts are automatically dairy free; again, read the ingredients carefully. Some of my testers had excellent results using nondairy yogurts made with rice and coconut milk, which is why the recipe will ask for vegan yogurt without further specification.

In recipe development, I used Tofutti brand sour cream and cream cheeses, Solgurt nondairy yogurt, Dandies and Sweet and Sara vegan marshmallows, and I am a fan of Daiya nondairy cheese. I have no affiliation with any of these companies, I just like their products. I encourage you to experiment with different brands until you find one you like, and if you know what you like, then use that for these recipes.

Tofu

Firm silken (or Japanese style, vacuum-packed) and soft regular (or Chinese style, water-packed) tofus are used quite frequently because of the special smoothness and creaminess they bring to a recipe. They also work to bind things together in small quantities. Where firm silken tofu is specified, I have used a vacuum-packed silken tofu (such as Mori-Nu) and have indicated whether it is interchangeable with water-packed (regular) soft tofu. I also use extra-firm regular (Chinese style, water-packed) tofu (*not* silken), mainly in savory recipes, so watch out for the recipes using that.

When measuring tofu, the easiest way I have found is to use a large, clear measuring cup and to start by filling with water to the ¼-cup line. Add your tofu until the water reaches the level of the amount of tofu you need plus ¼ cup. If you need ¼ cup of tofu, you'd add tofu until the water reaches the ½-cup line on your measuring cup! (It's obvious but let me say it anyway: When adding the tofu to your recipe, do not include the water used simply to measure it.)

As many of these recipes use only part of a package of tofu I think you'd like to know how to store the leftover portion, right? For all the types of tofu used in this book, that is firm silken (vacuum-packed), soft regular (water-packed), and extra-firm regular (water-packed), the storage method is the same. Place the leftover portion of tofu in a small sealable plastic container, and cover with clean, cold water. Seal the container and refrigerate. If saving for more than one day, replace the water with fresh clean, cold water daily. The tofu will stay fresh for up to a week if stored in this manner. If your tofu smells bad, or off, in any way when you open the container, please do not use it.

OTHER INGREDIENTS

You'll find other additional, less common ingredients in one or two recipes, such as some types of alcohol, tamarind paste, pomegranate molasses, nutritional yeast, liquid smoke, powdered egg replacer, cocoa nibs, goji berries, and panko. Suggestions for substitutions of the less common ingredients have been given in the respective notes for each recipe.

WHERE TO BUY?

As mentioned before, all the ingredients used aren't difficult to find if you know where to look, usually at better-stocked supermarkets, health food stores, Asian or Middle Eastern grocery stores, gourmet markets, and vegan specialty shops. If there aren't any stores like this where you live, or you just prefer to do your shopping online, you may like to try these sites for specialty items.

Vegan Specialty Stores

All the following stores offer vegan items shipped to your door. Browse and choose your favorite, or just use the one closest to you!

In the United States:

COSMO'S VEGAN SHOPPE
http://cosmosveganshoppe.com
Marietta, GA

FOOD FIGHT! VEGAN GROCERY
www.foodfightgrocery.com
Portland, OR

PANGEA, THE VEGAN STORE
www.veganstore.com
Rockville, MD

VEGAN ESSENTIALS
www.veganessentials.com
Waukesha, WI

And in Canada:

KARMAVORE, THE VEGAN SHOP
www.karmavore.ca
New Westminster, British Columbia
(near me!)

VIVA GRANOLA
http://www.vivagranola.com
Quebec, Canada—online orders only.

General Specialty Stores

Visit these for items you may not readily find on the shelves of your local supermarket.

AMAZON
www.amazon.com
The Groceries and Gourmet Food section seems to have almost everything!

BOB'S RED MILL
www.bobsredmill.com
For flours, grains, raising agents, and gluten-free mixes.

PENZEYS SPICES
www.penzeys.com
For spices! Obviously.

MOUNTAIN ROSE HERBS
www.mountainroseherbs.com
For organic herbs and spices.

Now that you've sorted out your kitchen cabinets, and gotten an idea as to what you are going to need to get baking, let's take a look at the steps involved!

Tropical Banana Cake with
Coconut Ice Icing • page 112

Vanilla Bean Cupcakes • page 114

Espresso Chocolate-Chip
Coffee Cake • page 98

Berry-Infused Cupcakes • page 94

Coffee and Caramel Cupcakes • page 96

Citrus Bundt Cake • page 95

Mango, Pineapple, and Mint
Upside-Down Cake • page 104

Apple Tea Loaf • page 75

Rich Brownie • page 68

Blueberry and Macadamia
Biscotti • page 54

Car Tire Cookies • page 119

No-Bake Chocolate Truffle–
Inspired Cookies • page 128

Chile and Cilantro Corn Bread • page 227

Hot Cross Buns • page 204

Rocky Road Brownies • page 69

Vanilla Crème Puffs • page 186

Everything Cookies • page 122

Plain Cookies • page 133

Seed Cookies • page 137

Pecan and Date Cookies • page 132

Spelt Jam Thumbprint Cookies • page 138

From-Scratch Cinnamon Straws • page 179

Roasted Garlic and Peppercorn Crackers • page 236

White Balsamic Fruit Tart with Jam Glaze
• page 187

Sticky Spice Buns • page 215   Sticky Nut Pie • page 184

How to Bake

THIS IS A beginners' guide to the basics of baking without yeast. For more information on baking with yeast, please refer to Yeasted Treats (page 191).

Read the Recipe All the Way Through

Twice is better, as is giving the recipe a good read a day in advance of when you want to bake, just so you have straight in your head what, if anything, you may need to do or purchase before proceeding, and so you can feel confident about following all the steps. This will give you an idea of the time required, both for the recipe itself and for any preparation that may need to be done first, or even the day before.

If you've chosen a recipe but you don't have everything required, and don't feel up to a substitution, write what you will need the next time on your shopping list. Keep a special running list on a pad in the kitchen at all times, so you won't forget later that you need to purchase things you've had to make do without now.

Assemble the Equipment

This (and the next step, too) is part of what is termed, in French by professional chefs everywhere, your *mise en place* (literally, "everything in its place"). It's where you gather together all the utensils and bowls and other kitchenware you will need to measure and make the recipe, so you can see if you're missing anything. Then everything is at your fingertips when you start to bake.

Assemble the Ingredients

More *mise en place* to make sure you have everything, and enough of it, before you start, so you don't run out halfway through and have to take an emergency trip to the store, or have to excavate through your cupboards looking for something at the point of needing to stir it in. It's always a good idea to measure first, or at least eyeball each quantity, once you're comfortable with how much each volume looks like, before proceeding.

When measuring dry ingredients, I use the scoop-and-scrape method: I scoop the flour with the measuring cup or spoon and then level off the top with the back of a knife or the side of my hand. To replicate the results in the recipes, it is best that you do the same. For liquid ingredients, use either a cup or spoon you can't overfill or a large, translucent liquid-measuring cup, fill just to the line required, then hold up to your line of sight to check the level.

The recipes in this book are broken down into ingredients needed per step, which sometimes translates to the same item appearing more than once within the complete ingredients list. It might be helpful for you to pre-measure every ingredient in advance and line up the items in order of use, to be absolutely sure that no item is omitted or inadvertently added in the wrong amount. Some gourmet and kitchenware shops sell small bowls perfect for this purpose.

Prep the Ingredients

Make sure the ingredients you have are in the form specified in the ingredient list. You may need to toast nuts, chop fruit, sauté vegetables, or soak dried fruit as well as make ad-ditional recipes, such as icing, so everything is ready to go. Getting this done in advance saves time once mixing starts. (Yes, it's more *mise en place!*)

Preheat the Oven

Now that you've got your equipment and ingredients assembled, you need to prepare your oven. First, check how the racks are positioned inside the oven and change their position, if necessary. Baking usually occurs in the center of the oven. Believe me, it is better to do it now, and not later on when the racks are hot, when your batter is mixed and ready to go.

Oven thermometers are small devices that clip onto the oven rack, showing the real temperature inside the oven. They are handy to have, as some ovens do not reflect accurately, on their external temperature gauge, the actual temperature inside. An oven thermometer lets you check the actual temperature at the end of the preheating time, so you can adjust the baking temperature accordingly before putting your batter or dough in the oven. So go out and buy one! They are relatively inexpensive and available from kitchen supply stores, department stores, and some well-stocked supermarkets.

My oven takes ages (more than 30 minutes) to come up to the desired temperature but holds it accurately once there. Generally speaking, most ovens take 15 to 20 minutes to preheat, so be sure to turn on your oven before starting the mixing, unless the recipe directs you otherwise.

The temperatures in this book are given in degrees Fahrenheit, as that is how they were tested. If you live where Celsius is the preferred measure of oven temperature, or you have an oven that uses gas marks, don't despair. I have included a handy little conversion table for you:

FAHRENHEIT	CELSIUS	GAS MARK
250°	130°	½
275°	140°	1
300°	150°	2
325°	165°	3
350°	177°	4
375°	190°	5
400°	200°	6
425°	220°	7
450°	230°	8

If you use a convection oven, consult the manufacturer's instructions and/or test with your oven thermometer—it may need to be set 25°F (roughly 14°C) lower than the recommended temperature. Also, if you are using a tempered glass baking pan or pie plate, such as Pyrex, reduce the oven temperature by 25°F. (If you are using a glass pan *in* a convection oven, lower the temperature just once, not by 50°F!)

Prepare the Pan(s)

Ready your pan(s) before you begin mixing your ingredients (typically at the start of the preheat stage) for the batter to go into later, so you don't end up with mixed batter sitting and wasting its chemical leavening power while you only then begin to prepare the pans. Makes sense, right?

Each recipe will guide you as to the preparation required, but generally speaking, loaf and brownie pans are lined by taking a piece of parchment paper larger than the overall shape of the pan. The pan is placed on top of the parchment, and the corners of the parchment are cut out where they would bunch if stuffed into the pan, creating a shape that fits in the bottom of the pan and up the sides, with just enough protruding to help you remove the baked item later.

For circular cake pans, an outline of the bottom of the pan is traced onto a piece of parchment paper, then this is cut around, leaving tabs 2 inches longer than the sides of the pan, high enough to facilitate easier removal. The sides of cake pans need to be greased with a little margarine or sprayed with non-stick cooking spray.

Pie plates and tart pans are usually greased with a little margarine, sprayed with nonstick cooking spray, or brushed with oil to prevent the crust from sticking. If using store-bought crusts in disposable pans, this is not an issue, as the pan peels off.

Baking sheets are the easiest of the lot. I will ask you to line with an appropriately sized piece of parchment paper, but, if you prefer, you can grease with a little margarine or spray with nonstick spray. If using parchment for these, please turn over and reuse the sheets for subsequent batches of cookies, as they really aren't soiled by one use.

A handy hint you may know, and if not, it's one of those "I should have thought of that" moments: Once your parchment is cut to size, flip it over when putting in the pan so it is not trying to fold back the way it was on the roll. This means less fights and mess when you are trying to place your batter on top.

Mix the Ingredients as Called for in the Recipe

See A Brief History of Baking (page 5) for more on the main methods of mixing. Before mixing, check your oven thermometer to ensure the oven is at the right temperature. Then, basically, you do what the recipe says, exactly in the order listed.

Sometimes, prior to the liquid ingredients being mixed, you are asked to mix the milk and the vinegar (or other acid) and set it aside (at room temperature) for 5 minutes. This is to curdle the milk, for activating the baking soda later and giving a lighter texture.

Some important terms you will encounter:

Sift: You are usually asked to sift the dry ingredients or, if they contain nut flours or cornmeal, you'll be asked to whisk them together. Why?

Well, sifting or whisking does a couple of things. First, it mixes all the dry ingredients together so you're not left with lumps of cocoa powder or baking soda, for example, in one part of the mixture and none in another. This is why you are asked to sift the dry ingredients "together," not one at a time through the sieve. In addition, the sifting/whisking action adds air to the dry ingredients, making them lighter, and then, when you gently mix in the wet ingredients, the air is trapped, aiding the action of the baking powder/soda.

You can't easily sift nut-based meals or cornmeal, as the particles are too large to fit through the sieve, hence the whisking. When sifting whole-grain flours, the bran portion often remains in the sieve once everything else has passed through; just add this back to the bowl and gently stir (or whisk) to recombine.

Toss additions: Once the dry ingredients are sifted or whisked, you may be asked to toss any number of additions in the flour mixture to coat them. This is done so all the additions will be less likely to sink to the bottom of the pan. It may also be that dry ingredients, which are too large to be sifted or too bulky to be whisked, need be mixed in with the dry ingredients before the wet ingredients are added, instead of being folded in afterward.

Alternate adding ingredients: You may be asked to alternate adding dry and wet ingredients to a creamed mixture. To do this, add one third of your dry ingredients and mix gently, add half of your wet ingredients and mix gently, then add another third of your dry ingredients and mix gently, and so on, until all is incorporated. You're trying to get everything mixed in while having lots of air in the batter, so please remember to mix gently.

Fold: Any additional bits and pieces that have not yet been added to one or other mixture are folded in at the end of the mixing process. To fold, you start by sprinkling the addition over the batter as evenly and lightly as you can. Then, with your wooden spoon or spatula, cut down through the center of the batter; draw it across the bottom and up the side of the bowl, and finally fold the batter over the additions on the top. Give the bowl a quarter turn and do it again. Repeat only until all the additions are distributed through the batter. You must work gently yet quickly, because the raising agents are now wet and working and you need to get your baking into the oven as soon as possible. Don't beat, because that will deflate the lightness of the batter.

Spoon or Pour Evenly into the Pan

Ensuring your batter is evenly distributed in its pan or pans will ensure your goods will bake evenly. Also, you will have an even-textured finished product with no lumps or bumps, and even quantities in each serving. Be sure to smooth out the tops of moist batters, and to roll out doughs to the same thickness throughout.

Add the Decoration/Topping

Some recipes have a specified decoration or topping that is to be sprinkled, spread, or otherwise placed on top prior to baking. Some get stirred in, some don't; just follow the individual directions. If dividing among pans or pan compartments, pace yourself so as to not run out of the topping midway through putting it on.

Bake

Your oven should be at the right temperature now—especially if you checked it before mixing. So, off you go! Place your filled pan(s) into the center of the oven. Set your oven timer for the minimum specified time and use this as a guide to doneness. (If your oven doesn't have a timer or it doesn't work, set the timer on your microwave or buy a cheap stand-alone one). As the time gets close, your kitchen should be filled with the delicious aroma. This is a good sign!

Baking more than one item at a time is not really recommended, as many ovens can't cope with the volume and also maintain the right temperature (but sometimes you do what you have to do). If you are doing this, make sure to rotate the oven racks from top to bottom, if the pans are on different racks, or from side to side, if on the same shelf, halfway through the baking time. Many ovens heat unevenly, and by doing this, you ensure that both batches get a chance to be in the "hot spot" if there is one. If you learn that your oven does bake unevenly, rotate your baking pan(s) halfway through the indicated baking time.

When baking items, such as loaves, with a long oven time, you may feel the top is browning quicker than you would like. In this instance, cover the top with a sheet of parchment paper; the browning will be slowed. The edges of pie crusts can be protected with a strip of tinfoil around the circumference if they are browning more quickly than the rest of the pie.

Test to Ensure Your Baking Is Done

Check that the item is fully baked at the shortest indicated baking time by using a toothpick (or something similar, such as a skewer or narrow knife). Quickly insert it into the center, then withdraw it to check if it is free of any batter. If it's clean, great, the item is done! Remove the pan from the oven.

If there is batter on your toothpick, it means that your item needs a little more baking, so return it to the oven for a little more time, 5 minutes or so, then retest. (In a few cases, a little moistness is intentional or the testing needs to be done in a different manner; this will be specified in the directions.)

Let Cool in the Pan

There will be guidelines in each recipe for the length of time a baked good should rest in its pan to cool after it has been removed from the oven. This resting time ensures things are not too hot to move, so you don't burn your fingers and so the tops and any toppings stay on. Also, cooling for a short time in the pan helps to retain moisture. Plus, you don't want to risk splitting a cake or loaf by inverting it too quickly onto a cooling rack; the dwindling warmth helps bake the item a tiny bit more solid. Sometimes complete cooling in the pan is necessary to maintain a shape, such as in the case of pies or when a topping needs to set firmly.

Take care when removing the item from its pan. If it looks like the top (in the case of muffins) or sides may have become stuck, despite your greasing or lining the pan, loosen gently with a butter knife (i.e., not a sharp one) before removing. If your pan is lined with parchment paper, you can just take hold of the sides of the paper overhanging the pan and lift everything out, with no need to invert onto a baking sheet to be able to set the cake upright again on a wire cooling rack. The recipe directions will guide you as to which cooling method to use.

Let Cool on a Wire Rack

Cooling is pretty self-explanatory. Leave on the rack until completely cool. If you will be icing or glazing the item(s) afterward, you might want to first set the rack on a baking sheet or piece of parchment paper to catch any drips.

Decorate

Each recipe will tell you what needs to be done, either before or after the baked item is fully cool. Use your own discretion here, too, and substitute or add your favorite icing or topping instead, if you prefer.

Store Once Completely Cool

Refer to Storage (page 41) and each individual recipe for information on what to do now! If what you've just baked lasts long enough to need storing, that is!

Hooray! You have graduated from Carla's Baking School! Now, there are just a few more housekeeping pages to get through, and then onward to the recipes!

Help!
A Troubleshooting Primer

THIS CHAPTER REFERS to common issues and problems that may occur when baking without yeast. Sometimes they happen and the recipe won't work as it should, so you might wish to curse my name and blacklist me on the Internet and in online forums. But please, before doing that, e-mail me and ask what might have gone wrong (see my blog, http://veganyear. blogspot.com) or post your question on the Vegan Bake Sale Facebook page. But even before doing that, first take a minute to check through this list and see if any of the following apply to your situation.

"Help! Carla, what did I do wrong? My baking is . . ."

Too Dry or Hard

* Did you use all the liquid required in the recipe? You don't have a bowl of soy milk and vinegar curdling in the corner? No? Good, then it isn't that and may be something else.
* Perhaps you got side-tracked or didn't set your timer and the item is a little overbaked, not burned, just left in the oven too long, and therefore a little dried out. Note to self for next time: Pay better attention to the clock.
* Maybe your oven was too hot. You are using your oven thermometer to make sure it's the right temperature though, aren't you?
* Perhaps you've subbed another flour for some or all of the all-purpose flour in the recipe. Whole-Wheat flour does tend to make items a little drier than all-purpose flour does. If switching things around, remember to reduce the amount of flour used, per Substitution Suggestions (page 37).

Too Moist or Sticky

✳ Did you use all the flour called for in the recipe? You didn't mean to replace that ¼ cup of quinoa flour with all-purpose and then forget to add either?

✳ It may be that the water content of your fruit puree/yogurt/fresh fruit differs from mine. It happens and it's pretty much outside anybody's control. You'll get to know what a batter should look like with experience, and will be able to add a tablespoon of flour, here or there, if it happens again.

✳ Or maybe you've put in more fruit to make everything more fruity, and while the result is super fruity, now it's also too moist. Try limiting fresh fruit to the recipe amount.

✳ Did you substitute all-purpose flour for whole wheat? It's the opposite of the above situation, under "too dry." Check Substitution Suggestions (page 37).

✳ Maybe your oven was too cool for the entire baking period, or not up to temperature when the items went in, so they're not completely baked. Again, did you use your handy-dandy oven thermometer to check?

✳ Did you use your "high-tech testing device" (the toothpick) to check that the item was done before you left it to cool? It may not be fully baked if you didn't.

Not Light Textured or Too Gummy

✳ Perhaps the batter was overmixed. Remember, and I'll say this again only once, *mix gently to just combine*, and fold in any additions.

✳ Be careful with items containing starchy vegetables such as pumpkin, sweet potato, or potato; these become gummy very easily. Just make a mental note for next time to mix lightly.

✳ Again, maybe your oven was too cool so the items are not completely baked. [Whispers:] Oven thermometer.

Sticking to the Pan or Liners

✳ Refer to "too gummy," above. If your batter is gummy, the baked item will often stick.

✳ Are you trying to remove the item from the pan or liner before it is completely cool? If you're not patient and don't wait, this is sometimes the result.

✳ Did you add extra "extra additions"? Perhaps you added chocolate chips as well as walnuts and raisins, without reducing the volume of either. The more you add to the batter, the more likely it is to stick, especially with moist additions that sink all the way down through the mixture.

✳ If you're not using liners and your baking is sticking to the pan, did you grease the pan with a little margarine or cooking spray first? Was it too little?

Coming Apart

✳ Are you (being impatient and) trying to get your baking out of the pan while it is still too hot? Wait 5 or 10 minutes as indicated, and it'll be easier to handle, and will have settled, making it less likely to come apart.

Too Large or Too Small

* You may be over- or under-filling the pan. Filling as described should result in the right-size result for the recipe, but this doesn't mean it is the right size for you. *Large* and *small* are pretty subjective.

* Perhaps you've added too much, or not enough, baking powder/ soda to the recipe. Were you not paying close attention and misread the quantity, or put one measure in twice? This would cause the item to over- or under-expand and not turn out as expected.

* Maybe your baking powder/soda is old and has lost some, or all, of its effectiveness. Test it as outlined in Ingredients for Baking (page 12), and replace if you need to, before starting a new recipe.

Looking a Little Charred Around the Edges

* Take extra care with baking times, especially for chocolate items as these can easily burn, especially at the edges. Test the items for doneness at the minimum baking time, as outlined on page 29.

* As I mentioned earlier (page 29), covering loaves with a sheet or parchment paper, or pie crusts with a small layer of tinfoil, will keep the tops of these items from browning too quickly.

* If you have used a glass baking pan or pie plate, you did remember to reduce the temperature by 25°F, didn't you? Failing to do this may result in charred edges.

* If fruit, especially dried fruit, is poking up from an item and appears charred, be sure to poke any exposed items into the batter prior to baking next time. (Mental note again!)

Pleased to be of service. My bill will be in the mail!

Adapting and Resizing Recipes

PERHAPS YOU FANCY the look of a loaf, but you're not sure you want a loaf? Fancy that cupcake, but prefer a big slice of cake? Once you are confident and proficient as a baker, you will find you can change the pan you bake in to get a differently shaped result. However, if you do so, you'll need to make adjustments to the baking time and, in some instances, the oven temperature. A good rule of thumb toward judging doneness is to test the baked item, as outlined in How to Bake (page 25), when it starts to smell delicious. If not baked thoroughly, test after a further 5 minutes.

Muffins and Quick Breads

In this book, each recipe that makes twelve standard-size muffins also makes (roughly):

Thirty-six mini muffins: The actual number depends on size of the mini pans. Generally, their cups are a third of the size of those in a standard pan. Mini muffins will usually take only 12 to 15 minutes to bake at the same temperature, compared to 20 to 25 minutes for standard-size muffins.

One 9-inch loaf: If you'd like to make the muffin recipe into a loaf, go right ahead. Reduce the oven temperature to between 350°F and 375°F, and at least double the baking time to 45 to 55 minutes, but keep a close eye on the loaf and test once it starts to smell good.

Eight mini loaves: Keep the baking temperature the same. You'll need to bake to the upper time limit and maybe add an extra 5 minutes. Again, keep an eye on them and test! The standard pan for making these loaves comes with eight cups or compartments, so these recipe are a perfect fit.

Six maxi muffins: These are *huge!* The standard batter only makes six of these. Leave the baking temperature the same but add at least 5 minutes to the baking time.

This rule of thumb guide also works in reverse, for using loaf recipes to create muffins or mini loaves!

Although I've aimed for standard-size muffin pans filled to the top and then baked, you'll find some of the recipes may fill the pans more than others. Also, not all standard muffin pans have exactly the same size cups; a ¼-inch difference in the diameter or depth when making twelve muffins could have an impact on your end product.

When you change the size or shape of the pans you are using, you may need a different amount of batter to fill each cup to the top. This may leave you with some spare cups; please remember to fill these with about half an inch of water to even out the moisture in the oven and prevent warping.

Cakes and Cupcakes

You'll find that a recipe of cupcake batter will make twelve large or eighteen small standard-size cupcakes. That is, I like my cupcake liners filled to the top to make twelve big cupcakes, but some of my testers preferred to fill them only two-thirds full and make eighteen smaller ones. This is why you see both yields listed on each recipe. This amount of batter also makes:

Thirty-six mini cupcakes: Times as noted above for muffins. Mini cupcakes will usually take only 12 to 15 minutes to bake at the same temperature. These are especially loved by children, and by all who prefer a higher icing-to-cake ratio.

One 9-inch layer cake: If you want a double layer cake with icing between the layers, then double the cupcake recipe. Each layer cake will need to bake for 20 to 25 minutes.

One 8-inch square cake: As this pan will fill a little more deeply than a 9-inch round layer cake pan, due to its having a different depth and shape, you'll need to bake for slightly longer than above; 25 to 30 minutes should be plenty.

Again, the rule of vice versa applies if you'd like to change a cake to cupcakes.

Bundt cakes: These require a larger amount of batter and a longer baking time than most normal cakes. You can split the batter from a Bundt cake recipe between two 9-inch layer cake pans and bake for the same time as a layer cake, which is 25 to 30 minutes.

Individually shaped pans of various sizes are also for sale in many stores and can be fun to use when baking. I have pans in the shape of hearts, flowers, stars, and butterflies, and have used them all with good results. These pans take a different amount of batter than standard-size pans do, by just how much varies. Often when you buy them, their label will state how many cups of batter they take, which is a good guide, if you remember that a batch of cupcakes (twelve large ones) is about 4 cups of batter. As specialty pans aren't standardized, you'll need to keep an eye open as the cake bakes, and test at the center once everything starts to smell good. Basically, the deeper the pan, the longer it may take for the batter to fully bake; also, using a pan with a central opening (like a large doughnut) will result in a quicker-baking cake than one that is baked as a solid disk.

Pies

Pies are made in a standard 9-inch pie plate, and tarts in a standard 11-inch loose-bottomed tart pan; one recipe of pie crust dough makes enough for either. One recipe will yield enough for two 5-inch pies if you have this sized pie plates.

Cookies

Cookies are shaped as stated. You can control how much larger or smaller you'd like them, and adjust the baking times up and down as necessary. If you want to change the cookie size, bake just a few as a test run before continuing with the rest of the dough. Keep in mind that thinner or smaller cookies bake more quickly than thicker or larger ones. Just be vigilant and check when your kitchen becomes aromatic!

The recipes in this book all halve or double quite easily. When doubling the recipe, remember that your oven may not cook evenly; rotating the pans halfway through is a very good idea. It's often better to make one batch at a time, time consuming though this may be.

Its fun baking in different shapes and sizes once you are confident in your abilities as a baker—so go wild!

Substitution Suggestions

SOMETIMES YOU DON'T have in the cupboard what the recipe calls for, but you really want to make it.

What to do?

Although it's always best to follow the recipe as written (at least the first time you make it), you can, with a little common sense and creativity, easily substitute what you have on hand and still get a good result.

If You Don't Have the Specified Flour

You can substitute spelt flour for all-purpose flour by adding 1¼ cup of spelt for every cup measure of all-purpose flour. Conversely, use 1 cup of all-purpose flour for every 1¼ cups of spelt. So to remember: 1 cup all-purpose flour = 1¼ cups spelt flour.

If you don't have enough whole-wheat pastry flour, which I use a lot, use instead half all-purpose flour and half whole wheat to make up the amount specified. So for 1 cup of whole-wheat pastry flour, you'd use ½ cup all-purpose and ½ cup whole wheat. When sifting the whole-wheat flour, discard the extra bran that won't sift, to make the flour lighter.

If you don't have whole-wheat pastry flour or whole-wheat flour, substitute all-purpose flour and add an extra tablespoon of flour per cup used.

If you want to substitute whole-wheat pastry flour for all-purpose, decrease the flour measurement by 1 tablespoon per cup used, because replacing all-purpose with whole-wheat pastry flour often makes the baked good a little dry; removing this small amount of flour helps.

If you don't have bread flour, substitute an equal amount of all-purpose flour and add 1 tablespoon of vital wheat gluten for each cup used.

To make a quick bread recipe gluten free, substitute a commercial gluten-free flour mix according to the instructions on the package. Many products may be substituted for all-purpose flour at a 1:1 ratio.

If You Don't Have the Specified Thickening Agent

Cornstarch, arrowroot, and tapioca powders can all be substituted at a 1:1 ratio without affecting the product too much. If used in a sauce, the result won't be clear if you use cornstarch instead of arrowroot, but it will still thicken.

If you don't have chia seeds, you can replace them on a 1:4 basis with flax seeds. That is, if the recipe specifies 1 teaspoon of ground chia seeds, 4 teaspoons of ground flax seeds will give you the same result, though the seeds will be more noticeable in the final product.

If You Don't Have the Specified Nondairy Milk

Use another one. Soy, rice, almond, and oat are fairly interchangeable; even use a combination, if that's what you have—the only proviso being, if the recipe calls for the milk to be curdled (using vinegar or citrus juice), soy or almond milk is your best substitute. Rice milk doesn't curdle in the same way, and then you don't get the desired buttermilk quality in the recipe.

If You Don't Have the Specified Liquid Sweetener

Try another one. Agave nectar and pure maple syrup stand in for each other pretty well, but if you don't have these (or if they are beyond your budget), you could use corn syrup or golden syrup in a pinch. Remember that doing this will change the taste of your results, but it shouldn't change the batter consistency.

Brown rice syrup or barley malt could be substitutes, too, but they are slightly thicker than the other syrups and you'll need to increase the other liquids (often the milk) by 1 tablespoon per cup of these sweeteners, to maintain the moisture balance. However, the converse isn't true. As these are thicker, they can act as binders in a recipe, in a way that agave or maple syrup can't.

I use blackstrap molasses as I like the dark color, rich taste, and little bit of extra nutrition it adds to baked goods, but it does have a slightly bitter taste that doesn't appeal to everyone. If you have another form of molasses you prefer then use it in place of the blackstrap; my testers did with good results.

If You Don't Have Apple Cider Vinegar to Curdle the Milk

Use another type of mild vinegar in its place. White wine vinegar would be your best bet, but malt vinegar would work if you had nothing else.

Or use citrus juice, preferably lemon, in place of the apple cider vinegar.

If You Don't Have the Specified Extract

Use vanilla extract instead. Extracts add an extra depth to whatever the flavor in question is, and vanilla is an all-purpose, works-with-anything extract.

If You Don't Have the Specified Fresh Fruit or Vegetable

Substitute a similarly textured fruit or vegetable. Apple would work as a substitute for a pear, whereas a peach most likely would not (unless it wasn't ripe, but then why would you use it?). Or, kale would substitute for spinach, if it was cooked longer, but broccoli probably wouldn't. Or, raspberries for blueberries would be good, but not watermelon cubes. Or, use sweet potato puree instead of pumpkin puree, but not beets (they're harder and so don't produce the same texture when pureed). You get the idea.

If You Don't Have the Specified Dried Fruit

This one is easy. Generally one dried fruit can be substituted easily for another. You may just have to cut larger ones (apple, date, or apricot for example) into smaller pieces if taking the place of raisins or cranberries.

If You Don't Have the Specified Nut

How much you can substitute will depend on how integral the nuts are to the recipe. If they are used, as say, ½ cup folded in as a flavor accent and to provide a pleasant crunch, then go ahead and substitute whatever nut you have or that take your fancy. However, if the nuts are one of the main ingredients and/or the recipe has many variations of the same nut in the recipe (ground/butter/whole), it will be harder to make a substitution without changing the whole recipe. It's doable, but you'll have to change all the nut items to be or to derive from the same replacement nut, or you won't get the result I was aiming for.

Generally speaking, pecans and walnuts substitute well for each other.

Be *very* careful of nut allergies, if baking for others!

If You Don't Have the Specified Fresh Herb

Use dried! If you're desperate, you can use 1 teaspoon of the dried herb for every tablespoon of the fresh herb specified. Don't change to a different fresh herb, it might have a very different flavor.

If You Don't Have the Specified Dried Herb/Spice

Use another one that is of a similar flavor, if you feel confident that you know your herbs/spices well enough. You could use pie spice for cinnamon, allspice for cloves, and so on, if you felt you had to. Remember, though, that any substitution in seasonings will change the flavor of the finished product; some are more strongly flavored than others, so tread carefully. Don't substitute a spice or herb if you don't know what it tastes like!

If only a small amount is required, leave it out. The omission will affect the final result, but only as a background flavor.

If You Can't Eat Chocolate

Oh, poor you. Can you eat carob? If so, simply substitute carob powder or chips where chocolate is specified, and you're on your way. If not, there are still loads of other tasty recipes without chocolate for you to enjoy. Carefully check any variety of carob you may use to be sure it's vegan, as many contain milk products!

If You Want to Limit the Oil

A lot of the recipes in this book are low in oil and fat already. At home, I have sometimes used applesauce, a selection of fruit purees, pureed tofu, or soy yogurt as a substitute for some or all of the oil that is in a recipe.

If you want to reduce the oil in my recipes even further, applesauce, mashed banana, fruit purees, fruit juices, vegan yogurt, blended silken tofu, or nondairy milks, used in equal quantities as the oil you are replacing, are your best bets for sweet recipes. They will change the mouthfeel and the moistness of the finished item.

For savory recipes, you can use an equal amount of quite moist mashed potato, plain vegan yogurt, blended silken tofu, or nondairy milk. Again, be aware the results may not be as pleasing as the original product.

If You Want to Limit Processed Sugar

As mentioned before, a number of the recipes in the book are sweetened with natural liquid sweeteners, and some with fruit puree. Maybe try one of those first, to see if their flavor is satisfying to you (see the list on page 257).

You can substitute natural (or artificial but I'm not keen on those) dry sweeteners on a 1:1 basis (or according to the package directions) for some or all of the granulated sugar in the recipe.

To substitute a liquid sweetener (such as pure maple syrup) for a dry one (usually granulated sugar), reduce the volume of the other liquid ingredients (usually the milk) by ¼ cup for every cup of sweetener used. As an example, if you replace ½ cup of granulated sugar with ½ cup of syrup, you'll need to reduce the amount of milk (or other liquid) in the recipe by 2 tablespoons (half of ¼ cup).

Substitutions for Eggs

I'd like to add a little note about eggs. Often, vegan cookbooks list a whole bunch of substitutions for eggs. I haven't seen the point, because, really, this is a vegan baking book and there are no eggs used in it anyway. If you want to veganize other recipes, I recommend the list in *Quick and Easy Vegan Comfort Food* by Alicia Simpson (The Experiment, 2009) as a starting point.

If you don't have something in the kitchen cupboards but want to make the recipe and don't feel comfortable with substituting, then now, *right now*, put what you need on your shopping list so you don't forget when it comes time to go to the store! Do it right away, or else something will come up and you will forget, and then the next time you're baking, you'll be in the same position.

Generally speaking, a small amount (e.g., up to 1 tablespoon) of extra liquid, dry ingredient, or other addition won't make too much difference to the product. Just use common sense, and you'll be creating your own variations in no time.

Storage

IF YOU'RE NOT eating your baked item immediately (what will-power!) or want to give it as a gift, you need to store it appropriately and then present it in a manner that suits the situation. In our house, unless a baked item is made specifically to give away, even when everyone gets told, under pain of death, not to touch it, it doesn't last long!

Store your baked goods only after they have been cooled completely. If you pop a hot or even warm item into a bag or sealed container, it will generate steam. That means it will go soggy and not stay fresh and tasty as you would like it to. All your hard work wasted. However, if anything needs to be stored for longer than a few hours, it must be placed in some form of a sealed container or it will start to dry out. There is nothing worse than a dry piece of cake or muffin that you have to choke down.

I have a selection of old-fashioned metal cake tins and also Tupperware-type plastic containers in which, lined with parchment paper, I keep my baked items, to keep everything moist and fresh and to prevent drying out. I prefer to use the tins as they have the added advantage of not letting in light; but to be honest, it's really just because they look so much better on my countertops. They also have the added advantage of not letting anyone see what is in them before I'm ready to serve! Most baked goods keep well for up to 2 to 3 days in these containers; see the specific recipes for more details about storage. If you're storing the goods for a longer period, or if there's a heat-sensitive icing or filling (does it really last that long at your house?), you'll need to pop them in the fridge.

If storing items in the fridge for more than a short period, as you would to set a topping, they need to be in a Tupperware-type container or covered with plastic wrap, to prevent the possible absorption of odors from other food in the fridge. I personally prefer not to keep some things in the fridge, as it can make them quite firm, or even hard, and sometimes dry. Some other items, such as pies, tarts, and cakes with icing, do need to be kept in the fridge for the sake of food safety. Any items stored in the fridge need to be returned to room temperature (or reheated if to be served warm) prior to serving for ease of slicing, and to ensure the best taste and texture. Baked goods will stay fresh for 3 to 5 days in the fridge.

An alternative for longer storage is freezing. Most of the recipes in this book will freeze well, but not Ganache-Style Chocolate, which, if frozen, is likely to cloud and discolor. Most icing does not freeze well, so if you are planning to freeze something that is to be served iced, plan to freeze the plain (not iced) item and ice it only after thawing.

To freeze baked items, wait until they are completely cool, place on a pan or large plate, then pop into your freezer, so items freeze individually and not all joined together. Once they are frozen, you'll need to transfer things such as cookies, muffins, and slices of loaves to individual freezer bags or wrap them in plastic wrap, so you can just put them into lunch boxes and work bags, as is, to thaw before lunchtime. Alternatively, you can use a larger freezer bag and place everything inside for removal, and thawing, one by one at home. Larger items, such as pies or cakes, can be put directly into their own well-sealed freezer bags. Don't blame me if you end up with freezer-burned items if you forget to wrap them well or pop them into a freezer (not just a regular plastic) bag. Most baked goods will keep well in the freezer for up to 3 months.

To thaw your frozen baked items, you can either allow them to thaw at room temperature over the period of a few hours or thaw them in your microwave on high in 10-second bursts, until soft. The microwave method is not recommended for pies, as it may make your crust go soggy!

If you want to reheat items to be served warm, however they have been stored, without using the microwave, turn your oven to 300°F, wrap the thawed item in tinfoil, and place in your oven for about 10 minutes. This gives a fresh, out-of-the-oven feel to reheated goods.

Presentation

YOU MAY BE baking to give your items as gifts, to sell in a bake sale (fancy that), to bring to a potluck, or to share with friends. If you are baking more than just a treat for your family, you may want to do more than pop the items in a resealable plastic bag (or similar), or leave them in a storage container. (Though I often give muffins to my children's teachers in small resealable plastic containers as "just-because" or "thank-you" gifts, and they never complain.)

Small plastic storage containers for individual portions of cake or pie, or cupcakes or muffins, are great. Place the piece or item on the inverted lid and use the base as the lid, essentially an upside-down container to preserve the item better. This also works for full-size cakes and pies in big containers: Place the item on the lid and cover with the base. This makes it so much easier to get the item out and present it neatly at the end of a journey.

If your baking is for someone other than your immediate family, you will most likely want to "fancy-up" your items, more than you would for eating at home. This means garnishes, extra icing drizzles or ganache, dipping chocolate, colored sugars, sprinkles, etc. Old squeeze bottles (such as those from agave nectar) that have been washed out make good drizzle icing bottles.

Remember, for home-baked items, no one is expecting something looking as if you've taken a cake decoration class or have just graduated from a culinary institute, so just do your best. If it looks good to you, it will look good to everyone else, too! Please don't make this into a stressful situation!

If the items are being given as individual gifts (say, at Christmastime) or sold in a bake sale, they'll need to be wrapped individually (for reasons of hygiene, if nothing else), or in the case of cookies, placed in a small package and then fancied up as much or as little as you like. If it's a school (or church, or sports team fund-raising, or . . .) bake sale, this may be enough, but if the goods are going to be gifts, or sold at a higher-end bake sale, you're limited only by your imagination and budget.

You can . . .

* Use paper bags with peekaboo cellophane compartments cut into them
* Box them in decorated, individual boxes, either store-bought or homemade
* Wrap in cellophane tied with a big ribbon
* Wrap in fabric and tie with a ribbon
* Wrap in gift wrap, as you would a birthday gift
* Tie a bow around the plastic wrap
* Secure with a tag with the recipient's name on it

Whatever takes your fancy and sparks your imagination!

A special note about cakes and pies at bake sales: I wouldn't recommend giving away, or selling, pie by the piece, as that would be far too messy unless it was being eaten there and then. I'd keep them whole and sell as a take-home-for-later item. With cakes, if selling by the slice, you'll need to precut and to place a cut-to-size piece of parchment paper between each slice, and have a cake server or other tool (such as a pancake turner) for serving hands free.

If you're taking your items to share and they don't need to be individually wrapped for either hygiene or decorative reasons (maybe you're going to a potluck or an extended family meal), you may choose to present your goods:

* On a cupcake display or the lid used for transport
* On a cake stand—one for cakes or cupcakes
* In a single layer on a decorative platter, pan or large plate
* Piled high in a pyramid, on something similar
* In a flat basket lined with fabric, cellophane, or parchment paper
* In a deep basket, similarly lined

Choose the method of presentation that works best for:

The type of item: Is it something less likely to break apart, or more likely to get squashed unless protected? Does it have icing? Can it be wrapped easily?

The transportation requirements: Are you traveling by bus, or car? Do you have a big box to carry everything in, or a cloth bag? How far are you traveling?

The availability of display materials: Do you have cellophane? Ribbon? A cupcake stand?

The specific situation: As touched on above, are you sharing with friends at a potluck, or selling to strangers to raise money for your favorite charity?

You'll also need to take into account:

The season: If it's for a summer picnic, you'll need a cover to keep out the bugs, but if you're going to a winter event, you'll need to keep the items covered so they don't freeze!

The time of day: Easy access at breakfast time is good for those who don't function well until after coffee; at the end of an evening meal, it's quite nice to unwrap an individual treat.

Who is eating the items: Is it family, who will only care how good they taste, or a boss or client you want to impress?

Allergies: Remember to label with ingredients if there may be any allergy issues, and to keep any unwrapped gluten-free items absolutely separate from those containing gluten, likewise keep items containing tree nuts or peanut butter separate from those that are nut free (don't mix them unwrapped on the same serving tray, don't use the same knife to cut everything, and so on). This is very important, as some people who have allergies can be made severely ill by even the tiniest contact with an allergen.

A note here about environmental friendliness: Although using plastic wrap is a handy way to keep things separate and covered, it's also not the best option for the environment. Think about using reusable containers and recyclable wrapping, such as paper bags, instead. If selling at a bake sale, ask people to bring their own bags and containers to take the goodies home, to save your having to provide plastic, or paper, bags. Remember, every little bit helps.

The main thing is that you get the items where they're going, looking good, so people eat them at their best and appreciate how good they taste, right? There are no hard-and-fast rules, so do what suits you best. I hope, these suggestions have given you some food for thought.

Baking Throughout the Year

SOME FOODS SEEM to fit at certain times of the year. Thanksgiving brunch? Fine, pick an autumnal sort of loaf or muffin, such as Pumpkin and Cranberry Muffins (page 160). Canada Day? Valentine's Day? There are recipes in this book to fit those days, too.

When you're using fresh produce, it follows that the best time of year to make certain recipes would be when ingredients are in season, when they are at their cheapest and their best. Although frozen produce works fine in a pinch, I really would recommend making the Berry-Infused Cupcakes (page 94) or Rhubarb and Strawberry Crumble-Top Pie (page 183) when berries are in season. Wait for a glut of zucchini at the grocer's or in your garden before making Zucchini and Currant Muffins (page 162). Your taste buds will thank you.

A year offers so much by way of seasonal produce and days to celebrate, as I said, that there's likely a recipe here to fit them all. Just to get you on the right track, let's take a quick trip through the year and see what we can come up with.

Apologies to my family, and book purchasers, in the Southern Hemisphere. For the purposes of this stroll through the seasons, I have used the Northern Hemisphere timings, so Easter is in spring (where it really belongs), not autumn as I grew up with. Speaking of spring, let's start there.

SPRING

As the days get warmer, things start to grow, and soon fresh produce starts to hit the stores. If you have a garden, lucky you—you'll be really busy getting things planted, and you'll soon find yourself overwhelmed with fresh bounty! It's great to have some recipes up your sleeve to use up some of these spring fruits and vegetables; giving these as gifts is always welcome. Try the Asparagus, Pine Nut, and Roasted Garlic Quiche (page 226) or Rhubarb Squares (page 67).

Also, spring has some celebration days, as if celebrating the return of the warm weather isn't enough! Make a dish to share with family and friends to mark these days. At Easter, try the Individual New World Simnel Cakes (page 101) or make the Hot Cross Buns (page 204). You could be decidedly secular about it and go wild with one or more of the chocolate muffins, pies, cupcakes, or cakes.

If you want to be especially sneaky on April Fool's Day, bake a Secret-Ingredient Chocolate Cake (page 108) and see if you can fool everyone with the secret ingredients. Can they guess what they are?

For Mum's special day, get her to flip through this book and choose her favorite recipe, then make that for her. What says "I love you, Mum" more than home baking?

If you're in New Zealand or Australia, on April 25, remember the brave ANZACs with a batch of their biscuits (that would be cookies, to North Americans) after the Dawn Parade. See the recipe (page 122) for my take on that, the Coconut and Oatmeal Cookies.

Celebrate all the bounty the Earth has to offer on Earth Day by making a fruit or vegetable loaded muffin, such as Carrot and Pistachio Muffins (page 150) or Arugula and Pine Nut Muffins (page 225) and share with your family, friends, neighbors or workmates after you complete your neighborhood litter cleanup.

Also in late spring the Worldwide Vegan Bakesale takes place, raising money for a variety of great causes, by selling great baked goods. Check out www.veganbakesale.org for more information on setting up your own sale or finding out where one is in your area!

SUMMER

As spring becomes summer, all the gorgeous summer fruits and vegetables come into the stores: berries, cherries, peaches and other stone fruit, zucchini, and leeks, to name a few. Yum! If you have too many to eat, or you want to share the bounty in a different format, then make some summertime dishes such as Rosemary and Zucchini Focaccia (page 209) or Raspberry Clafouti Tart (page 182).

Summer brings sunshine and outdoor cooking, so to accompany your barbecue, or go into your picnic basket, how about a savory treat such as Spanikopita Loaf (page 239), Pesto Muffins (page 235), or Spicy Corn Biscotti (page 240)? You could even make a sweet dessert, such as Pinkalicious Cookies (page 132) or Vanilla Bean Cupcakes (page 114).

There are days to be celebrated in summer, too, not the least of which are the days that mark the founding of nations. If you're in Canada, try taking the Maple Crosshatch Cookies (page 126) or a loaf of Canadian Anniversary Bread (page 196) for your Canada Day celebration, the cookies being just as tasty and better for you than that cream and strawberry–covered cake that always seems to appear. If you're celebrating July 4th in the USA, how about the White Balsamic Fruit Tarts with Jam Glaze (page 187), or the Berry Infused Cupcakes (page 94)? As a different option, try the

Agave Crackle Cups (page 53), which are like the very American marshmallow-laden Rice Krispie Treats, as a tasty, if unusual, gesture.

Spoil Dad rotten on Father's Day with his favorite treat (Why should Mums get all the home baked goodies?) or make our dad's favorite, Father's Day Muffins (page 155).

AUTUMN

As the days get cooler and shorter, when the leaves fall from the trees and the children head back to school, you'll find wonderful autumn produce in the stores. The season is perfect for spending time indoors, baking things with your family that showcase the flavors that fit the season. Choose recipes containing autumnal fruits and vegetables, such as Cranberry Scones (page 78), Apple Tea Loaf (page 75), or Blackberry and Apple Crumble Muffins (page 148).

If you have children and are sending them back to school in a new grade, how about baking them a batch of muffins or cookies, to share with their class and to impress their new teacher? Be careful to label with *all* the ingredients (not just the most obvious ones such as peanuts), in case of allergies, and always check with the school that this is an appropriate gesture. The Chocolate Crackle Cups (page 56) would be a great choice—kids love them!

Fall seems to abound in special-food related days. Instead of candy for your Halloween Party, serve or take along the Jaffa (Chocolate and Orange Marble) Loaf (page 81), perfectly decked out in the colors of the season.

Then there is a Thanksgiving (or two) to bake for, especially if you have a mixed American/Canadian household! Why not gather for a brunch the day before, after, or just sometime in the time around the holiday, and con-

tinue to give thanks, with such recipes as Earl Grey Tea Muffins (page 154), Spiced Raisin Breakfast Cake (page 110), or Lemon and Blueberry Biscuits (page 83). Why not make Oven Potato Farls (page 234), Dinner Biscuits (page 228), or Irish-Inspired Soda Bread (page 230), to go alongside the main meal itself, just to add a touch of a little something different and special?

I must also make mention of World Vegan Day, November 1. What a perfect opportunity to share tasty baked goods and prove to the world how cruelty-free and health-filled treats can also taste divine! Choose your favorite combination to share at work, at school, or in your neighborhood. Have a bake sale! Spread the love.

WINTER

Winter really seems to kick in once Christmas arrives, or vice versa. Baking makes perfect gifts to give, homemade with love, showing how much you do care. Good traditional and nontraditional choices include Sweet Potato Pie (page 185), Gingerbread (page 81), and Reindeer Squares (page 66). These all look super cute if wrapped in cellophane with a bright ribbon, or in holiday-themed wrapping paper.

Produce in winter tends to be either from very far away (not a good option), a storage type of fruit or vegetable (e.g., apples, potatoes, or squash), or limited. Make the most of what you have by using that which is available in a recipe such as Parsnip and Orange Muffins (page 158). You could try one of the recipes in the Savory Goodies section (starting on page 223), for a change at dinnertime.

Frozen berries are great in some of the berry muffin recipes, for a touch of summer, or try dried fruit for a different type of goodness, in such recipes as Date Pinwheels (page 200) or Spiced Raisin Whole-Wheat Scones (page 86).

As we move into the New Year, many people find themselves looking to shed a few pounds, and as many of the recipes in this book are lower in fat, you could find your skills in demand! Indulgence with all of the taste and less of the guilt, the Whole-Wheat Rum Raisin Cookies (page 140) are especially good and were loved by my testers.

As winter draws to a close and the days start to get brighter, it's time for chocolate and love. Surprise your Valentine with an array of homemade treats made with the love baked right in. Choose a recipe you know your loved one will like, or choose one of the many chocolate recipes, such as (You'll Never Guess What's in This) Chocolate Pie (page 174) or Cola Chocolate Cupcakes (page 97), for a traditional Valentine's Day taste.

We've been through the year, so that all brings us back to where we started. There are more options included in this book than I have given suggestions for, and they are just that, suggestions. Do with these recipes what you will, when you will, and create your own food traditions!

Bars, Slices, and Squares

THESE ARE THE cookies that are baked in pans (or use other methods of shaping), unlike traditional dropped or rolled cookies. They're still sweet and good, and come in single-size servings; they just look, and are made, differently.

You may call them bar cookies, or slices, or squares, or pan bakes, depending on where you come from and what the item is. But they're all cookies, so all those terms work and have been used relatively interchangeably, depending on how I feel about the name!

I've also included in this section treats that are not made by rolling or dropping, even if technically they aren't baked in a pan or sliced into bars or squares. They just seemed to fit better here than with the rest of the cookies.

Please make sure your bars are completely cold prior to icing, so the icing doesn't run everywhere. Sometimes these are iced in the pan to help the icing hold its shape as it cools, so it will stay in place once cut.

A handy tip: Make sure your batter for the bars (and any topping) is spread evenly across the whole pan, for uniformity when the bars are sliced. Someone will complain if another's piece is bigger, or has more topping or more icing. I have children, and being the eldest of five, I know this to be true!

Agave Crackle Cups

MAKES 12 TREATS

▶ **NO NUTS • NO SUGAR • NO WHEAT**

My grandmother used to make us Honey Bubble Cakes all the time when we were kids. Sort of like Krispie Squares, but not as you'd know them in North America. I never knew that such things often contain marshmallows until I moved here. Anyhow, this is my updated and veganized version of the treats Gran used to make.

I've given an option for adding marshmallows into these no-bake treats for those who like them that way.

⅓ cup vegan margarine

¼ cup agave nectar

2 tablespoons brown rice syrup

2 tablespoons coconut oil (see Notes)

½ teaspoon vanilla extract

Pinch of salt (optional)

4 cups vegan puffed rice cereal, in the style of Rice Krispies

¼ cup vegan marshmallows, chopped small (optional; see Notes)

1. Line a twelve-cup muffin pan with cupcake liners. (See Notes).

2. In a medium saucepan, combine the margarine, agave nectar, brown rice syrup, coconut oil, vanilla, and salt, if using, over medium heat. Stir while everything dissolves. Bring to a boil and cook, still at a boil, stirring occasionally, for 2 minutes.

3. Remove from the heat and stir in the cereal, and the marshmallows, if using, ensuring they are well coated with the melted mixture.

4. Spoon the mixture into the prepared pan and press down with the back of a wooden spoon or spatula to compact the treats.

5. Chill until set, about 2 hours, then store in a covered container in the fridge.

NOTES:

❖ The coconut oil is to help the treats set firmly, not to add flavor. These treats don't taste coconutty.

❖ Vegan mini marshmallows, such as the ones from Sweet & Sara, don't need chopping. If using full-size vegan marshmallows, you'll need to cut them smaller. Kitchen shears sprayed with nonstick cooking spray are perfect for this.

❖ If you have a set of Krispie Treat molds or other shaped molds, you could use them to shape these treats.

- -

Banana and Chocolate Chip Biscotti

MAKES ABOUT 16 BISCOTTI

▶ **NO NUTS • NO SOY**

These are like banana bread, only crunchy. Seriously good, they are lovely by themselves or served alongside ice cream.

These biscotti are quite long, so if you would prefer shorter pieces, cut the long strips in half before the second baking. You'll need to bake the biscotti halves for a slightly shorter time (5 minutes or so) in the second baking so they don't over-crisp.

If you want to "fancy-up" these or any of the other sweet biscotti for any reason, you can dip one-half into Ganache-Style Chocolate (page 252) or decorate with a little Drizzle Icing (page 251).

2¾ cups all-purpose flour

¾ cup granulated sugar

2 tablespoons cornstarch

¾ teaspoon baking soda

½ teaspoon salt

½ cup vegan chocolate chips, mini size
   preferred

2 frozen bananas, cut into chunks (about
   2 cups) (see Notes)

1 cup rice milk

1 teaspoon vanilla extract

½ teaspoon banana extract, or more vanilla extract

1. Preheat the oven to 350°F and line a baking sheet with parchment paper.

2. Sift together the dry ingredients (from flour through salt), into a large bowl, then add the chocolate chips and toss to coat with the flour mixture.

3. In a blender or food processor, blend the bananas, milk, and extracts until very smooth and creamy.

4. Add the liquid from the blender to the dry ingredients and mix to combine. The dough will be wet.

5. With dampened hands and a rubber spatula, shape the dough into a 13 by 4-inch flattened log, about 1½ inches high, on the prepared sheet.

6. Bake for 30 minutes, until lightly browned and firm to the touch. Remove from the oven and let cool on the sheet for at least 1 hour. Turn off the heat if not using the oven for something else. Reheat to 350°F when needed.

7. Transfer the cooled log to a cutting board and slice, on a long diagonal, into 6-inch long strips ½ to ¾ inch thick.

8. Place the slices back on the baking sheet, standing on their short edge, if possible, and bake for a further 30 minutes, until browned and dry looking. (See Notes.)

9. Turn off the heat, open the oven door slightly, and leave the biscotti in the cooling oven for 30 minutes.

10. Remove from the oven, let cool on the sheet for 5 minutes, then transfer to a wire rack and let cool completely.

11. Store in a covered container.

NOTES:

❖ Freeze any excess ripe bananas you may have, already peeled and cut into 1-inch chunks, in freezer bags, for ease of access for such recipes as this, and for smoothies.

❖ If you can't fit all the slices on the baking sheet (or they fall over), put them cut side down. Flip halfway through the second baking to ensure even browning.

Variations

Banana Carob Chip Biscotti
Replace the chocolate chips with vegan carob chips, if you'd prefer.

Nutty Banana Biscotti
Instead of the chocolate chips, use an equal amount of your favorite nuts, finely chopped. I like walnuts in these.

Blueberry and Macadamia Biscotti 📷

MAKES ABOUT 16 BISCOTTI

This is a great combination, perfect with tea or coffee. The blueberries are sweet but a little tart; the nuts provide a creamy textured crunch.

These, too, are quite long biscotti, so if you would prefer shorter pieces, cut the long strips in half before the second baking. You'll need to bake them for slightly less time (5 minutes or so) in the second baking so they don't over-crisp.

2 cups all-purpose flour
½ cup cornmeal (see page 15)
¾ cup + 2 tablespoons granulated sugar
2 tablespoons cornstarch
¾ teaspoon baking soda
½ teaspoon salt

⅓ cup dried blueberries
⅓ cup chopped macadamia nuts

¾ cup + 2 tablespoons soy milk
¼ cup (2½ ounces) tofu, soft regular (water-packed) or firm silken (vacuum-packed)
1 teaspoon vanilla extract

1. Preheat the oven to 350°F and line a large baking sheet with parchment paper.

2. Sift together the dry ingredients (from flour through salt), into a large bowl. Add the blueberries and nuts, and toss to coat.

3. Using a blender or food processor, blend the milk, tofu, and vanilla until smooth and creamy, pour the blended mixture into the dry ingredients, and mix to just combine.

4. Using dampened hands and a rubber spatula, shape the dough into a 13 by 4-inch flattened log, about 1 inch high, on the prepared baking sheet.

5. Bake for 30 minutes, until lightly browned and firm to the touch. Remove from the oven and let cool on the sheet for at least 1 hour. Turn off the heat if not using the oven for something else. Reheat to 350°F when needed.

6. Transfer the cooled log to a cutting board and slice, on a long diagonal, into 6-inch long strips ½ to ¾ inch thick.

7. Place the slices back on the baking sheet, standing on their short edge, if possible, and bake for a further 30 minutes, until browned and dry looking. (See Notes.)

8. Turn off the heat, open the oven door slightly, and leave the biscotti in the cooling oven for 30 minutes.

9. Remove from the oven, leave on the sheet for 5 minutes, then transfer to a wire rack and let cool completely. Store in a covered container.

NOTE:
❖ If you can't stand all the slices on the baking sheet (or they fall), put them cut side down. Flip halfway through the second baking, to ensure even browning.

Variations

Blueberry and White Chocolate Biscotti
Use vegan white chocolate chips instead of the macadamia nuts, for a really decadent version!

Other Dried Fruit and Macadamia Nut Biscotti
If you don't have, or can't get, dried blueberries, use another dried fruit; for example, raisins or cranberries.

Blueberry and Other Nut Biscotti
Is finding reasonably priced macadamias a challenge? Use your favorite nut in its place. I like pistachio as second choice option here, followed by pecan, but really it's up to you.

Fruity Blueberry Biscotti
For an all-fruit, nut-free affair, use your favorite other dried fruit instead of the macadamia nuts. I think dried cranberries or currants pair exceptionally well with blueberries, but that's just me.

Chocolate Cereal Squares

▶ **NO NUTS** if baked without optional walnuts

Growing up, I knew these as "Afghans"—but I never knew the reason for this name, and Google has been no help. Calling these squares by their ingredients is more descriptive, but less evocative of my childhood.

These are quite rich bars, you'll notice there's not much baking powder, so not a lot of rising going on, but that's how I remember them!

The walnuts are entirely optional. They are, for some reason lost in the mist of time, traditional, but if you don't like them or there is another "no nut" reason, leave them out and top with chocolate shavings instead.

¾ cup granulated sugar
⅓ cup vegan margarine
¼ cup canola oil
¼ cup vegan shortening

½ teaspoon vanilla extract

1¼ cups all-purpose flour
¼ cup unsweetened cocoa powder
½ teaspoon baking powder
¼ teaspoon ground cinnamon
¼ teaspoon salt

1½ cups vegan cornflakes-style cereal

1 recipe Ganache-Style Chocolate (page 252)
18 walnut halves (or shaved vegan chocolate), for garnish (optional)

1. Preheat the oven to 350°F and line a 7 by 11-inch brownie pan with parchment paper.

2. Cream together the sugar, margarine, oil, and shortening until fluffy. Add the vanilla and stir well to combine.

3. Sift together the flour, cocoa powder, baking powder, cinnamon, and salt into this bowl and mix in, along with the cereal. Some cereal will get crushed, but that is fine.

4. Firmly press the mixture into your prepared pan, with the back of a wooden spoon or moist fingers. Bake for 20 to 22 minutes, until it looks puffy, with the edges firm and pulling from the sides of the pan slightly.

5. While still warm, mark with a knife into eighteen pieces (three columns by six rows). Do not cut all the way through. Allow to cool in the pan, then drizzle with Ganache-Style Chocolate.

6. Top the center of each piece with a walnut half (if using), backed with a little ganache to help it stick, or sprinkle on a small amount of shaved chocolate before the ganache sets.

7. Remove from the pan, using the parchment liner to lift out all in one piece, but only after the Ganache-Style Chocolate has set. Finish slicing, and store in a covered container at room temperature.

Chocolate Crackle Cups

▶ **NO NUTS • NO SOY • NO WHEAT**

I remember making these as a kid with Mum, using a recipe very similar to this one. I think it's a rite of passage for every seven-year-old in New Zealand. It's a recipe I've had to tweak a little here in North America so my children could make them, too. The vegetable shortening sold here is less solid than that in NZ. But, no worries, coconut oil to the rescue!

These no-bake treats are good made with puffed rice cereal, flaked corn cereal, and those little round cheery ones (check that the cereal is vegan). I sneak the hemp seeds in for texture and also to add essential fatty acids to these treats, but consider those optional.

½ cup confectioners' sugar

2 tablespoons unsweetened cocoa powder, plain or Dutch-processed

¼ cup vegan shortening

2 tablespoons coconut oil

3½ cups vegan breakfast cereal, as noted above

¼ cup vegan chocolate chips

2 tablespoons hemp seeds (optional)

1. Line a twelve-cup muffin pan with cupcake liners.

2. Sift together the confectioners' sugar and cocoa powder.

3. In a medium saucepan, melt the shortening and coconut oil over medium heat. Once melted, remove from the heat and add the cocoa mixture.

4. Once that is mixed smooth, add all the remaining ingredients and stir to ensure everything is well coated.

5. Spoon the mixture into the lined pan. The cups will be just full. Refrigerate until firm, about 1 hour.

Variations

Carob Crackle Cups
Use vegan carob chips and powder if you are avoiding chocolate.

Chocolate Crackle Cups with Add-Ins
Add up to 2 tablespoons of your choice of nuts, seeds, dried fruit, and/or shredded coconut with the cereal, to create a personalized treat.

Currant Squares

MAKES 16 SQUARES

▶ **NO NUTS**

I've updated the traditional currant square and brought it into the new century, and new hemisphere, with the addition of dried cranberries and blueberries. I've also gone for a softer crust that the fruit can sink into.

BASE AND TOPPING

¾ cup granulated sugar

¼ cup + 2 tablespoons canola oil

3 tablespoons vegan margarine

2 tablespoons vegan shortening

1 teaspoon vanilla extract

3 cups all-purpose flour

2½ teaspoons baking powder

½ teaspoon ground cinnamon

¼ teaspoon salt

¼ teaspoon ground ginger

¼ cup soy creamer + 2 tablespoons, if required (see page 16)

FILLING

¼ cup + 1 tablespoon vegan margarine

¼ cup light brown sugar, packed

2 tablespoons soy creamer (see page 16)

½ teaspoon vanilla extract

1 cup dried currants

¼ cup bread crumbs

¼ cup vegan panko (see Note)

2 tablespoons dried cranberries

2 tablespoons dried blueberries

1. Preheat the oven to 375°F and line an 8-inch square cake (brownie) pan with parchment paper.

Make the base and topping

2. Cream together the granulated sugar, oil, margarine, and shortening until smooth. Add the vanilla and mix well.

3. Sift in the flour, baking powder, cinnamon, salt, and ground ginger. Mix to form a crumbly dough.

4. Add the soy milk and mix until a firm dough is formed that holds together when pressed. If at this point you feel the dough is too stiff, add the additional soy milk, by the teaspoon, until the dough just holds together when pressed.

Prepare the filling

5. In a small saucepan, over medium-high heat, combine the margarine, brown sugar, creamer, and vanilla. Stir constantly until the margarine is melted, then boil over medium heat, stirring occasionally, for 3 minutes, until the mixture is slightly thickened.

6. Remove from the heat, add the remaining filling ingredients to the saucepan, and stir well.

7. Place half of the dough mixture into the bottom of the pan and press lightly into place.

8. Pour the filling over the base in the cake pan, spreading to cover evenly.

9. Cover the fruit filling with the remaining dough and then press firmly into place, sandwiching the filling between the layers of dough.

10. Bake for 20 to 25 minutes, until lightly golden, with browned edges pulling away from the sides of the pan slightly.

11. Remove from the oven and let cool in the pan until completely cooled. Cut into sixteen equal squares.

12. Remove from the pan, using the parchment liner to lift out all in one piece. Store at room temperature in a covered container.

NOTE:

❖ Panko is a Japanese type of bread crumb that stays crisp during baking. Available in most supermarkets, health food stores, and Asian food stores, it is not hard to find.

Elvis Blondies

MAKES 16 BLONDIES

▶ **PEANUT ALERT!**

I asked my recipe testers what they wanted to see in the book that I hadn't covered. Jamie very quickly e-mailed me back asking for something combining bananas, peanut butter, and chocolate. She even suggested calling it the "Elvis something."

As written, these are heavy on the banana, and quite moist because of it. If you'd prefer a more peanut-heavy blondie, go with the variation. So here we have it, for Jamie.

1½ cups all-purpose flour
1½ teaspoons baking powder
½ teaspoon salt
¼ teaspoon baking soda

1 ripe medium banana, very well mashed
½ cup almond milk
1 teaspoon vanilla extract
¼ teaspoon almond extract

½ cup light brown sugar, packed
¼ cup smooth or crunchy peanut butter
¼ cup vegan shortening
¼ cup vegan margarine
¼ cup granulated sugar

½ cup vegan chocolate chips
1 ripe medium banana, roughly chopped into ¼- to ½-inch pieces

1 recipe Peanut Buttercream (page 107) (optional)
1 recipe Ganache-Style Chocolate (page 252) (optional)
Roasted, salted peanuts, for garnish (optional)

1. Preheat the oven to 375°F and line an 8-inch square cake (brownie) pan with parchment paper.

2. Sift together the dry ingredients (from flour through baking soda), into a medium bowl.

3. In another bowl, whisk together the banana, milk, and extracts until smooth. In a large bowl, cream together the brown sugar, peanut butter, shortening, and margarine until light and fluffy. Add the banana milk mixture and stir really well to combine.

4. Add the sifted dry ingredients, mix, then fold in the chocolate chips and chopped banana.

5. Pour the batter into the prepared pan and smooth the top. Bake for 35 to 40 minutes, until the edges are golden, the middle is just firm to the touch, and a toothpick comes out almost clean.

6. Remove from the oven and let cool in the pan until completely cool, then for the full-on "Vegas Elvis" experience, ice with a layer of Peanut Buttercream, drizzle with Ganache-Style Chocolate, and sprinkle with nuts. For a less full-on experience, omit the Peanut Buttercream and/or peanuts.

7. Slice into sixteen equal squares.

Variations

Peanut-Intense Elvis Blondies

To make this less banana flavored and more peanut intense, instead of the chopped banana, add ½ cup of roasted, salted peanuts.

Not Elvis Blondies

Use a different nut butter for a change, such as almond or cashew! Make the icing using this nut butter and top with the kind of nuts used in the butter.

Ginger Crunch

MAKES 18 BARS

▶ **NO NUTS**

My sister Sonia was our family expert at making Ginger Crunch. I've taken the recipe she always used (from the *Edmonds Cookery Book*, a New Zealand institution) and given it a vegan makeover and a modernization.

If you are a ginger lover, you'll enjoy this as written; but if you are a true ginger fiend, you'll need to try the variation!

BASE

    2 tablespoons vegan margarine
    2 tablespoons vegan shortening
    3 tablespoons canola oil
    ½ cup granulated sugar
    ½ teaspoon vanilla extract

    1½ cups all-purpose flour
    1 teaspoon baking powder
    1 teaspoon ground ginger
    ¼ teaspoon salt
    ¼ teaspoon ground nutmeg

    ¼ cup crystallized ginger, chopped finely

TOPPING

    ¼ cup vegan margarine
    ¾ cup confectioners' sugar
    2 tablespoons brown rice syrup
    2 teaspoons grated fresh ginger

1. Preheat the oven to 375°F and line a 7 by 11-inch brownie pan with parchment paper.

Make the base

2. Cream together the margarine, shortening, oil, and granulated sugar until light and fluffy. Add the vanilla and mix well.

3. Sift in the flour, baking powder, and spices. Stir in the crystallized ginger. Mix to form a crumbly dough that holds together if pressed. (See Note.)

4. Press firmly and evenly into the prepared pan, prick with a fork a few times, then bake for 20 to 25 minutes, until lightly browned.

5. During the last 5 minutes of baking, make the topping.

6. In a small saucepan, combine all the topping ingredients over medium heat, stirring frequently until the mixture comes to a boil. Remove from the heat and, while still hot, pour over the hot base.

7. Let cool for about 15 minutes, then cut into eighteen pieces (three columns by six rows works well). You need to cut the bars before they set fully or they are likely to crack. Let cool completely in the pan.

8. Once fully cool, cut again. Remove from the pan, using the parchment liner to lift out. Store in a covered container at room temperature.

NOTE:

❖ If you find the base is too crumbly before pressing into the pan (humidity can affect the flour), add vegan milk by the tablespoonful until the base holds together better.

Variation

Super-Ginger Crunch
Add a further ¼ cup of finely chopped crystallized ginger to the topping mixture, if you really love ginger!

Lemon Bars

MAKES 16 BARS

▶ **NO NUTS**

This was a last-minute request from my testers. It's sticky and messy, and very, very, very more-ish. Don't eat too much in one go or you'll feel a bit sick. I speak from experience. It's good! I don't know if it is exactly what they had in mind when it was requested, but it's my take on the lemon bar.

For this one, you'll need the zest and juice from two medium lemons.

BASE
> ¼ **cup vegan margarine**
> 3 **tablespoons canola oil**
> ½ **cup granulated sugar**
>
> 2 **tablespoons soy milk**
> 1 **tablespoon freshly squeezed lemon juice (½ medium lemon) (see Note)**
> 1 **teaspoon lemon zest**
> ½ **teaspoon lemon extract**
> ½ **teaspoon vanilla extract**
>
> 1½ **cups all-purpose flour**
> 1 **teaspoon baking powder**
> ¼ **teaspoon salt**
> ¼ **teaspoon ground nutmeg**

TOPPING
> ¾ **cup granulated sugar**
> ¼ **cup vegan margarine**
> ¼ **cup freshly squeezed lemon juice (2 medium lemons) (see Note)**
> 4 **teaspoons lemon zest**
> ½ **teaspoon agar powder**

1. Preheat the oven to 375°F and line a 7 by 11-inch brownie pan with parchment paper.

Make the base

2. Cream together the margarine, oil, and sugar until light and fluffy.

3. Add the soy milk, lemon juice, zest, and extracts, then mix well.

4. Sift in the flour, baking powder, salt, and nutmeg. Mix to form a soft dough that holds together if pressed.

5. Press the base firmly and evenly into the prepared pan, prick with a fork a few times, and bake for 18 to 22 minutes, until lightly browned.

6. Remove from the oven and turn off the heat. Allow to cool in the pan for 30 minutes and then make the topping.

7. In a small saucepan, combine all the topping ingredients over medium heat, stirring frequently, until the sugar and margarine are dissolved and the mixture comes to a boil. Remove from the heat and set aside for 5 minutes.

8. After 5 minutes, whisk the topping to recombine and thicken. While still hot, pour over the warm base.

9. Place the brownie pan in the fridge for the topping to set completely. Cut into sixteen rectangles (two columns by eight rows works well).

10. Remove from the pan, using the parchment liner to lift out. Store in a covered container at room temperature.

NOTE:

❖ Although I specify freshly squeezed lemon juice, feel free to top up the juice you get from your lemon with bottled if your lemon doesn't provide enough. I used only bottled juice when making the lime variation—when I cut open my limes, they were all completely dry inside! The result was fine using bottled juice.

Variations

Lime Bars
Replace the lemon juice and zest with those from limes. Replace the lemon extract with more vanilla extract.

Grapefruit Bars
Replace the lemon juice and zest with those from grapefruit. Replace the lemon extract with more vanilla extract.

Lemon Cookies
Instead of pressing the base into the tin and baking to make bar cookies, roll into a 2-inch-diameter log, wrap in plastic wrap, and chill for an hour. Slice the log into disks between ¼ and ½ inch wide to form cookies and place on a parchment-lined baking sheet. Bake at 375°F for 10 to 12 minutes, until the bottoms are browned, then ice with Drizzle Icing (page 251). This variation will also work with any of the flavor variations listed above.

Mini Lavender Bites with Sour Cream Icing

MAKES 24 MINI BITES

▶ NO NUTS

Near where I live there's a garden with a lavender bush growing wild. I have permission to take what I need, so I do! If you, or anyone you know, have lavender in the garden, it is fine for culinary use, but take care as "cosmetic-use" lavender is treated. Health food stores sometimes carry culinary lavender.

As lavender is not available all the year round I have included a variation with mint for when there is no lavender to be found.

¼ **cup packed fresh culinary lavender flowers, stripped from stems and flower heads (see Notes)**

¾ **cup soy milk**

1 **cup granulated sugar**

¼ **cup (2½ ounces) tofu, soft regular (water-packed) or firm silken (vacuum-packed)**

¼ **cup + 2 tablespoons canola oil**

½ **teaspoon vanilla extract**

1¾ **cups all-purpose flour**

1½ **teaspoons baking powder**

½ **teaspoon salt**

1 **recipe Sour Cream Icing (recipe follows)**

1. In a small saucepan, combine the lavender and milk. Heat gently over medium heat and, stirring occasionally, bring to a boil. Remove from the heat, cover, and set aside for 15 minutes to allow the flavor to infuse. Strain out and discard the lavender flowers.

2. While the lavender is infusing, preheat the oven to 350°F and spray a twenty-four-cup mini-muffin pan with nonstick spray.

3. Using your blender or food processor, blend together the lavender-infused milk, sugar, tofu, oil, and vanilla until smooth and creamy.

4. Sift together the flour, baking powder, and salt into a large bowl. Directly from the blender, add the lavender mixture to the dry ingredients, then mix to combine.

5. Spoon into prepared mini-muffin pan. The cups will be full. Smooth the tops and bake for 15 to 18 minutes, until the tops are puffy, the sides are browned, and a toothpick comes out clean.

6. Remove from the oven and let cool in the pan for 5 minutes, before transferring to a wire rack to let cool completely.

7. Once completely cool, ice with the Sour Cream Icing.

NOTES:

❖ Culinary lavender is fresh-from-the-garden lavender that has not been treated in any way that could make it harmful if ingested.

❖ If fresh culinary lavender is not available, use 4 teaspoons of dried culinary lavender. Look for it in the spice section at gourmet groceries and health food stores, where it is sometimes sold in bulk. Do not bake with dried lavender that is sold for any purpose other than culinary use (such as display, cosmetics, or potpourri).

Variation

Mini Mint Bites
Instead of lavender flowers, use an equal amount of mint leaves, and replace the vanilla extract with mint extract.

⭐ Sour Cream Icing

MAKES ABOUT 1½ CUPS ICING

▶ **NO NUTS • NO WHEAT**

Instead of a cream cheese–based icing I have a sour cream–based one! Too simple for words, this shouldn't count as a recipe. This is also great wherever I've recommended Buttercream, More or Less (page 249).

¼ **cup vegan sour cream**

½ **tablespoon freshly squeezed lemon juice (¼ medium lemon)**

½ **teaspoon vanilla extract**

2 **cups confectioners' sugar, sifted if lumpy**

1. In a large bowl, whisk together the sour cream, lemon juice, and vanilla until smooth.

2. Add the confectioners' sugar and mix to combine. The icing will be quite thick but spreadable.

3. If too thick for your purposes, thin with ½ teaspoon of water at a time until the desired consistency is reached.

Nanaimo Bars

MAKES 18 BARS

▶ NO NUTS

Based on the superfamous recipe available all over the Internet, though really nontraditional with all the changes I've made to get it perfected. I just had to put these quintessential British Columbian treats in the book!

The bottom layer is a little crumbly, but not too crumbly; the custard layer firm, yet still creamy; and the chocolate, a rich topping. You could call them Chocolate-Coconut-Custard Squares if you can't bring yourself to call them Nanaimo Bars.

This one is another no-bake recipe for those of you who think you can't bake!

BASE

1½ cups vegan graham cracker crumbs (see Notes)
1 cup unsweetened shredded coconut
⅓ cup unsweetened Dutch-processed cocoa powder, sifted if lumpy
½ cup granulated sugar
¼ cup vegan margarine
¼ cup canola oil
2 tablespoons coconut oil
1 teaspoon vanilla extract

FILLING

1⅓ cups confectioners' sugar
1 cup all-purpose flour
¼ cup vegan custard powder (see Notes)

½ cup canned coconut milk
¼ cup vegan margarine
2 tablespoons coconut oil
1 teaspoon vanilla extract

TOPPING

2 recipes Ganache-Style Chocolate (page 252)
Shredded coconut (optional)

1. Line a 7 by 11-inch brownie pan with parchment paper.

Make the base

2. Start by combining the cookie crumbs, coconut, and cocoa powder in a large bowl.

3. In medium saucepan over medium heat, heat together the granulated sugar, margarine, canola and coconut oils, and vanilla. Stir constantly to combine and continue stirring frequently until completely melted and smooth, about 5 minutes.

4. Add the melted mixture to the cookie-crumb mixture, and mix in really well to combine.

5. Firmly and evenly press the mixture into the prepared pan. Chill the base while preparing the filling.

Make the filling

6. Sift together the confectioners' sugar, flour, and custard powder into a large bowl.

7. Using a medium saucepan over medium heat (I give the one used above a wipe and use it again), combine the coconut milk, margarine, coconut oil, and vanilla and stir while it heats, until completely melted.

8. Pour the melted mixture into the sifted dry ingredients and mix until smooth and thick.

9. Carefully spread the filling over the prepared base and chill in the fridge for 1 hour, until firm.

10. Once set, top with a layer of warm Ganache-Style Chocolate, sprinkle with coconut (if desired), then chill for 20 minutes before slicing.

11. Using a hot knife (heated under hot running water is enough), slice into eighteen pieces (three columns by six rows) before the ganache is fully set.

12. Return to the fridge and chill for at least a further 30 minutes, prior to lifting out of the pan using the parchment liner. Store in a covered container in the fridge. The bars will get firmer the longer they are kept in the fridge prior to serving.

NOTES:

❖ Bird's Custard Powder is the most commonly available brand, and, at time of writing, is vegan—as always, check the ingredients.

❖ If you cannot find any vegan custard powder, replace each tablespoon of custard powder needed with 1 tablespoon of cornstarch, along with ⅛ teaspoon of vanilla extract for flavor, and a pinch of turmeric (about 1/16 teaspoon) for color.

❖ If you can't find vegan graham crackers where you live, replace the graham cracker crumbs with vegan digestive biscuit crumbs or other plain vegan cookie crumbs.

Nutty Blondies

MAKES 18 BLONDIES

I don't know what to say about these. I made up the recipe to use some leftover hazelnut coffee syrup I had in the cupboard, then I dis-

covered they're good with maple syrup, too. My husband took these into work and all the feedback he got was, "Mmmmhhhmhm," so I guess they got approval!

1½ cups all-purpose flour

½ cup ground almonds

2 teaspoons baking powder

½ teaspoon salt

1 cup chopped mixed nuts of your choice, toasted

6 ounces tofu, firm silken (vacuum-packed, half of a 12-ounce package)

½ cup almond milk

½ cup light brown sugar, packed

⅓ cup pure maple syrup, or hazelnut or almond coffee syrup

¼ cup canola oil

1 teaspoon vanilla extract

1 recipe Drizzle Icing (page 251), Ganache-Style Chocolate (page 252), or Sugar Glaze (page 252), if desired

1. Preheat the oven to 375°F and line a 7 by 11-inch brownie pan with parchment paper.

2. Sift together the dry ingredients (from flour through salt), into a large bowl, then add the nuts and toss to coat.

3. Using your blender or food processor, blend together the tofu, milk, brown sugar, syrup, oil, and vanilla until smooth and creamy, scraping down the sides as required.

4. Pour the liquids from the blender into the dry ingredients and mix to just combine.

5. Pour the batter into the prepared pan, smooth the top, and bake for 18 to 22 minutes, until the edges are firm, the top is golden and puffy, and a toothpick comes out clean. Bake for the shorter time if you like your brownies underbaked and gooey, for about

20 minutes for just done, or 22 minutes for a more cakelike brownie.

6. Remove from the oven and let cool in the pan for 5 minutes, then lift out using the parchment liner and transfer to a wire rack and let cool completely.

7. Once completely cool, slice into eighteen pieces (three columns by six rows is easiest), and ice or decorate, if desired.

Orange and Almond Biscotti

MAKES ABOUT 16 BISCOTTI

This one is a tasty combination that went over well with the mothers at preschool!

Making biscotti is a longish process but not hard and there is a lot of downtime. I tend to plan to bake something at the same temperature during the cooling time, or do the first baking before I have to go out and the second baking after I come back.

If you want to "fancy-up" these or any of the other sweet biscotti for any reason, you can dip one half in Ganache-Style Chocolate (page 252) or decorate with a little Drizzle Icing (page 251).

½ **cup almonds, chopped roughly**
1½ **tablespoons agave nectar**

1½ **cups all-purpose flour**
½ **cup ground almonds**
¾ **cup granulated sugar**
2 **tablespoons cornstarch**
¾ **teaspoon baking soda**
½ **teaspoon salt**

1 **tablespoon orange zest (1 medium orange)**

¼ **cup + 1 tablespoon almond milk**
¼ **cup orange juice**
¼ **cup vegan yogurt**
½ **teaspoon almond extract**
½ **teaspoon vanilla extract**

1. Preheat the oven to 350°F and line a large baking sheet with parchment paper. Set aside a sheet of parchment for the nuts.

2. In a medium skillet over medium heat, toast the almonds for about 4 minutes, until just golden. Add the agave nectar, stir to coat, and allow the mixture to caramelize for about a minute. Spread in a thin layer on the reserved parchment and allow to cool for 5 minutes. Break up into small pieces.

3. Sift together the dry ingredients (from flour through salt), into a large bowl. Add the caramelized nuts and zest, and toss to coat with the flour mixture.

4. Using a blender or food processor, blend the milk, juice, yogurt, and extracts until smooth and creamy. You can whisk these together if you'd prefer to do it by hand.

5. Pour the blended mixture into the dry ingredients and mix to just combine.

6. Using dampened hands and a rubber spatula, shape the dough into a 12 by 3-inch log, about 1½ inches high, on the prepared baking sheet.

7. Bake for 30 to 35 minutes, until lightly browned and firm to the touch. Remove from the oven and let cool on the sheet for at least 1 hour. Turn off the heat if not using the oven for something else. Reheat to 350°F when needed.

8. Transfer the cooled log to a cutting board and slice, on a long diagonal, into 6-inch-long strips ½ to ¾ inch thick, with a heavy knife.

9. Place the slices back on the baking sheet, standing on their short edge, if possible,

and bake for a further 25 to 30 minutes, until browned and dry looking. (See Note.)

10. Turn off the heat, open the oven door slightly, and leave the biscotti in the cooling oven for 30 minutes.

11. Remove from the oven, let cool on the sheet for 5 minutes, then transfer to a wire rack and let cool completely. Store in a covered container.

NOTE:

❖ If you can't stand all the slices on the baking sheet (or they fall), put them cut side down. Flip halfway through the second baking, to ensure even browning.

● ●

Reindeer Squares

MAKES 18 SQUARES

▶ NO SOY • NO WHEAT

Do you leave out rolled oats, colored with glitter, for Santa's reindeer on Christmas Eve? We do, and we call it "Reindeer Food." While there's no glitter in these flourless bars, they sure do look pretty with all the colorful add-ins. I'm sure Santa's reindeer would love them and have lots of energy for their long flight afterward!

I know goji berries are pretty pricey and can be hard to find, but they add an interesting flavor dimension to this recipe, being a little more tart than sweet. Not many are called for, so leave them out if you don't have or don't like them. They are apparently one of the best antioxidant providers, so if you can, do.

Also, hemp seeds are another thing you might not have around the house and can get pricey. These wee seeds are loaded with omega-3 and omega-6 essential fatty acids, so include if you can. If not, replace with sesame seeds.

⅓ cup canola oil

⅓ cup apricot jam

¼ cup light brown sugar, packed

¼ cup brown rice syrup

1 teaspoon vanilla extract

2½ cups quick-cooking or old-fashioned rolled oats (not instant)

½ cup sunflower seeds

½ cup golden raisins

¼ cup sesame seeds

¼ cup hemp seeds

¼ cup pumpkin seeds

¼ cup raisins

¼ cup chopped dried apricots

2 tablespoons goji berries (optional)

2 tablespoons ground flax seeds

2 teaspoons pie spice (see page 19)

½ teaspoon salt

1. Preheat the oven to 350°F and line a 7 by 11-inch brownie pan with parchment paper.

2. In a small saucepan, combine the sugar, jam, rice syrup, oil, and vanilla. Heat over medium heat until the brown sugar is melted, 8 to 10 minutes, and everything is well combined. The oil may not completely mix in, but that's fine.

3. While the jam mixture is melting, combine the remaining ingredients in a large bowl. Once the jam mixture is melted, pour into the seed mixture and stir well to combine and distribute the liquids.

4. Press the mixture firmly into your prepared pan, using a damp spatula or dampened hands (the dampness makes this easier), then bake for 32 to 35 minutes, until lightly golden.

5. Allow to cool slightly, about 5 minutes, in the pan before marking into eighteen bars (three columns by six rows is easiest). The best way I have found to do this is to use a sharp knife that has been rinsed under hot water.

You need to mark the bars immediately; if you wait for these to cool, it is near impossible to cut into them without bits coming out.

6. Remove from the oven and let cool in the pan for 30 minutes, then lift out using the parchment liner and let cool completely on a wire rack.

7. Once completely cool, slice all the way through your markings. Store the bars in a covered container.

NOTES:

❖ If you're feeling really decadent, these bars are very more-ish when drizzled with Ganache-Style Chocolate (page 252).

Rhubarb Squares

MAKES 16 SQUARES

▶ NO NUTS

I got the idea for these from an old magazine in a dentist's office somewhere. I love rhubarb, so they appealed on all sorts of levels. The eggs and cream they were loaded with appealed less, so I took the idea and changed it just for me!

BASE
½ cup canola oil
¼ cup light brown sugar, packed

1½ cups all-purpose flour
½ cup whole-wheat pastry flour
½ teaspoon ground ginger
½ teaspoon ground cinnamon
½ teaspoon baking powder
¼ teaspoon salt

TOPPING
2 tablespoons turbinado sugar

2 tablespoons vegan panko (see Notes)

1 cup granulated sugar
½ cup (5 ounces) tofu, firm silken (vacuum-packed)
3 tablespoons cornstarch
2 tablespoons soy milk
2 teaspoons baking powder
1½ teaspoons vanilla extract
½ teaspoon salt

3 cups finely chopped rhubarb, about 4 medium stalks (see Notes)

1. Preheat the oven to 350°F and line an 8-inch square cake (brownie) pan with parchment paper.

Make the base

2. In a large bowl, mix together the brown sugar and oil.

3. Sift in the ingredients from flour through salt and mix to combine. The mixture will look crumbly but will hold together if squeezed.

4. Press the base evenly and firmly into the bottom of the prepared pan, then bake for 8 minutes, until very lightly golden.

Make the topping

5. In a small bowl, combine the turbinado sugar and panko.

6. Using your blender or food processor, blend the ingredients from granulated sugar through salt for the topping until smooth and creamy. Scrape down the sides of the bowl as necessary.

7. Transfer the blended mixture to a large bowl and stir in the rhubarb.

8. Pour this mixture on top of the hot base, and sprinkle with the panko mixture.

9. Bake for a further 45 minutes, until the topping is golden brown with a crisp-looking sugar crust.

10. Remove from the oven and let cool in the pan. Slice into sixteen equal squares, and remove from the pan once completely cool.

11. Store, covered, in the fridge.

NOTES:

❖ Panko is a Japanese type of bread crumb that stays crisp during baking. Available in most supermarkets, health food stores, and Asian food stores, it is not hard to find.

❖ Ensure the rhubarb is chopped into small enough pieces to enable it to cook in the oven as the squares bake. Always remove any leaves or leaf bases from the stalks, as these are poisonous.

Variations

Gingered Rhubarb Squares
Add 2 tablespoons of finely chopped crystallized ginger with the rhubarb.

Nutty Rhubarb Squares
Add 2 tablespoons of finely chopped walnuts with the rhubarb.

Strawberry Rhubarb Squares
Replace ½ cup of the rhubarb with sliced strawberries.

Rich Brownies 📷

MAKES 16 BROWNIES

▶ NO SOY • NO WHEAT

I was coming to the end of recipe creation for this book, when I realized I hadn't included a full-size brownie recipe! Now, the one I used as my go-to recipe was Isa and Terry's in *Vegan Cookies Invade Your Cookie Jar* (Da Capo Lifelong Books, 2009), and it had been since I first made it while being a tester for that book. The recipe(s) I was using before that just didn't cut it anymore. I decided that I would revamp them and create something both soy- and wheat-free, while still being super delicious and an alternative to Isa and Terry's. It took a few tries to get it right, but here we have it!

The coconut milk doesn't make the brownies taste of coconut, it just adds a creamy richness.

1 cup spelt flour
3 tablespoons unsweetened Dutch-processed cocoa powder
3 tablespoons cornstarch
1 teaspoon baking powder
½ teaspoon salt
½ teaspoon ground cinnamon (see Notes)
½ teaspoon ancho chile powder (see Notes)

1½ cups raw cashews, soaked in water for at least 8 hours, or overnight, then drained and rinsed
½ cup canned coconut milk
¼ cup almond milk

1½ cups vegan chocolate chips
½ cup granulated sugar
¼ cup canned coconut milk
½ teaspoon vanilla extract
½ teaspoon chocolate extract, or more vanilla extract

½ cup vegan chocolate chips (optional)

1 recipe Ganache-Style Chocolate (page 252) (optional; see Notes)

1. Preheat the oven to 375°F and line an 8-inch square cake (brownie) pan with parchment paper.

2. Sift together the ingredients from flour through chile powder, into a large bowl.

3. In a blender or food processor, pulse together the nuts and milk until thick and creamy. Scrape down the sides as required to ensure everything is well mixed and very smooth.

4. In a medium saucepan over medium-low heat, melt the chocolate chips, sugar, coconut milk, and extracts, stirring frequently. Once melted, with no lumps, add to the blender and blend until smooth.

5. Pour the blended mixture into the flour mixture and fold in, with the chocolate chips (if using).

6. Pour the batter into the prepared pan and smooth the top. Bake for 25 to 28 minutes, until the edges are lightly browned, the middle is just firm to the touch, and a toothpick comes out clean when inserted near the edge and nearly clean when inserted near the middle.

7. Remove from the oven and let cool in the pan for 10 minutes, then lift out using the parchment liner and transfer to a wire rack and let cool completely.

8. Ice with Ganache-Style Chocolate, if desired, then slice into sixteen squares.

NOTES:

❖ If you'd prefer your brownies without the "Mexican Hot Chocolate vibe" going on (quoting one of my testers, Laura), leave the spices out of the brownie. Still rich and chocolaty!

❖ An alternative topping is a sprinkle of confectioners' sugar, which has the bonus of making these less rich.

Rocky Road Brownies 📷

MAKES 16 BROWNIES

▶ **PEANUT ALERT!**

I had some leftover marshmallows and dried cherries one day and was trying to think of a way to use them up. In an "a-ha" type moment—you'd have been able to see the shining lightbulb above my head if I were a cartoon character—I thought, "Rocky Road!" In a subsequent "a-ha" moment, I thought about making it into brownies. The result is a very more-ish, goodie-laden chocolate treat! Dessert with vanilla ice cream, anyone?

¼ **cup vegan margarine**
¼ **cup canola oil**
¾ **cup granulated sugar**

¼ **cup + 2 tablespoons soy milk**
½ **teaspoon chocolate extract (see Note)**
½ **teaspoon vanilla extract**

1½ **cups all-purpose flour**
¼ **cup unsweetened Dutch-processed cocoa powder**
2 **teaspoons baking powder**
½ **teaspoon salt**

½ **cup vegan chocolate chips**
½ **cup peanuts**
⅓ **cup vegan mini marshmallows, or large ones cut into ½-inch pieces**
¼ **cup dried cherries, chopped finely**

1 **recipe Ganache-Style Chocolate (page 252) (optional)**

1. Preheat the oven to 375°F and line a 7 by 11-inch brownie pan with parchment paper.

2. Cream together the margarine, oil, and sugar until light and fluffy.

3. Add the soy milk and extracts, then mix well.

4. Sift in the flour, cocoa powder, baking powder, and salt. Mix well.

5. Add the chocolate chips, peanuts, marshmallows, and dried cherries, and stir well to distribute evenly.

6. Pour into the prepared pan, spread evenly, then bake for 22 to 28 minutes, until puffy, just firm to the touch, and a toothpick comes out clean.

7. Remove from the oven and let cool in the pan for 10 minutes, then lift out using the parchment liner and transfer to a wire rack and let cool completely.

8. Once completely cool, drizzle with Ganache-Style Chocolate, if desired, and slice into sixteen pieces.

NOTE:

❖ If you don't have chocolate extract, substitute more vanilla extract.

Shortbread

MAKES 8, 10, OR 12 SLICES

▶ **NO NUTS**

In testing this recipe I made it many times, just to check it was fine. In all honesty, it was fine the first time—I just love shortbread! If you're a traditionalist, you may not like this recipe; the result is a soft, melt-in-your-mouth texture, none of that hard, crisp shortbread you may prefer. Though in saying that, if you do want a harder-textured shortbread, when I ask you to just knead the dough lightly for a minute, ignore that and knead for as long as

you please! My dad's cousin Jane swears by fifteen minutes!

¾ cup vegan margarine, at room temperature

¼ cup vegan shortening

½ cup confectioners' sugar, sifted if lumpy

½ cup granulated sugar

1 cup all-purpose flour

¾ cup white rice flour

¼ cup cornstarch

1 teaspoon baking powder

1 tablespoon soy milk, if needed (see Notes)

1. Preheat the oven to 350°F and spray a 9-inch pie plate with nonstick cooking spray.

2. Cream the margarine and shortening together until very light and fluffy. If you have an electric mixer, use it now, otherwise use a whisk and a lot of elbow grease.

3. Add the sugars, and cream some more. You want this mixture very light and fluffy.

4. Sift in the cornstarch, flour, and baking powder, then mix well. It will look crumbly, but should hold together if pressed.

5. If the dough is too crumbly, add the soy milk a teaspoonful at a time, until the dough holds together when pressed.

6. Lightly knead the dough a few times (maybe for 1 minute) in the bowl or on a floured board, to encourage the dough to hold together (see Notes).

7. Press the dough very firmly into the prepared pie plate. Ensure it is pressed down as far as it can be. Press your two forefingers around the edge to give it a crustlike appearance, if you like.

8. With a knife or pizza cutter, cut the dough into equal wedges, like slicing a pizza.

You choose how many pieces; for me, cutting into eight gives pieces that are too large and into twelve gives pieces that are too small, so I slice down the middle, then divide each side into five equal slices.

9. Prick the slices with a fork.

10. Bake for about 30 minutes, until very lightly golden, with lightly browned, firm edges that have pulled away from the sides.

11. Remove from the oven and let cool in the pie plate until completely cool. After 20 minutes of cooling, carefully reslice along the lines you made earlier. When fully cool, remove carefully from the pie plate, using a thin metal spatula. Store in a covered container.

NOTES:

❖ If your fat has been creamed enough, you should not need the soy milk. If the dough holds together when pressed without it, you are fine to continue without adding any.

❖ With regard to the kneading of the dough, as discussed above, I prefer my shortbread to have a light and airy texture, but I know this is not traditional. If you prefer a harder, crisper shortbread, then you need to knead. The kneading activates the gluten in the wheat and makes the finished shortbread a firmer product. I push the dough together a few times for maybe a minute and that is all, but you can knead for up to 5 minutes, until the dough is soft and smooth.

Variations

Thyme Orange Shortbread
Add 1 tablespoon of orange zest (from 1 medium orange), and 1 tablespoon of finely chopped fresh thyme with the margarine and shortening.

Lemon and Lemongrass Shortbread
Finely chop the soft inside part of a lemongrass stalk (about 1 teaspoon) and add, with 1 teaspoon of lemon zest, with the margarine and shortening.

Lavender Shortbread
Add 1 tablespoon of finely chopped fresh culinary lavender (see Notes, page 62) with the margarine and shortening.

Rosemary Shortbread
Add 1 tablespoon of finely chopped fresh rosemary with the margarine and shortening.

Mint Shortbread
Add 1 tablespoon of very finely chopped fresh mint and ½ teaspoon of mint extract with the margarine and shortening.

Cocoa (or Carob) Shortbread
Replace 3 tablespoons of the flour with an equal amount of unsweetened cocoa or vegan carob powder.

Coffee Shortbread
Add 1 teaspoon of instant coffee granules with the flour.

Mocha Shortbread
Replace 1 tablespoon of the flour with unsweetened cocoa powder, and add 1 teaspoon instant coffee granules.

Green Tea Shortbread
Add 1 teaspoon of matcha green tea powder (see Notes, page 100) with the dry ingredients.

Two-Bite Chocolate Chunk Brownies

MAKES 24 BROWNIES

▶ **NO NUTS**

I was at Highland dance class with my girls one day and I asked some of the other dancers what their favorite treat was. Most said, "Chocolate chip cookies," but one girl in particular was adamant that "two-bite brownies" were the best thing ever. After that, I just had to make some.

The applesauce taste is apparent if you eat these warm. If you're a little more patient and wait until they have cooled it is not noticeable. They're not too sweet, but nice and chocolaty.

⅔ **cup granulated sugar**

½ **cup (5 ounces) tofu, firm silken (vacuum-packed)**

¼ **cup canola oil**

¼ **cup unsweetened applesauce**

1 teaspoon vanilla extract

1 cup all-purpose flour

3 tablespoons unsweetened cocoa powder

1 teaspoon baking powder

⅓ **cup vegan chocolate chunks, large chips, or just a chopped-up bar**

1 recipe Ganache-Style Chocolate (page 252)

1. Preheat the oven to 350°F and spray a twenty-four-cup mini-muffin pan with nonstick spray.

2. Using your blender or food processor, blend together the sugar, tofu, oil, applesauce, and vanilla until smooth and creamy.

3. Sift together the flour, cocoa, and baking powder into a bowl, add the blended mixture and mix, then add the chocolate and fold in.

4. Spoon into prepared pan. The cups will be full. Bake for 11 to 13 minutes, until the tops are puffy and have a few cracks and bounce back when lightly pressed. If you test them, the toothpick should not come out totally clean; brownies are best when slightly underbaked.

5. Remove from the oven and let cool for 5 minutes in the pan before transferring to a wire rack to let cool completely.

6. Top with Ganache-Style Chocolate, if desired.

Biscuits, Scones, and Loaves

QUICK BREADS, AS you may have read before, are really everything raised by the action of baking powder and/or baking soda. I've given muffins, cookies, bars, slices and squares, as well as cakes and cupcakes, their own sections, so in this section you'll find a selection of sweet biscuits, scones, and loaves, basically everything not savory that was left! All of the recipes here make fine breakfast and snack foods. Dress them up with an icing or topping and you could even use some of them as an emergency dessert.

I'd like to note here that when mixing the batter for these recipes, you really do need a gentle touch, so no electric mixers, please. Where the recipe directs you to mix until just combined, it really does mean just: Small lumps in the batter are okay, as are small patches of flour that have not been mixed in—it will all bake out fine in the oven, I promise you that.

You may not think so, but loaves do qualify as "quick and easy." Easier than quick, admittedly, but the mixing time is generally the same, if not less, than the time needed to mix a batch of muffins, cookies, or a cake. The main thing most of these loaves need is baking time. Think of this as bonus time—use it to do chores, make or eat a quick and easy vegan dinner, have a bath, watch your favorite TV show—you know, multitask! All the while, your house will gradually fill with the gorgeous smell of what you have in the oven.

Note: Loaves often crack. It's nothing you've done wrong. Nothing I've done wrong, either. It happens as the outer crust of the loaf sets in the heat of the oven, and then the inside rises. It's not necessarily a bad thing. Any nooks and crannies your loaf has on top are just more space for absorption of any glaze or drizzle icing that you're using!

In case you're wondering what the difference is between a loaf and a tea loaf (I use both terms), the answer is height and weight. Tea loaves are generally not as highly risen as loaves, and are often loaded with extra add-ins, and so are denser. Other times, it's just random.

The easiest way to serve your loaves is to wait until they are completely cool, cut slices of your desired width, present, and serve. It is almost impossible to cut a hot loaf nicely or accurately. If you have a highly risen loaf, it may be easier to slice wider, say, up to 2 inches, then in half down the middle of the slice, giving you a more manageably shaped serving.

These items are best on the day they're made or the day after. Store at room temperature, unless the room is very hot and humid, in which case the fridge would be better, in a covered container or wrapped in plastic wrap to maintain freshness and moistness. If you'd like to store something for a later date, it should be sliced, frozen, and then thawed, either in the microwave or on the countertop.

To end, there's the whole *scones* and *biscuits* debate. Its super confusing for me, being originally from New Zealand. Biscuits are what we call cookies over there. What a biscuit is here in North America would probably be called a scone, too; that term covers a wide range of baking. What to do? For the purposes of recipe-naming clarity, and so as not to lose my sanity, I have used the term *scone* if the item in question was made by dropping the dough onto a prepared sheet, so it bakes a little free form and in a random shape. If the dough was patted out and a cookie cutter used, then I have called the items *biscuits*, with one exception, which you'll notice as you go through the chapter. Please don't all shout at me at once.

Apple Tea Loaf 📷

MAKES ONE 9-INCH LOAF

▶ **NO NUTS**

This deliciously apple-loaded bread came into being one day after I chopped up a few apples for the children for a morning snack. They decided they'd rather be hungry than eat apple on that particular day, so I was left with a pile of slowly browning apple slices. To use them up, I quickly threw together and baked this loaf. By lunchtime the children were asking about the delicious smell coming from what I was baking. I told them that if they ate all their lunch, they could have some. They all gobbled their lunch and promptly ate three slices each. Who had the last laugh that day, I wonder?

½ cup soy milk
½ cup unsweetened applesauce
1 teaspoon apple cider vinegar

1½ cups cored and grated dessert apple (e.g., Ambrosia, Fuji, Pacific Rose, or even Gala), packed (roughly 2 apples) (see Notes)
¾ cup light brown sugar, packed
¼ cup canola oil
3 tablespoons freshly squeezed lemon juice (1 to 1½ medium lemons)
1 tablespoon lemon zest (1 medium lemon)
½ teaspoon vanilla extract

3 cups all-purpose flour
1 tablespoon baking powder
1¼ teaspoons ground cinnamon
½ teaspoon salt
½ teaspoon baking soda
¼ teaspoon ground cloves

½ cup add-ins (optional) (see Notes)

1. Preheat the oven to 375°F and line a 9-inch loaf pan with parchment paper.

2. In a large bowl, combine the soy milk, applesauce, and vinegar. Set aside for 5 minutes to curdle and then add the apple, brown sugar, oil, juice, zest, and vanilla. Mix well.

3. Sift the dry ingredients into this bowl, and mix to combine. Fold in any add-ins if using.

4. Pour the mixture into the prepared pan and bake for about 1 hour, until golden brown and a toothpick comes out clean. (There may be a little residue on the toothpick, as the grated apple will stay moist.)

5. Remove from the oven and let cool for 10 minutes in the pan, then lift out using the parchment paper and let cool completely on a wire rack.

NOTES:
- ❖ I like to leave the skin on the apples; it adds pretty color flecks and a little extra fiber. You can choose to leave it on or to peel your apples.
- ❖ For the add-ins, you are limited only by your imagination, but you may like to try:
  - ✦ Nuts, toasted or untoasted (e.g., walnuts, hazelnuts, pistachios, or pecans)
  - ✦ Dried fruit (e.g., raisins, currants, or cranberries)
  - ✦ Seeds, toasted or untoasted (e.g., sunflower)

- Dry quick-cooking or old-fashioned rolled oats (not instant) or bran cereal
- Cooked grains that are not too moist; millet, quinoa, or rice would work nicely.

Variations

Pear Tea Loaf

Use pears instead of apples if you have loads of pears available. If your pears are too ripe to grate, then finely chop as best you can.

Healthier Apple Tea Loaf

Change the flour, half or all, to whole-wheat pastry flour, for a little extra nutritional value.

British Scones

MAKES ABOUT 14 SCONES

▶ **NO NUTS**

Plain British-style, "no fancy add-ins" scones. Denser and smaller than you may be expecting, these are lovely with a smear of vegan margarine, your favorite jam, and a dollop of Crazy Whip Topping (page 249).

You may be wondering what it is that makes these British, and how that differs from American scones. Well, for a start, these are smaller and denser, as noted above, and what makes them that way (apart from the cutter used) is the kneading. I see you throwing your hands up in horror, as kneading a scone probably goes against everything the Food Network has ever told you! It's not a making-bread-knead-for-20-minutes knead that would make these tough and unappetizing. It is, instead, just a quick knead to incorporate all the loose

flour and make a smooth dough. Try it; you'll be amazed.

You can make these using only shortening, if you wish, but I like the touch of butteriness the margarine imparts.

2½ cups all-purpose flour
½ cup whole-wheat pastry flour
¼ cup + 1 tablespoon granulated sugar
1 tablespoon baking powder
½ teaspoon salt

¼ cup cold vegan shortening
2 tablespoons cold vegan margarine

1 cup plain soy milk

1. Preheat the oven to 400°F and line a baking sheet with parchment paper.
2. Sift together the flour, baking powder, sugar, and salt into a large bowl.
3. Using a pastry cutter (or two knives held together), cut the shortening and margarine into the dry ingredients until the mixture resembles pebbly sand.
4. Make a well, add the soy milk, and mix with a fork or your hands to form a loose dough. Turn out onto a lightly floured board and knead lightly for 30 to 60 seconds to incorporate all the loose flour and get smooth textured dough. As I noted above, it's not a long kneading, nor too vigorous.
5. Pat out the dough to 1 inch thick and, using a 2-inch-diameter cookie cutter, cut out your scones. Place about 1 inch apart on the prepared baking sheet. Re-form any leftover dough and continue cutting until all the scones are formed.
6. Bake for 12 to 15 minutes, until nicely risen and the bottoms are golden brown.
7. Remove from the oven and let cool on the sheet for 5 minutes and, if not serving warm, transfer to a wire rack to let cool completely.

Variations

Currant Scones

Soak ½ cup of dried currants in boiling water for 10 minutes, drain, and add only the currants with the soy milk.

Cinnamon Scones

Add 1 teaspoon of ground cinnamon with the flour.

Vanilla Scones

Add 1 teaspoon of vanilla extract, or the scrapings from half a vanilla bean, for more gourmet scones, with the soy milk.

Carrot and Pineapple Scones

MAKES 8 SCONES

▶ **NO NUTS**

Like a gentle version of carrot cake, these scones are great for breakfast and snacks, as they are not too sweet. They're also a handy way to use up that last little bit of leftover canned pineapple in your fridge (from the Tropical Banana Cake on page 112, for example).

2¼ cups all-purpose flour

¼ cup + 2 tablespoons granulated sugar

2 teaspoons baking powder

½ teaspoon baking soda

¼ teaspoon ground nutmeg

¼ teaspoon ground allspice

¼ teaspoon salt

¾ cup + 2 tablespoons soy creamer or soy milk (see page 16)

⅓ cup canola oil

½ teaspoon vanilla extract

¼ cup drained, canned crushed pineapple

¼ cup finely grated carrot

1. Preheat the oven to 375°F and line a baking sheet with parchment paper.

2. Sift together the ingredients from flour through salt, into a large bowl.

3. In another bowl, use a fork to whisk together the creamer, oil, and vanilla. Stir in the pineapple and carrot.

4. Add the wet ingredients to the dry and gently combine.

5. Using a ⅓-cup measuring scoop sprayed with nonstick spray, drop the scones onto the prepared baking sheet.

6. Bake for 15 to 18 minutes, until golden and lightly browned on the bottom.

7. Remove from the oven and let cool for 5 minutes on the sheet, then transfer to a wire rack to let cool completely.

Remember...

Chai Chocolate Mini Loaves

MAKES 8 MINI LOAVES

▶ **NO NUTS**

Combining the warmth of chai spices and the sweet richness of chocolate lends these cute little loaves a feeling of being a perfect combination. It's something whole and new, a divine addition to your morning cup of tea or coffee.

2 cups all-purpose flour

2 plain black tea bags, contents only

2 teaspoons baking powder

1 teaspoon ground cinnamon

½ teaspoon baking soda

½ teaspoon salt

½ teaspoon ground cardamom

½ teaspoon ground ginger

¼ teaspoon ground allspice

⅛ teaspoon freshly ground black pepper

⅛ teaspoon ground cloves

½ cup soy creamer (see page 16)

¾ cup soy milk

⅔ cup light brown sugar, packed

1 teaspoon vanilla extract

⅓ cup plain or vanilla vegan yogurt

¾ to 1 cup grated semisweet vegan chocolate (100 g bar) (see Notes)

1. Preheat the oven to 375°F and prepare the mini-loaf pans (see page 8) by spraying with nonstick spray.

2. Sift together the dry ingredients (from flour through cloves), into a large bowl.

3. In a separate bowl, whisk together the creamer, milk, brown sugar, and vanilla, then gently stir in the yogurt (lumps here are fine).

4. Add the wet ingredients to the dry and mix carefully to just combine. Fold in the grated chocolate.

5. Spoon the mixture into the prepared pans. The cups will be almost full. Bake for 20 to 25 minutes, until golden and a toothpick comes out clean. The chocolate will have melted and may stick to the toothpick, so be aware when checking.

6. Remove from the oven and let cool in the pans for 5 minutes, then transfer to a wire rack to let cool completely.

NOTES:

❖ You can also chop the chocolate very, very finely instead of grating; you want tiny little pieces so the result appears speckled with the chocolate, the tea, and the spices. Use a box grater for easiest and fastest results. It goes more easily if you grate a line of chocolate squares at a time instead of trying to grate the whole bar at once.

❖ If you don't have mini-loaf pans bake these as 12 standard-sized muffins for 18 to 22 minutes so you don't miss out on a taste sensation.

Cranberry Scones

MAKES ABOUT 10 SCONES

▶ **NO NUTS**

I usually have cranberries in the freezer to use in baking. If you buy them fresh when they're in season and freeze them yourself, they're better value than buying frozen!

The combination of creamer and coconut milk makes these a little richer and sweeter than using only soy milk. That combination counteracts the natural tartness of the cranberries.

These taste best if you allow them to cool a little, so they're still warm, just not super warm. Alternatively, serve these cold with vegan margarine and jam.

1¼ cups spelt flour
1 cup + 2 tablespoons all-purpose flour
⅓ cup granulated sugar
2 tablespoons cornstarch
2½ teaspoons baking powder
½ teaspoon baking soda
½ teaspoon salt
¼ teaspoon ground allspice

½ cup + 2 tablespoons soy creamer or soy milk (see page 16)
⅓ cup canola oil
¼ cup canned coconut milk
½ teaspoon vanilla extract

½ cup fresh or frozen cranberries
2 tablespoons dried cranberries

1. Preheat the oven to 350°F and line a baking sheet with parchment paper.

2. Combine the ingredients from flour through allspice in a large bowl and whisk together.

3. In another bowl, whisk together the creamer, oil, milk, and vanilla.

4. Add the wet ingredients to the dry and gently combine. Fold in the cranberries.

5. Using a ¼-cup measuring scoop sprayed with nonstick spray, drop the scones onto the prepared baking sheet.

6. Bake for 15 to 18 minutes, until golden and lightly browned on the bottom.

7. Remove from the oven and let cool for 5 minutes on the sheet, then transfer to a wire rack to let cool completely.

Date Biscuits

MAKES ABOUT 10 BISCUITS

▶ **NO NUTS • NO SUGAR**

These are healthy tasting and good for you, too! They're not too sweet, as all the sweetening power comes from the dates. That's right, no added sugar in these biscuits. They still have a delicate taste, even with the whole wheat they contain, and they are great with a little vegan margarine.

1¼ cups all-purpose flour
1 cup whole-wheat pastry flour
1 tablespoon baking powder
¾ teaspoon ground ginger
½ teaspoon ground cinnamon
½ teaspoon salt

3 tablespoons vegan shortening
3 tablespoons vegan margarine

½ cup rice milk
½ cup Date Paste (page 250) (see Note)

1. Preheat the oven to 425°F and line a baking sheet with parchment paper.

2. Sift together the flour, baking powder, and salt, into a large bowl.

3. Using a pastry cutter (or two knives held together), cut in the shortening and margarine, until the mixture resembles pebbly sand.

4. In a small bowl, whisk together the milk and date paste, add to dry ingredients, and mix to just combine.

5. Lightly flour a work surface and turn out the mixture. Gently shape into a rough circle about 1 inch thick. Using a 2½-inch cookie cutter, or a glass of about the same diameter,

cut out your biscuits. Gently reshape any remaining dough and repeat.

6. Transfer to the prepared baking sheet and bake for 12 to 14 minutes, until the bottoms are lightly browned and the tops firm.

7. Remove from the oven and let cool on the sheet for 5 minutes, then serve hot, or transfer to a wire rack to let cool completely. Serve cold.

NOTE:

❖ Two of my testers found the perfect way to prepare the date paste for making the biscuits! Make it the night before and leave in the fridge overnight; it is then super quick and easy to throw the biscuits together in the morning for a not-too-sweet breakfast. Thanks, Melissa and Elizabeth!

Dundee Loaf

MAKES ONE 9-INCH LOAF

▶ NO SOY

The city of Dundee, in central Scotland, is traditionally known as the city of the three J's—journalism, jute, and jam. The jam in this instance is marmalade (traditionally Seville Orange). Over time, "Dundee" in the title of a recipe has come to indicate there's marmalade in there somewhere! This loaf is lighter than Dundee Cake (a traditional Scottish fruit cake), which it is loosely based on, but the same flavors still come shining through.

Dundee Cake is traditionally made with a single-malt scotch whiskey, but I don't want you to blow your budget, so use whatever whisky you have on hand.

1¼ **cups all-purpose flour**

1 **cup whole-wheat pastry flour**
¾ **cup granulated sugar**
½ **cup ground almonds**
2 **teaspoons baking powder**
¾ **teaspoon baking soda**

¼ **cup candied mixed peel**
¼ **cup dried currants**

1 **cup rice milk**
¼ **cup canola oil**
¼ **cup three-fruit or any other marmalade**
2 **tablespoons whisky (see Note)**
2 **tablespoons freshly squeezed lemon juice (1 medium lemon)**

10 **to 12 blanched whole almonds, for garnish**

1. Preheat the oven to 375°F and line a 9-inch loaf pan with parchment paper.

2. In a large bowl, whisk together the dry ingredients (from flour through baking soda). Add the peel and currants and toss to coat.

3. In a separate bowl, whisk together the milk, oil, marmalade, whisky, and lemon juice until smooth with no big lumps of marmalade.

4. Add the wet ingredients to the dry and stir to just combine.

5. Scrape into the prepared pan and place the whole blanched almonds decoratively on the top of the loaf.

6. Bake for 45 to 50 minutes, until a toothpick comes out clean. Remove from the oven and let cool in the pan for 10 minutes, then transfer to a wire rack to let cool completely. Slice once cool.

NOTE:

❖ For a nonalcoholic version, use apple juice in place of the whisky.

Gingerbread

MAKES ONE 9-INCH LOAF

▶ NO NUTS

This spicy, warm loaf is also good made as mini loaves or muffins (extra festive, too), and just screams "Christmastime" at you. Slices of this are perfect for sharing with friends or using as edible gifts. If you don't like crystallized ginger, leave it out; the recipe works well that way, too. My younger daughter prefers it that way.

To make as muffins or mini loaves please refer to page 34 for guidelines.

> 1½ cups all-purpose flour
> ¾ cup whole-wheat pastry flour
> 2 tablespoons cornstarch
> 1½ teaspoons ground ginger
> 1 teaspoon baking soda
> 1 teaspoon baking powder
> 1 teaspoon ground cinnamon
> ¼ teaspoon salt
>
> ½ cup crystallized ginger, chopped finely (optional)
>
> 1 cup soy milk
> ⅓ cup light brown sugar, packed
> ⅓ cup canola oil
> ⅓ cup pure maple syrup
> ⅓ cup blackstrap molasses (see Note)
> 1 tablespoon grated fresh ginger
>
> 1 recipe Sugar Glaze (page 252), ginger variation (optional)

1. Preheat the oven to 375°F and line a 9-inch loaf pan with parchment paper.

2. Sift together the ingredients from flour through salt, into a large bowl. Add the crystallized ginger and toss to coat.

3. In a large bowl, whisk together the soy milk, brown sugar, oil, maple syrup, molasses, and grated ginger until smooth.

4. Add the wet ingredients to the dry and mix to just combine.

5. Pour the mixture into the prepared pan and bake for 50 to 55 minutes, until a toothpick comes out clean.

6. Remove from the oven and let cool in the pan for 10 minutes before turning out onto a wire rack.

7. Glaze when warm for a thin, crustlike glaze; or once cool for a more icinglike glaze.

NOTE:
- ❖ I love the flavor and color blackstrap molasses brings to this. If you prefer a different grade of molasses, use that instead.

Jaffa (Chocolate and Orange Marble) Loaf

MAKES ONE 9-INCH LOAF

▶ NO NUTS

If you're not from New Zealand, maybe you've never had a Jaffa, a round ball of chocolate encased in an orange-flavored candy shell—used for rolling down the aisles in movie theaters and for bribing children to be on their best behavior. They taste good but, alas, are not vegan, unlike this loaf, which tastes great and, as a bonus, looks perfect for Halloween!

This may seem like a lot of work with the two batters, but really, the most time-consuming part of the loaf is the baking. Mixing more than one load of batter doesn't take much more time, just a little more memory.

This is great with no topping—my children prefer it that way—but if you want to decorate it a little, a drizzle of Ganache-Style Chocolate (page 252) or Drizzle Icing (page 251), or even some of both, works really well.

ORANGE BATTER

1 cup soy milk

1 teaspoon apple cider vinegar

¾ cup + 2 tablespoons all-purpose flour

¾ cup granulated sugar

¼ cup whole-wheat pastry flour

1 teaspoon baking powder

½ teaspoon salt

2 tablespoons canola oil

1 tablespoon orange zest (1 medium orange)

1½ teaspoons orange extract

A few drops of vegan orange food coloring (optional)

CHOCOLATE BATTER

1 cup + 2 tablespoons soy milk

1 teaspoon apple cider vinegar

¾ cup all-purpose flour

½ cup + 2 tablespoons granulated sugar

¼ cup whole-wheat pastry flour

3 tablespoons unsweetened cocoa powder

1 teaspoon baking powder

½ teaspoon salt

2 tablespoons canola oil

1 teaspoon vanilla extract

½ teaspoon chocolate extract, or more vanilla extract

1. Preheat the oven to 350°F and line a 9-inch loaf pan with parchment paper.

2. Using two small bowls, stir together the soy milk and vinegar for each batter and set aside, to curdle.

3. Sift the dry ingredients for each mixture into its own respective bowl: for the orange batter, the flour, baking powder, salt, and sugar; for the chocolate batter, the flour, cocoa powder, baking powder, salt, and sugar.

4. To one of the bowls with the soy milk mixture, add the oil, orange extract, zest, and food coloring for the orange batter, and mix well.

5. To the second soy milk mixture, add the oil, vanilla, and chocolate extracts and mix well.

6. Mix the liquid ingredients for the orange batter into the dry ingredients for the same, stirring to just combine.

7. Mix the liquid ingredients for the chocolate batter into the dry ingredients for the same, stirring to just combine.

8. Using a large spoon or a measuring cup, spoon half of the orange batter into one end of the loaf pan. Spoon half of the chocolate batter in the other end of the loaf pan, using a spoon if necessary to hold the orange half back so the batters remain separate.

9. Spoon the remaining orange batter on top of the chocolate already in the pan, and the remaining chocolate batter on top of the orange, in a checkerboard-type pattern.

10. Once the pan is filled, use a chopstick or knife to lightly swirl or marble the batter. I like to start at one corner and go up and down the pan lengthwise four or five times, then finish with a random swirl.

11. Bake for 55 to 60 minutes, until a toothpick comes out clean.

12. Remove from the oven and let cool in the pan for 10 minutes, then turn out onto a wire rack to let cool completely.

Variations

Mint Marble Loaf

In the orange batter, substitute mint extract for the orange, and finely chopped mint leaves for the orange zest. Instead of the orange color, use a few drops of vegan green food coloring.

Berry Marble Loaf

In the orange batter, use only ¾ cup soy milk, adding ¼ cup of Strawberry Sauce (page 94) when the oil is added. Also, substitute strawberry extract for the orange, and leave out the zest and the food coloring.

• •

Lemon and Blueberry Biscuits

MAKES 12 BISCUITS

▶ NO NUTS

Slightly sour, slightly sweet, and always good, make these biscuits into shortcake to impress with the addition of Crazy Whip Topping (page 249), and Blueberry Sauce (page 109). Add fresh blueberries as a garnish if they're in season!

> 2 cups all-purpose flour
> ½ cup granulated sugar
> ¼ cup cornmeal (see page 15)
> 1 tablespoon baking powder
> ½ teaspoon baking soda
> ½ teaspoon salt

> ¼ cup vegan margarine
> 3 tablespoons vegan shortening

> 1 tablespoon lemon zest (1 medium lemon)
> ¼ cup fresh or frozen blueberries (try to get the small wild ones)

> 2 tablespoons freshly squeezed lemon juice (1 medium lemon)
> ½ cup soy creamer or soy milk (see page 16)

> Soy creamer or milk, for brushing (optional)
> Granulated Sugar, for sprinkling (optional)

1. Preheat the oven to 425°F and line a baking sheet with parchment paper.

2. Sift together the ingredients from flour through salt into a large bowl.

3. Using a pastry cutter (or two knives held together), cut in the margarine and shortening until the mixture resembles coarse bread crumbs. Add the zest and berries, and toss to coat.

4. Form a well in the dry ingredients; add the lemon juice and creamer and mix gently to form a loose dough.

5. Gently pat out the dough on a lightly floured board to about 1½ inches thick. Using a 2-inch cookie cutter, cut out rounds and place on the prepared baking sheet. Gather together the leftover dough, gently re-form, and cut out.

6. Once all dough is cut out, brush the tops of the biscuits with the creamer, and sprinkle with a little sugar, if desired.

7. Bake for 10 to 12 minutes, or until golden with lightly browned bottoms.

8. Remove from the oven and let cool on the sheet for 5 minutes before serving hot or letting cool on a wire rack.

Lemon and Blueberry Shortcake

Once biscuits are completely cool, cut in half and place the bottom section on a plate. Spoon on a decent amount of Crazy Whip Topping (page 249) (use your discretion, but I think a rounded tablespoon is a good amount), drizzle with a little Blueberry Sauce (page 109), and place the top section on at a jaunty angle.

Lime and Poppy Seed Loaf

MAKES ONE 9-INCH LOAF

▶ **NO NUTS**

Zippy, zesty, not too sweet with a pleasant crunch, this is a nice anytime loaf. I think it's especially perfect in the summer with a long cool drink, sitting in a lazy chair, on the deck while you enjoy the sunshine. Shut your eyes, you're there.

I haven't put a glaze or icing to go with this one, as I don't think it needs it. If you want to add something, some Drizzle Icing (page 251) or Sugar Glaze (page 252) would do the trick.

⅔ cup granulated sugar

½ cup soy creamer (see page 16)

½ cup soy milk

¼ cup unsweetened applesauce

¼ cup lime juice (see Note)

3 tablespoons canola oil

1 tablespoon lime zest (see Note)

1 cup all-purpose flour

1 cup whole-wheat pastry flour

2 teaspoons baking powder

1 teaspoon baking soda

½ teaspoon salt

⅓ cup poppy seeds

1. Preheat the oven to 350°F and line a 9-inch loaf pan with parchment paper.

2. In a large bowl, combine sugar, creamer, soy milk, applesauce, juice, oil, and zest and mix well.

3. Sift together the flour, baking powder, baking soda, and salt into another bowl. Add the poppy seeds and toss to coat.

4. Pour the dry ingredients into the wet and gently fold in to just combine.

5. Pour the mixture into the prepared pan and bake for 40 to 45 minutes, or until a toothpick comes out clean.

6. Remove from the oven and let cool for 10 minutes in the pan, then turn out onto a wire rack to let cool completely..

7. If using a glaze or icing, ensure the loaf is completely cool first.

NOTE:

❖ For the zest and juice, you'll need 1 or 2 medium limes, depending on their size and how juicy they are.

Variation

Other Citrus and Poppy Seed Loaf

Needless to say, you can change this one any way you want by changing the citrus fruit. Orange, lemon, or even grapefruit would all be nice.

Rhubarb, Walnut, and Ginger Tea Loaf

MAKES ONE 9-INCH LOAF

I'm a rhubarb fan. If you've read my blog at all, you may have noticed. I've found it's one of those things you either love or you hate, and I'm a firm lover. In this recipe, the tartness of the rhubarb with the sweet sharpness of the ginger and the crunch of the walnuts come together. It's a combination that works for me!

This is a very dense, heavy, filling loaf with a lovely texture, if that's possible. Really good warm, or cold with a smear of vegan margarine.

1 cup all-purpose flour

¾ cup whole-wheat pastry flour

½ cup granulated sugar

2½ teaspoons baking powder

½ teaspoon baking soda

1½ teaspoons ground ginger

½ teaspoon ground cinnamon

½ teaspoon salt

1 medium stalk rhubarb, rinsed, trimmed, and chopped finely (about ¾ cup) (see Note)

½ cup roughly chopped walnuts

⅓ cup roughly chopped crystallized ginger (optional)

1 cup soy milk

½ cup vegan sour cream

¼ cup agave nectar

½ teaspoon vanilla extract

1 recipe Sugar Glaze (page 252) (optional)

1. Preheat the oven to 375°F and line a 9-inch loaf pan with parchment paper.

2. Sift together the dry ingredients (from flour through salt), into a large bowl. Toss in the rhubarb, walnuts, and ginger (if using), to coat.

3. In a separate bowl, whisk together the soy milk, sour cream, agave nectar, and vanilla. This won't be entirely smooth.

4. Add the mixed liquid ingredients to the dry and mix to just combine.

5. Pour into the prepared pan and smooth top. Bake for 40 to 45 minutes, until a toothpick comes out clean.

6. Remove from the oven and let cool in pan for 10 minutes, then turn out onto a wire rack to let cool completely.

7. Glaze, if desired, as the loaf cools.

NOTE:

❖ Ensure the rhubarb is chopped into small enough pieces to enable it to cook in the oven as the loaf bakes. Always remove any leaves or leaf bases from the stalks, as these are poisonous.

Spelt Coconut Chip Biscuits

MAKES ABOUT 9 BISCUITS

▶ NO NUTS • NO WHEAT

I've found that I really like the combination of spelt flour and coconut oil. Maybe it's the slight nutty sweetness of both that seems to complement each other, or maybe it's just that they are fated to be together. Anyhow, this pairing works well in all sorts of recipes, including this one! These biscuits are sweet without being overly so, and are lovely hot out of the oven or cool; either way, a little vegan margarine doesn't hurt. They also reheat well:

Wrap in tinfoil and place in a 350°F oven for about 10 minutes.

If you'd prefer to make these as drop biscuits, proceed as directed until the recipe asks you to turn the mixture onto the floured work surface. Instead, using a ⅓-cup measuring scoop, drop onto the prepared baking sheet. You should get the same yield and use the same baking time.

½ cup unsweetened shredded coconut

2 cups spelt flour
2 tablespoons light brown sugar, packed
1 tablespoon baking powder
¼ teaspoon salt

3 tablespoons solid coconut oil, room temperature
3 tablespoons vegan margarine

½ cup vegan mini chocolate chips

½ cup + 2 tablespoons soy milk
1 tablespoon brown rice syrup

1. Preheat the oven to 400°F and line a baking sheet with parchment paper.

2. In a small nonstick skillet over medium heat, toast the coconut for 3 to 5 minutes, until lightly golden. Stir frequently, and if it starts to look brown, remove from the heat immediately. Transfer to a small bowl and put into the fridge for 5 minutes to cool (otherwise it will melt the fat too soon!)

3. In a large bowl, whisk together the flour, salt, brown sugar, and baking powder, ensuring there are no sugar lumps. Add the cooled coconut and whisk to combine.

4. Using a pastry cutter (or two knives held together), cut in the oil and margarine, until the mixture resembles pebbly sand.

5. Stir in the chocolate chips to distribute evenly.

6. Make a well in the center of the mixture and pour in the milk and rice syrup. Mix to just combine.

7. Lightly flour a work surface and turn out the mixture. Shape into a circle about 1 inch thick. Use a 2-inch cookie cutter (or the top of a cup/glass or what-have-you) to cut out your biscuits. Gently reshape any remaining dough and repeat.

8. Transfer to the prepared baking sheet and bake for 12 to 14 minutes, until the bottoms are lightly browned and the tops are firm.

9. Remove from the oven and let cool on the sheet for 5 minutes, then turn out onto a wire rack. Serve hot or cold.

NOTE:

❖ Some of my testers made these without toasting the coconut first. I prefer it toasted as the flavor is richer somehow, but if you are pushed for time or would rather not, it's okay to leave out that step and just add the plain coconut.

Spiced Raisin Whole-Wheat Scones

MAKES ABOUT 9 SCONES

▶ **NO NUTS • NO SOY**

Don't be frightened by the ancho chile powder you see listed as an ingredient in these. It's a very mild powder made by grinding up dried ancho chiles and is spicy as opposed to hot. It adds a nice background dimension to the scones, complementing the pie spice without adding heat.

These are great either hot out of the oven, or cold, smeared with a little vegan margarine.

3 tablespoons raisins

3 tablespoons golden raisins

⅓ cup boiling water

2 cups whole-wheat pastry flour

3 tablespoons granulated sugar (see Note)

2½ teaspoons baking powder

¼ teaspoon baking soda

½ teaspoon pie spice (see page 19)

¼ teaspoon ancho chile powder

¼ teaspoon salt

½ cup + 1 tablespoon rice milk

3 tablespoons canola oil

½ teaspoon vanilla extract

Turbinado sugar, for sprinkling (optional)

1. Preheat the oven to 375°F and line a baking sheet with parchment paper.

2. Soak the raisins, covered, in the water for 15 minutes, then drain, reserving the raisins and 3 tablespoons of the soaking water.

3. Sift together the ingredients from flour through salt, into a large bowl.

4. In another bowl, whisk together the reserved raisin-soaking water, milk, oil, and vanilla. Stir in the drained raisins. Add the wet ingredients to the dry and gently combine.

5. Using a ¼-cup measuring scoop sprayed with nonstick spray, drop the scones onto the prepared baking sheet. If desired, sprinkle with a little turbinado sugar.

6. Bake for 15 to 18 minutes, until golden and lightly browned on the bottom.

7. Remove from the oven and let cool for 5 minutes on the sheet prior to removing.

NOTE:

❖ The stated amount of sugar assumes you are sprinkling the scones with turbinado sugar. If you prefer not to do this, or know you like sweeter scones, increase the granulated sugar to ¼ cup.

Straight-Up Spelt Banana Bread

MAKES ONE 9-INCH LOAF

▶ **NO NUTS • NO WHEAT**

My children always want add-ins in their banana bread, usually chocolate chips but sometimes blueberries, and although I sometimes add them, this time I haven't. I don't think this bread needs any. If you mash the bananas roughly so there are still some pea-size chunks, you get banana as the add-in. Although, if your preference is for smooth banana bread, then keep mashing. If you want to add up to ½ cup of chocolate chips, nuts, raisins or something similar, then who am I to stop you?

If you're anything like me, you often have ripe bananas frozen in chunks, waiting for a smoothie with their name on it. If not, it's a good habit to get into, for this banana bread as well as smoothies! This use of the frozen banana makes the liquid portion of the mixture smooth, creamy, and airy, which translates into a light and airy final product; it does, however, make the batter a little colder, hence the slightly longer baking time and the help of a little more baking powder.

3 cups spelt flour

3½ teaspoons baking powder

½ teaspoon salt

½ teaspoon ground cinnamon

¼ teaspoon ground nutmeg

2 frozen ripe bananas (chunks are easier on your blender) (see Note)

½ cup canola oil

½ cup soy milk

1½ teaspoons vanilla extract

½ teaspoon banana extract, if you have it, otherwise more vanilla extract

⅓ cup granulated sugar

⅓ cup light brown sugar, packed

2 very ripe bananas, mashed roughly

1. Preheat the oven to 350°F and line a 9-inch loaf pan with parchment paper.

2. Sift together the ingredients from flour through nutmeg, into a large bowl. Make a well in the center and set aside.

3. Blend the frozen banana chunks, oil, milk, and extracts until smooth and very fluffy. Add the sugars and blend again to incorporate.

4. Pour the blended mixture (scrape the blender out to get everything) into the well in the dry ingredients, add the mashed banana, and fold to just combine.

5. Pour the batter into the prepared pan and bake for about 1 hour, or until a tooth-pick comes out clean. If you find the top of your loaf is browning too quickly, cover with a sheet of parchment paper.

6. Remove from the oven and let the loaf cool for 10 minutes, then turn out onto a wire rack to cool completely prior to slicing.

NOTE:

❖ Freeze any excess ripe bananas you may have, peeled and cut into 1-inch chunks, in little plastic bags, for ease of access for recipes like this and for smoothies.

Sunny Sunflower Tea Loaf

MAKES ONE 9-INCH LOAF

▶ **NO NUTS • NO SOY**

Sunflower seeds are great. They're a source of protein, healthy fats, and zinc, and they taste good, too! This loaf makes it easier to eat more of them. This is sunny like a glorious summer day, filled with fields of yellow flowers nodding in the warm breeze.

½ cup toasted sunflower seeds

⅓ cup sunflower or canola oil
½ cup granulated sugar
2 tablespoons agave nectar
1¼ cups rice milk

1 cup all-purpose flour
¾ cup whole-wheat pastry flour
½ cup yellow corn flour
2 tablespoons cornstarch
2 teaspoons baking powder
1 teaspoon ground cinnamon
½ teaspoon baking soda
½ teaspoon salt

¼ cup sunflower seeds (see Note)
¼ cup raisins
¼ cup finely chopped dried apricots

2 tablespoons sunflower seeds, for sprinkling (optional)

1. Preheat the oven to 375°F and line 9-inch loaf pan with parchment paper.

2. Grind the ½ cup of the sunflower seeds to a fine meal in your food processor (or in batches in a spice grinder). Keep a close eye on this, or you'll have seed butter!

3. In a large bowl, combine the ground seeds, oil, sugar, agave nectar, and milk. Mix well to combine.

4. Sift together the dry ingredients (from flour through salt) into the milk mixture and mix.

5. Fold in the dried fruit and seeds, and spoon the mixture into prepared pan. Sprinkle with sunflower seeds, if desired.

6. Bake for 45 to 50 minutes, until golden and a toothpick comes out clean.

7. Remove from the oven and let cool in the pan for 10 minutes, then turn out onto a wire rack to let cool completely.

NOTE:

❖ If you'd like to toast your seeds prior to adding to the loaf, go right ahead. I prefer them to be toasted, but many of my testers left them plain and enjoyed the loaf perfectly as it was.

Variation

Pumpkin-Patch Tea Loaf

Instead of sunflower seeds, use pumpkin seeds. Replace the sunflower oil with canola (or use it anyway; it's pretty mild), replace the agave with blackstrap molasses. In the dry ingredients, replace the yellow corn flour with another ¼ cup of all-purpose flour and ¼ cup of whole-wheat pastry flour, and use pie spice (see page 19) instead of the cinnamon. Finish by substituting dried cranberries for the dried apricots. How very seasonal!

Cakes and Cupcakes

Balsamic Berry Bundt Cake

Berry-Infused Cupcakes 📷

Citrus Bundt Cake 📷

Coffee and Caramel Cupcakes 📷

Cola Chocolate Cupcakes

Espresso Chocolate-Chip Coffee Cake 📷

Green Tea and Pistachio Cake

Individual New World Simnel Cakes

Lamingtons

Mango, Pineapple, and Mint Upside-Down Cake 📷

Nut-Topped Almond and Hazelnut Bundt Cake

PB&J Marble Cupcakes with Peanut Buttercream

Secret-Ingredient Chocolate Cake with Blueberry Cream

Spiced Raisin Breakfast Cake

Sticky Toffee Pudding Cake

Tropical Banana Cake with Coconut Ice Icing 📷

Vanilla Bean Cupcakes 📷

Zebra Cake

BIG CAKES, SMALL cakes, whatever your preference I've tried to include something that will tickle your fancy, and the fancy of whoever you're baking for, if it's not yourself.

Cupcakes are more than just mini cakes, and more than fancy muffins! So let no one tell you otherwise. These individual portioned cakes have a higher icing-to-cake ratio than does a large cake, perfect for you icing lovers, and are nowhere near as healthy as muffins. As I said previously, I like my cupcake liners filled to the top to make twelve large cupcakes, but some of my testers preferred to fill them only two-thirds full and make eighteen small ones, which is why you see both yields listed on each recipe.

Bundt cakes are fun! These circular cakes with the hole in the middle look pretty and need very little by way of icing to make them look fancy. If you don't have a Bundt pan and if the recipe calls for one, bake the mixture in two 9-inch layer cake pans instead. You could even bake the cake this way if you wanted to add icing to a Bundt recipe to make it even fancier for an occasion.

Most of these cakes are made for serving cold, usually with icing of some description (see each individual recipe, or mix and match as desired), though can be served warm out of the oven. If reheating to serve a cake warm, a microwave works just fine.

Most nonvegan cakes are made by the creaming method (page 6) so the fats and the eggs, which are used for both binding and leavening, combine properly. As there are no eggs in vegan baking, vegan cakes turn out just as well if made with oil and the blending method. Both methods were used with great success in creating the items in this chapter.

Cakes and cupcakes are best stored covered, at room temperature, once completely cooled and iced. If the icing is temperature sensitive (many are), the weather or room is hot, or the cake is not being served for a while, then it would be sensible to put it in the fridge to save all your hard work from becoming a mess. If your cake has been stored in the fridge, return it to room temperature prior to serving, for ease of slicing and for the best taste and texture.

Balsamic Berry Bundt Cake

SERVES 10 TO 12

▶ **NO NUTS**

How often do you see posh restaurants serving berries doused in a balsamic vinegar reduction and sugar, as a special summer dessert? I'm sure loads of great chefs have done it on the Food Network, too, so why not a variation on the theme in my book?

I ask you to grease the pan for this cake (maybe the only time in the whole book), as the berries tend to stick! Also, please ensure you place a baking sheet under your Bundt pan to catch any unintentional spillage. I didn't have any, but one of my testers was cursing my name as she cleaned her oven!

2 cups fresh or frozen mixed berries
½ cup granulated sugar
2 tablespoons water
1 tablespoon white balsamic vinegar

2 cups soy milk
2 tablespoons white balsamic vinegar

2½ cups all-purpose flour
½ cup cornmeal (see page 15)
1 cup granulated sugar
4 teaspoons baking powder
½ teaspoon salt
½ teaspoon ground cardamom

½ cup canola oil
2 teaspoons vanilla extract

Confectioners' sugar, for dusting (optional)

1. Preheat the oven to 350°F and thoroughly grease a 10-inch Bundt pan with vegan margarine or shortening. Place the Bundt pan on a baking sheet.

2. Combine the berries, granulated sugar, water, and vinegar in a medium saucepan and bring to a boil, stirring until the granulated sugar is dissolved. Lower the heat to medium and boil, stirring occasionally, for about 12 minutes, until the mixture has reduced by half and thickened. Remove from the heat and let cool for 5 minutes prior to pouring evenly into the bottom of the prepared Bundt pan.

3. In a small bowl, combine the soy milk and vinegar, and set aside to curdle for 5 minutes.

4. Sift together the ingredients from flour through cardamom, into a large bowl.

5. Add the oil and vanilla to the soy milk mixture, and then add this to the dry ingredients. Mix to just combine.

6. Carefully pour the batter into prepared pan, on top of the berries. Using a chopstick or knife, gently swirl the batter to incorporate the berries into the batter. You're not wanting big fruit swirls through the batter, just to incorporate the fruit layer a little. Smooth the top.

7. Bake for 45 to 50 minutes, until well risen, golden, and a toothpick comes out clean, though if the berry mixture sticks to your toothpick, ignore it—only test the batter.

8. Remove from the oven and let cool in the pan for 10 minutes, then invert to let cool on a wire rack. If any of the berry mixture remains in the bottom of the Bundt pan, spoon it onto any bald patches on top of the cake and allow to cool.

9. Once completely cool, and prior to serving, dust with a little confectioners' sugar, if desired.

Berry-Infused Cupcakes 📷

MAKES 12 LARGE OR 18 SMALL CUPCAKES

▶ **NO NUTS**

I've made these using strawberries, as they give the prettiest results. You can make them with blueberries, too, but the result does tend to look a little greenish purple. If you'd like to substitute raspberries, that would be a nice option, as well.

1 cup soy milk
1 tablespoon apple cider vinegar

2 cups all-purpose flour
2 tablespoons cornstarch
2 teaspoons baking powder
½ teaspoon baking soda
½ teaspoon salt

⅔ cup granulated sugar
½ cup Strawberry Sauce (recipe follows), at room temperature
3 tablespoons canola oil
1 teaspoon vanilla extract
½ teaspoon strawberry extract, or more vanilla extract

1 recipe Buttercream, More or Less (page 249) (see Note)
6 strawberries, cut, for garnish

1. Preheat the oven to 375°F and line twelve or eighteen cups of your muffin pan with cupcake liners, as desired. (If not using some of the cups, fill them halfway with water so the pan won't warp.)

2. In a large bowl, combine the soy milk and vinegar, and set aside to curdle for 5 minutes.

3. Sift the dry ingredients (from flour through salt), into another bowl.

4. Whisk the sugar, sauce, oil, and extracts into the soy milk mixture.

5. Add the dry ingredients to the wet, fold in to just combine, breaking up any large lumps.

6. Spoon into the prepared muffin pans. If using twelve cups, they will be full. Bake for 20 to 22 minutes, until a toothpick comes out clean. For more slightly smaller cupcakes, fill eighteen liners two-thirds of the way and bake for 18 to 20 minutes.

7. Remove from the oven and let cool in the pans for 5 minutes, then transfer to a wire rack to let cool completely.

8. Once they are completely cool, pipe a swirl of buttercream on each cupcake, and decorate the tops with sliced strawberries in an attractive pattern, or decorate as you wish.

NOTE:

❖ If you make the Buttercream, More or Less (page 249) with strawberry sauce substituted for both the extracts, you get a lovely pretty pale pink icing that is also subtly flavored.

Strawberry Sauce

MAKES ABOUT 1¼ TO 1½ CUPS SAUCE

▶ **NO NUTS • NO SOY • NO SUGAR • NO WHEAT**

Perfect as a topping for ice cream or oatmeal, as well as in these cupcakes!

4 cups frozen or fresh strawberries
¼ cup water
¼ cup agave nectar

1. Combine all the ingredients in a medium saucepan and heat over medium to high heat, then boil, stirring occasionally, until thick and syrupy and the volume has reduced to half (about 20 minutes after the berries have started to boil).

2. Let cool to room temperature and blend until smooth. Pass through a sieve to remove the seeds, if desired. Store the sauce in a covered container in the fridge until required. Return any refrigerated sauce to room temperature prior to using.

Variation

Raspberry Sauce
As for strawberry sauce, but with fresh or frozen raspberries.

Citrus Bundt Cake 📷

SERVES 10 TO 12

▶ **NO NUTS**

It's like a two-layer cake, baked in layers! This is a fresh-tasting, light-textured cake, perfect for afternoon tea or as a light dessert. You can dress it up, if you like, with some glaze or icing, but I prefer to leave it plain, or to just shake a little confectioners' sugar on top.

¼ cup candied mixed peel

ORANGE LAYER
1½ cups all-purpose flour
¾ cup granulated sugar
2 teaspoons baking powder
½ teaspoon salt
¼ teaspoon ground nutmeg

1 cup soy milk
¼ cup canola oil
¼ cup orange juice
1 tablespoon orange zest (½ medium orange)

1 teaspoon vanilla extract
1 teaspoon orange extract

¼ cup three-fruit or other marmalade, melted (see Notes)

LEMON LAYER
1½ cups all-purpose flour
¾ cup granulated sugar
2 teaspoons baking powder
½ teaspoon salt

1¼ cups + 1 tablespoon soy milk
¼ cup canola oil
2 tablespoons freshly squeezed lemon juice (1 medium lemon)
1 tablespoon lemon zest (1 medium lemon)
1 teaspoon vanilla extract
1 teaspoon lemon extract

1 recipe Drizzle Icing (page 251) or Sugar Glaze (page 252), or confectioners' sugar, for dusting (optional)

1. Preheat the oven to 350°F and grease a 10-inch Bundt pan with canola oil or vegan margarine (the candied peel may stick).

2. Sprinkle the mixed peel evenly around the bottom of the pan.

Prepare the orange layer

3. Sift together the ingredients from flour through nutmeg, into a large bowl.

4. In a smaller bowl, whisk together the ingredients from soy milk through orange extract.

5. Pour the wet ingredients into the dry ingredients and mix to just combine.

6. Pour the batter into the prepared pan and smooth the top.

7. Drizzle the warm melted marmalade randomly over the batter. It won't cover the whole area, so spread it as evenly as you can.

Prepare the lemon layer

8. Work quickly, so the orange layer doesn't sit for too long:

9. Sift together the ingredients from flour through salt, into a large bowl.

10. In a small bowl, whisk together the ingredients from soy milk through lemon extract.

11. Pour the wet ingredients into the dry ingredients and mix to just combine.

12. Pour the lemon mixture into the half-filled Bundt pan and smooth the top.

13. Bake for 45 to 50 minutes, until the cake looks golden, the edges are pulling away from the sides and look lightly browned, and a toothpick comes out clean.

14. Remove from the oven and let cool in the pan for 10 minutes, then turn out onto a wire rack to let cool completely.

15. Once cool, ice with Drizzle Icing or Sugar Glaze, or dust with a little confectioners' sugar.

NOTES:

❖ To melt the marmalade, either heat gently in a small pan over medium heat, stirring constantly, or heat in 15-second bursts on high in the microwave, until liquid. Make sure it is not too hot when you drizzle it over the orange layer. Just warm is best, otherwise the marmalade will sink to the bottom and not be suspended between the layers.

❖ One of my testers, Kate, had great success with baking this in two 9-inch layer cake pans and sandwiching the cakes together with marmalade. She notes, however, that the layers took differing times to bake when made this way, and asked that I tell you that more care would be needed if you decided to make it this way, too.

Coffee and Caramel Cupcakes 📷

MAKES 12 LARGE OR 18 SMALL CUPCAKES

▶ **NO NUTS**

I had to make this recipe five times to get it right, changing the format, the topping, the cake part—everything. I couldn't seem to get it to work, but I persevered and finally ended up here! My tasters really enjoyed it (even the failures), so it has been worthwhile! Try it and let me know what you think!

> 1 cup dark brown sugar, packed
> ¾ cup vegan margarine, room temperature
>
> ¼ cup (2½ ounces) tofu, firm silken (vacuum-packed)
> 5 tablespoons instant coffee dissolved in ½ cup boiling water, or ½ cup very strong espresso
> ¼ cup soy creamer (see page 16)
> 1 teaspoon caramel or vanilla extract
>
> 2 cups all-purpose flour
> 2 tablespoons cornstarch
> ½ teaspoon salt
> 2½ teaspoons baking powder
> 1 teaspoon ground cinnamon
>
> 1 recipe Caramel Sauce (recipe follows)
>
> 1 recipe Buttercream, More or Less (page 249), made with coffee instead of extracts, if desired

1. Preheat the oven to 375°F and line twelve or eighteen cups of your muffin pan with cupcake liners, as desired. (If not using some of the cups, fill them halfway with water so the pan won't warp.)

2. In a large bowl, cream the brown sugar and margarine until fluffy.

3. Using a blender or food processor, blend together the tofu, coffee, creamer, and caramel extract. Add the blended ingredients to the creamed mixture and stir to combine. It will look curdled at this point but that's fine.

4. Sift together the ingredients from flour through cinnamon into the creamed mixture and stir until smooth, to form the batter.

5. Spoon into the prepared muffin pan. If using twelve cups, they will be full. Bake for 20 to 25 minutes, until a toothpick comes out clean. For more slightly smaller cupcakes, fill eighteen liners two-thirds of the way and bake for 18 to 20 minutes.

6. Remove from the oven and let cool in the pans for 5 minutes, then transfer to a wire rack to let cool completely.

7. Spread the top of the cooled cupcakes with a generous spread of the Buttercream, More or Less and drizzle with the Caramel Sauce in a decorative crosshatch pattern.

8. Store the cupcakes in the fridge to set the icing and caramel. Dust with a little confectioners' sugar, prior to serving, if desired.

★ Caramel Sauce

MAKES ABOUT ⅓ CUP SAUCE

▶ NO NUTS • NO WHEAT

Although this sauce is specifically for the Coffee and Caramel Cupcakes, please don't limit it to just those! It's perfect for drizzling on cakes in place of Ganache-Style Chocolate or Drizzle Icing or for using as an ice-cream topping!

2 tablespoons vegan margarine
2 tablespoons dark brown sugar, packed
1 tablespoon brown rice syrup
1½ tablespoons soy creamer (see page 16)

1. Combine all ingredients for the sauce in a small saucepan over medium-high heat, stirring constantly until everything is melted.

2. Bring to a boil, lower the heat to medium-low, and boil, stirring frequently, for 8 to 10 minutes, until thickened and syrupy.

3. Keep warm until required. This sauce may be made in advance, and gently rewarmed over low heat when required.

Cola Chocolate Cupcakes

MAKES 12 LARGE OR 18 SMALL CUPCAKES

▶ NO NUTS

This is a bit of an homage to Nigella Lawson, the "Cola Cooking Queen" of Europe! It isn't a veganization of any recipe of hers or anything quite so stalkerlike; I just took for inspiration the idea of using cola in baking.

Don't feed to anyone who can't handle the caffeine or the sugar!

1½ cups cola (see Notes)
1½ cups + 2 tablespoons all-purpose flour
¼ cup unsweetened cocoa powder
3 tablespoons cornstarch
2 teaspoons baking powder
1 teaspoon baking soda
½ teaspoon salt

¾ cup granulated sugar
⅓ cup vegan margarine

1 teaspoon vanilla extract

1 recipe Ganache-Style Chocolate (page 252) or Buttercream, More or Less (page 249) (optional)

1. If not using half-flat leftovers (see Notes), pour out your cola, stir around a bit, and sit on the counter at room temperature for about 30 minutes to go a little flat. You still need some bubbles, but not as many as when first poured.

2. Preheat the oven to 375°F and line twelve or eighteen cups of your muffin pan with cupcake liners, as desired. (If not using some of the cups, fill them halfway with water so the pan won't warp.)

3. Sift the dry ingredients (from flour through salt) into a bowl.

4. In a large bowl, cream together the margarine and sugar until light and fluffy. Add the vanilla and mix well.

5. Add the remaining ingredients by alternating folding in the dry ingredients and cola. Start and end with an addition of dry ingredients, per the instructions on page 28. Make sure everything is well folded in, between each addition.

6. Spoon into the prepared muffin pan. If using twelve cups, they will be full. Bake for 20 to 25 minutes, until a toothpick comes out clean. For more slightly smaller cupcakes, fill eighteen liners two-thirds of the way and bake for 18 to 20 minutes.

7. Remove from the oven and let cool for 5 minutes in the pan, then transfer to a wire rack to let cool completely.

8. Once completely cool, ice as desired. These look great finished with chocolate shavings.

NOTES:

❖ If you've got a half-empty bottle of cola slowly going flat in the fridge, that is perfect; you don't want the cola super bubbly! I don't usually have this in the house—the children aren't allowed to drink it—but sometimes we'll have it for mixing with other beverages if other adults are over. Sure, you could just throw it out if it's gone flat, but this is much tastier.

❖ My testers and I have made this with big-brand, store-brand, natural-brand, artificially sweetened low-calorie, and decaffeinated cola; they all work.

❖ A fun idea for presentation is to save the cola bottle lids (if you drink that much) and place a lid on top of each cupcake after icing, instead of the chocolate shavings—but don't eat them!

Espresso Chocolate-Chip Coffee Cake 📷

MAKES 12 LARGE OR 16 SMALL PIECES

▶ NO NUTS

Like a cup of coffee, laced with chocolate, in a portable, easily held format. Who needs to go to Starbucks or Tim Hortons?

1 cup + 2 tablespoons soy milk
1 teaspoon apple cider vinegar

2½ cups all-purpose flour
¾ cup granulated sugar
2½ teaspoons baking powder
¾ teaspoon baking soda
½ teaspoon salt

½ cup vegan chocolate chips

⅓ cup strong espresso, at room temperature (see Notes)
¼ cup canola oil
1 teaspoon vanilla extract

1 recipe Coffee Streusel Topping (recipe follows)

1 recipe Ganache-Style Chocolate (page 252)
12 or 16 vegan chocolate-covered coffee beans, for garnish (optional)

1. Preheat the oven to 375°F and line an 8-inch square cake (brownie) pan with parchment paper.

2. In a small bowl, combine the soy milk and vinegar, and set aside for 5 minutes to curdle.

3. Sift together the flour, sugar, baking powder, baking soda, and salt into a large bowl. Toss in the chocolate chips.

4. Form a well, then add the soy milk mixture, espresso, oil, and vanilla to the dry ingredients and mix to just combine.

5. Spoon the mixture into the prepared pan, sprinkle the topping evenly on top, and gently press into the cake.

6. Bake for 35 to 40 minutes, until golden, the edges are lightly pulling from the edges of the pan, and a toothpick comes out clean.

7. Remove from the oven and let cool in the pan for 10 minutes, then lift out using the parchment liner and transfer to a wire rack and let cool completely.

8. Once cool, slice into twelve or sixteen equal pieces, depending on how large you want them. Drizzle Ganache-Style Chocolate over the top (pre- or postslicing) and decorate each slice with a chocolate-covered coffee bean, if desired.

· ·

★ Coffee Streusel Topping

MAKES ENOUGH TOPPING FOR ONE 8-INCH CAKE

Although created specifically for this cake, the streusel topping is a nice addition to any chocolate, coffee, mocha, or vanilla cupcake, or a muffin, if you're wanting a change.

¼ cup all-purpose flour
2 teaspoons instant coffee granules
½ teaspoon baking powder
½ teaspoon ground cinnamon
⅓ cup quick-cooking or old-fashioned rolled oats (not instant)
⅓ cup vegan panko (see Notes)
3 tablespoons turbinado sugar

3 tablespoons canola oil

1. Sift together the ingredients from flour through cinnamon, into a large bowl.

2. Mix in the panko, oats, and turbinado sugar.

3. Add the oil, and with clean hands or a fork, mix until crumbly looking.

4. Use as directed above.

NOTES:

❖ If you don't have an espresso machine at home, you can either buy some strong espresso from your local coffee shop and take it home for this, or make some strong instant coffee. Three tablespoons of instant coffee mixed into ⅓ cup of boiling water is strong enough, and if you don't want the caffeine, use decaf!

❖ Panko is a Japanese type of bread crumb that stays crisp during baking. Available in most supermarkets, health food stores, and Asian food stores, it is not hard to find.

· ·

Green Tea and Pistachio Cake

SERVES 10 TO 12

Japan meets the Middle East, and peace breaks out all over this cake. That's pretty corny, but don't let it put you off! There's only a little green tea powder to provide color and a hint of flavor; the pistachios are the stars, and boy, do they shine!

The cake is a little delicate, so you need to take care when cooling and removing from the pans.

2½ cups all-purpose flour

1 cup finely ground raw pistachios (see Notes)

¼ cup + 2 tablespoons cornstarch

3½ teaspoons baking powder

2 teaspoons matcha green tea powder (see Notes)

½ teaspoon baking soda

¼ teaspoon salt

1¼ cups granulated sugar

½ cup vegan margarine, at room temperature

¼ cup canola oil

1 cup soy milk

1 cup soy creamer (see page 16)

1 teaspoon vanilla extract

½ cup toasted, chopped pistachios

2 recipes Buttercream, More or Less (page 249), made with rose water in place of both extracts and tinted pink with the tiniest drop of vegan red food coloring (see Notes)

Whole and chopped pistachio nuts, for garnish

1. Preheat the oven to 375°F and prepare two 9-inch layer cake pans by lining the bottoms with parchment (as outlined on page 27), then spraying the sides with nonstick cooking spray.

2. In a medium bowl, whisk together the ingredients from flour through salt.

3. In a large bowl, cream together the sugar, margarine, and oil until soft, light, and fluffy. Add the soy milk, creamer, and vanilla. Mix to combine well; it will look curdled at this point, but carry on.

4. Add the dry ingredients and toasted nuts to the creamed mixture, stirring to combine.

5. Divide the batter evenly between the two pans (I use a measuring cup and the "one for you, one for the other you" method) and then bake for 25 to 30 minutes until a toothpick comes out clean.

6. Remove from the oven and let cool for 10 minutes in the pans, then invert onto a wire rack, remove the parchment paper, and let cool completely. The cake is quite delicate while warm, so be gentle.

7. Once completely cool, sandwich the two layers together with the Buttercream, More or Less as modified above. Spread the buttercream over the top and sides of the cake as desired and decorate the top with chopped and whole pistachios.

NOTES:

❖ For the pistachios, grind an equal amount of whole pistachios in your food processor, blender, or spice grinder until fine and flourlike; a pulse option is good. Keep an eye on these, as you don't want to end up with nut butter.

❖ Try to get raw nuts, unsalted, unroasted, and undyed. If you can't, the recipe will work, but please leave out the salt.

❖ If you don't have or can't find matcha powder, leave it out. Your cake simply won't be as vibrantly green. Matcha powder is often available in small cans from Asian grocery stores, or at health food stores, or at supermarkets with a large tea selection.

❖ If you don't want to rose-flavor your icing, use a vanilla-flavored buttercream.

❖ If you have rose extract and not rose water, add a drop to a teaspoon of water and use that in place of the stated extracts.

❖ Ensure your red food coloring is vegan. Many varieties are made with cochineal, which comes from crushed-up beetles. There are, however, a number of plant-based alternatives available.

Individual New World Simnel Cakes

MAKES 6 SERVING-SIZE CAKES

The traditional English Easter Cake in mini format, with a New World twist. If you can find marzipan without eggs, use it, otherwise there is a recipe for making your own. Not just for Easter, but anytime you'd like a fruit-filled treat.

I have made these in maxi-muffin pans, which are available at supermarkets and kitchen supply stores.

1 recipe Marzipan (recipe follows)

3 tablespoons water
1 teaspoon ground chia seeds (see Notes)

2 cups all-purpose flour
½ cup ground almonds
1 tablespoon baking powder
½ teaspoon salt

¾ cup granulated sugar
¼ cup vegan margarine
¼ cup canola oil

½ cup + 3 tablespoons soy creamer (see page 16)
¼ cup (2½ ounces) tofu, firm silken (vacuum-packed)
1 teaspoon almond extract
½ teaspoon vanilla extract

¼ cup raisins
¼ cup dried currants
¼ cup pecans, chopped roughly
2 tablespoons golden raisins
2 tablespoons dried blueberries (see Notes)
2 tablespoons dried cranberries (see Notes)

Soy creamer, for brushing (optional)

1. Preheat the oven to 375°F and prepare the maxi-muffin pans by spraying with non-stick spray.

2. On a lightly floured board, roll out the marzipan to ¼-inch thickness, then cut out twelve 3-inch circles, rerolling as required. With the remaining marzipan, shape eighteen small balls. Cover with plastic wrap and set aside.

3. In a small bowl, mix the chia seeds with the water and set aside for 5 minutes.

4. Sift together the flour, ground almonds, baking powder, and salt into a medium bowl.

5. In a large bowl, cream together the sugar, margarine, and oil until light and fluffy.

6. Blend together the chia mixture, tofu, creamer, and extracts until smooth and creamy. Add to the creamed mixture, stirring until smooth and well combined.

7. Add the dry ingredients to the creamed mixture and mix well. Fold in all the dried fruit and nuts.

8. Put 2 tablespoons of batter in each muffin cup. Place one of the marzipan circles on top of each.

9. Fill the pans with the remaining batter. They will be just full. Bake for 25 to 30 minutes, until the edges are light brown and a toothpick comes out nearly clean (there will be a little batter on the toothpick. It's fine, and even desirable, for the cake to be a touch underdone at this point).

10. Remove from the oven and lay the other marzipan circles on the hot cakes. Top each with three small marzipan balls, using a little water or creamer to help them stick in place. Brush lightly with creamer, if desired, and return to the oven for 10 to 12 minutes to lightly brown the marzipan and complete baking the cake.

11. Remove from the oven and let cool in the pans for 15 minutes before transferring to a wire rack to let cool completely.

NOTES:

❖ If you don't have chia seeds, use 4 teaspoons of ground flax seeds instead.

❖ If you don't have the dried blueberries, or cranberries, then substitute with your choice of dried fruit.

⭐ ## Marzipan

MAKES 1½ CUPS MARZIPAN

Most store-bought marzipan contains egg whites, so it's not much use to me being vegan. I made up this recipe specifically for the Individual New World Simnel Cakes, but also use it in the Fancy Almond Bread (page 202). It's very almond-y, not as thick and heavy as store-bought marzipan, and is great to eat as it is! But don't tell anyone I told you that!

½ **cup ground almonds**
½ **cup all-purpose flour**
½ **cup confectioners' sugar**
2 tablespoons cornstarch

¼ **cup + 2 tablespoons vegan margarine**
¼ **teaspoon almond extract**

1. Sift together the almonds, flour, confectioners' sugar, and cornstarch into a medium bowl.
2. Stir in the margarine and almond extract, rubbing with the back of a wooden spoon until a crumbly mixture is formed. Knead gently in the bowl to form a firm dough.
3. Turn onto a lightly floured board and knead for about 2 minutes, until smooth. Wrap in plastic wrap and refrigerate until required.

Lamingtons

MAKES 16 LAMINGTONS

▶ **NO NUTS**

Lamingtons are a traditional Australasian treat. Both New Zealand and Australia claim them as their own, but I call dibs on these! Usually made from "light as air" sponge cake, these are a little heavier than the originals while still capturing the essence of the treat.

The chocolate coating is the more traditional, but these often come with a strawberry coating, too. Options for both are given.

This is one of the few recipes that call for powdered egg replacer. I don't use it very often, but to get a cake as sponge cake–like as possible, I needed to use it. I found that other egg replacers made the cake too heavy, and didn't give the result I was looking for. Ener-G brand is widely available in most health food stores and many well-stocked supermarkets.

1 cup plain soy milk
1 cup granulated sugar
¼ **cup canola oil**
3 tablespoons water
1 tablespoon powdered egg replacer (such as Ener-G)
1 teaspoon vanilla extract

1½ **cups all-purpose flour**
¼ **cup cornstarch**
2 teaspoons baking powder
¾ **teaspoon baking soda**
½ **teaspoon salt**

1 recipe Chocolate and Coconut Coating or Strawberry and Coconut Coating (recipes follow)

1. Preheat the oven to 375°F and line an 8-inch square cake (brownie) pan with parchment paper.

2. In a blender or food processor, blend the ingredients from soy milk through vanilla until really smooth and creamy. Scrape down the sides every now and then.

3. Sift together the remaining ingredients (from flour through salt), into a large bowl. Add the liquid ingredients from your blender and fold until just combined.

4. Pour the mixture into prepared pan and bake for 25 to 30 minutes, until it is golden and bounces back when lightly pressed, and a toothpick comes out clean.

5. Remove from the oven and let cool for 5 minutes in the pan, then transfer to a wire rack and let cool completely.

6. Once completely cool, thinly slice off the hard side edges, using a sharp knife. Slice the remaining inside portion into sixteen squares and coat with coating of your choice.

To coat the Lamingtons

7. There may be drips, so place a wire rack over a piece of parchment paper for ease of counter cleanup.

8. Prepare the coating of your choice, from the two that follow, and have warm in a small bowl. Place the coconut in a bowl to one side, ready for dipping.

9. Take your square of cake and, holding carefully with one hand, dip each side in turn into the coating. Allow the coating to soak in a little, but don't leave the cake in for too long, as you don't want it to fall apart, or for the coating to be used up before you run out of cake.

10. Once all sides are coated, place cake into the coconut. Using the same hand, turn the cake to coat all sides with the coconut. It will stick to the coating.

11. Use your clean hand to place each Lamington on the wire rack to allow the coating to set.

12. You'll need to wash your hands frequently!

Chocolate and Coconut Coating

ENOUGH FOR 16 LAMINGTONS

1½ to 2 cups unsweetened shredded coconut

¼ cup boiling water
1½ tablespoons unsweetened cocoa powder
1½ tablespoons canola oil
½ teaspoon chocolate or vanilla extract

1½ cups confectioners' sugar, sifted if lumpy

1. Place the coconut in a small, deep bowl and set aside until required.

2. Mix the water, cocoa powder, oil, and chocolate extract together in another small, deep bowl. Add the confectioners' sugar and whisk with a fork until smooth.

3. Use as directed in the above recipe.

Strawberry and Coconut Coating

ENOUGH FOR 16 LAMINGTONS

1½ to 2 cups unsweetened shredded coconut

¼ cup Strawberry Sauce (page 96)
¼ cup water
1 tablespoon canola oil
1 teaspoon strawberry or vanilla extract

1 cup confectioners' sugar, sifted if lumpy

1. Place the coconut in a small, deep bowl and set aside until required.

2. Mix the sauce, water, oil, and strawberry extract in a small saucepan. Over medium heat, gently bring to just before a boil.

3. Remove from the heat and add the confectioners' sugar and mix until smooth. Let cool until warm to the touch.

4. Use as directed in the recipe.

Mango, Pineapple, and Mint Upside-Down Cake 📷

MAKES 12 OR 16 SERVING-SIZE CAKES

I was looking for an alternative to the standard Pineapple Upside-Down Cake and came up with this lovely flavor combination. If you love mango, this will be a treat in your house!

I prefer to use frozen and thawed mango pieces, mainly because I am useless at chopping fresh mangoes! It also means that I can make this year-round without paying too much for the mango.

2 cups mango chunks, fresh or frozen and thawed, no more than ½ inch across (about 2 medium mangoes, if using fresh)

1 cup canned pineapple chunks, drained and chopped to no more than ½ inch across

¼ cup light brown sugar, packed

¼ cup vegan margarine, melted

1 cup soy milk

1½ teaspoons apple cider vinegar

2 cups all-purpose flour

¾ cup ground almonds

¾ cup granulated sugar

2½ teaspoons baking powder

½ teaspoon baking soda

½ teaspoon salt

¾ cup soy creamer (see page 16)

⅓ cup canola oil

¼ cup very finely chopped fresh mint, packed

1 teaspoon vanilla extract

¼ teaspoon mint extract

1. Preheat the oven to 375°F and prepare an 8-inch square cake (brownie) pan by lining with parchment paper and then spraying the parchment with nonstick spray. The "top" of the cake is prone to sticking.

2. In a small bowl, mix together the mango, pineapple, melted margarine, and brown sugar, then spread in the bottom of the pan.

3. In a medium bowl, combine the soy milk and vinegar. Set aside for 5 minutes to curdle.

4. In a large bowl, whisk together the ingredients from flour through salt.

5. Add the ingredients from soy creamer through mint extract to the soy-milk mixture, and stir to combine.

6. Fold the wet ingredients into the dry until just combined.

7. Using a large serving spoon, carefully place the batter over the mango mixture, then spread to even the top. Take care not to disturb the fruit or it will be up the sides instead of on the "top" of the cake.

8. Bake for 40 to 45 minutes, until golden and a toothpick comes out clean. Be careful when testing, as the fruit will make the "top" of the cake very moist and will come off on the toothpick even if the rest of the cake is done.

9. Remove from the oven and let cool in the pan for 10 minutes, then hold a wire rack over the top of the cake pan, invert the pan onto the rack, and allow to cool upside down for a further 5 minutes before removing the pan. (Place a tea towel under the rack before removing the pan, as juice from the fruit is likely to run off.)

10. Allow to cool completely prior to slicing into twelve or sixteen equal pieces, depending on how large you want the servings to be.

Variation

Boozy Mango, Pineapple, and Mint Upside-Down Cake

Add 1 tablespoon of dark rum to the fruit mixture for an adult take on this cake! And/or, replace the mint extract with crème de menthe! Thanks to my testers, Ann and Kate, for this variation!

• •

Nut-Topped Almond and Hazelnut Bundt Cake

SERVES 10 TO 12

This looks super fancy, between the shape from the Bundt pan and the caramel toffee–nut topping! Don't save for a special occasion, though. The cake is lovely and moist, loaded with great nut flavors.

2 cups soy milk

2 teaspoons apple cider vinegar

2½ cups all-purpose flour

1 cup granulated sugar

½ cup ground almonds

4 teaspoons baking powder

1 teaspoon salt

1 teaspoon unsweetened Dutch-processed cocoa powder

½ teaspoon ground nutmeg

½ teaspoon instant coffee granules

½ teaspoon ground allspice

⅛ teaspoon ground cinnamon

¼ cup finely chopped almonds, toasted if desired

¼ cup finely chopped hazelnuts, toasted if desired

½ cup hazelnut- or almond-flavored coffee syrup (see Note)

½ cup canola oil

1 teaspoon vanilla extract

½ teaspoon almond extract

Topping

½ cup chopped mixed almonds and hazelnuts

¼ cup light brown sugar, packed

2 tablespoons soy creamer (see page 16)

2 tablespoons vegan margarine

1. Preheat the oven to 350°F and spray a 10-inch Bundt pan with nonstick spray.

2. In a small bowl, combine the soy milk and vinegar, and set aside for 5 minutes to curdle.

3. Sift together the ingredients from flour through cinnamon, into a large bowl. Add the nuts and toss to coat with the flour.

4. Add the coffee syrup, oil, and extracts to the soy milk mixture and stir in.

5. Pour the wet ingredients into the dry and mix to just combine.

6. Pour into prepared Bundt pan, smooth the top, and bake for about 50 minutes, until the cake is golden and well risen, and a toothpick comes out clean.

7. Remove from the oven and let cool in the pan for 10 minutes before inverting onto a wire rack to let cool completely.

8. Once completely cool, make the topping. In a medium skillet, over medium heat, toast the nuts for 5 minutes, stirring frequently to avoid burning. Add the brown sugar, creamer, and margarine, stirring while the sugar and margarine melt. Allow to boil for 2 minutes and thicken to coat the nuts. Remove from the heat and let cool for

a further 2 minutes prior to spooning the warm topping over the cool cake. Allow to set at room temperature.

NOTE:

❖ If you don't have coffee syrup, substitute agave nectar or pure maple syrup.

· ·

PB&J Marble Cupcakes with Peanut Buttercream

MAKES 12 LARGE OR 18 SMALL CUPCAKES

▶ NO SOY • PEANUT ALERT!

Ask anyone, "What do vegans eat for lunch?" Are you told, "Peanut butter and jelly sandwiches"? I'll bet many of you are! Although sometimes we may eat that for lunch, there's a new kid in town, and it's dessert! It's the classic flavor combination in a cupcake. Which side is your favorite?

To avoid confusion with the two batters, I work with one, wet and dry, to my right and the other to my left. This works for me.

"PB" BATTER

1 cup all-purpose flour
¼ cup + 1 tablespoon granulated sugar
1 teaspoon baking powder
½ teaspoon salt
¼ teaspoon baking soda
⅛ teaspoon ground nutmeg

¾ cup + 3 tablespoons almond milk
3 tablespoons crunchy natural peanut butter

2 tablespoons canola oil
½ teaspoon vanilla extract

"J" BATTER

1 cup all-purpose flour
¼ cup granulated sugar
1 teaspoon baking powder
¼ teaspoon baking soda
½ teaspoon salt

½ cup + 2 tablespoons almond milk
3 tablespoons canola oil
3 tablespoons strawberry or raspberry jam
½ teaspoon strawberry or raspberry extract (see Note)

TO ICE (OPTIONAL)

2 tablespoons strawberry or raspberry jam, as above
1 teaspoon agave nectar

1 recipe Peanut Buttercream (recipe follows)

1. Preheat the oven to 375°F and line twelve or eighteen cups of your muffin pan with cupcake liners, as desired. (If not using some of the cups, fill them halfway with water so the pan won't warp.)

2. Prepare two disposable piping bags with large circular nozzles (nothing fancy, just big) and have on hand two clips or rubber bands, to secure these when required.

3. Using two small bowls, sift the dry ingredients for each mixture into each respective bowl. For the PB batter, sift in the flour, baking powder, baking soda, salt, sugar, and nutmeg. For the J batter, sift in the flour, baking powder, baking soda, salt, and sugar.

4. In a third small bowl, whisk together the milk, oil, vanilla, and peanut butter until as smooth as possible. Set aside until required for the PB batter.

5. In another small bowl, mix together the milk, oil, extract, and jelly and whisk well. You'll have some small lumps of jelly, but that's great.

6. Mix the liquid ingredients for the PB batter into the dry ingredients for the PB batter, and stir to combine. Fill the first piping bag by turning up the nozzle (so the batter doesn't run out) and, using a soup ladle, scoop the batter into the bag. Secure the open end with a clip or rubber band. Place to one side, nozzle facing up, until required.

7. Mix the liquid ingredients for the J batter into the dry ingredients for the J batter, and stir to combine. Rinse your soup ladle and fill the second piping bag as above.

8. Taking one piping bag in each hand, and piping simultaneously, fill the twelve liners to the brim or, for eighteen slightly smaller cupcakes, fill the liners two-thirds of the way. This method is a little messy, and takes a little coordination and practice, but it is fast!

9. Alternately, drop spoonfuls of each mixture into opposite sides of each muffin pan. If you have another person to help, you can do this simultaneously; otherwise you'll need to do one and then the other.

10. Once all liners are filled, use a chopstick or wooden skewer to lightly swirl or marble the batter.

11. Bake the larger cupcakes for 20 to 22 minutes, or the smaller ones for 18 to 20 minutes, or until a toothpick comes out clean.

12. Remove from the oven and let cool in the pans for 5 minutes, transfer to a wire rack and let cool completely prior to icing.

13. To ice, if desired

14. In a small bowl, warm the jam and agave nectar in the microwave on high for about 15 seconds. Stir to combine. It won't be completely smooth.

15. Either spread this mixture on each cupcake and pipe Peanut Buttercream on top, or (and this is my preferred method) place a small blob of the jelly mixture roughly in the center of the cupcake and pipe a swirl of the Peanut Buttercream to one side. This allows you to see both, as well as the pretty cupcake underneath.

NOTE:
 ❖ If you don't have access to berry extracts, use vanilla instead.

. . . .

Peanut Buttercream

MAKES ABOUT 1½ CUPS ICING

▶ **NO WHEAT • PEANUT ALERT!**

Specifically created for the PB&J Marble Cupcakes, this icing is also good for making sandwich cookies out of the Peanut Butter Cookies (page 131) and for adding "Vegas Elvis" power to the Elvis Blondies (page 58). It is very peanut buttery and good!

¼ cup vegan margarine
1 tablespoon smooth natural peanut butter (see Note)

½ teaspoon vanilla extract
¼ teaspoon salt

1 cup confectioners' sugar, sifted if lumpy
1 to 2 tablespoons almond milk

1. In a bowl, cream together the margarine and peanut butter until smooth. Add the vanilla and salt, and mix well.

2. Add the confectioners' sugar and mix until smooth. Add the almond milk a teaspoonful at a time and mix until the icing is soft but not runny.

NOTE:
 ❖ Smooth peanut butter is easier for piping, but if you have crunchy, then use what you have.

Secret-Ingredient Chocolate Cake with Blueberry Cream

SERVES 10 TO 12

▶ **NO NUTS**

Can they guess? Let everyone try to guess the three secret ingredients—the blueberry puree, the black pepper, and the balsamic vinegar—after they've eaten a slice; they'll be pleasantly surprised. The black pepper is more apparent at the end of each bite. This is a supermoist cake, decorated with a lovely, vibrant filling, Blueberry Cream, which needs to be refrigerated. Buttercream, More or Less (page 249) would be an alternative icing (good but *much* richer), if you'd prefer.

1 recipe Blueberry Cream (recipe follows)

¾ cup Blueberry Sauce (recipe follows), at room temperature (see Notes)

1 cup plain soy milk

2 tablespoons balsamic vinegar (see Notes)

1½ cups all-purpose flour

⅓ cup unsweetened cocoa powder

¼ cup cornstarch

2½ teaspoons baking powder

1 teaspoon baking soda

¾ to 1 teaspoon freshly ground black pepper (see Notes)

¼ teaspoon salt

1 cup granulated sugar

½ cup vegan margarine, softened

1 teaspoon vanilla extract

1 recipe Ganache-Style Chocolate (page 252) (optional)

1. Preheat the oven to 375°F and prepare two 9-inch layer cake pans by lining the bottoms with parchment, then spraying the sides with nonstick cooking spray.

2. In a medium bowl, whisk together the sauce, milk, and vinegar.

3. Sift together the dry ingredients (from flour through salt), into a medium bowl.

4. In a large bowl, cream together the sugar and margarine until soft, light, and fluffy. Add the vanilla and mix well.

5. Alternate adding the dry and wet ingredients to the creamed mixture, starting and ending with the dry ingredients (as described on page 28).

6. Divide the batter evenly between the two pans (I use a measuring cup and the "one for you, one for other you" method) and bake 25 to 30 minutes, until a toothpick comes out clean.

7. Remove from the oven and let cool 15 minutes in the pans, then invert onto a wire rack to let cool completely.

8. Once completely cool, sandwich the two layers together with the Blueberry Cream. Spread the cream in the center of the cake, leaving a ½-inch margin around the edge (it will squish out once the top layer is placed on).

9. Spread a layer of Ganache-Style Chocolate on top of the cake (and down the sides, too, if you wish). I find this cake quite rich, so use only a smear, and top with shaved chocolate.

10. Please store this cake in the fridge to allow the filling to remain set.

NOTES:

❖ If you are planning to decorate the finished cake with Blueberry Cream, make it after you have your Blueberry Sauce ready. This is to give the cream time to sit in the fridge and thicken while the cake is baking and cooling.

❖ On occasion I have made this with either regular dark or white balsamic vinegar, depending on what I had available at the time. I prefer it with the dark balsamic, but the white is a perfectly acceptable alternative!

❖ Add the lesser amount of black pepper and taste; if you'd like more kick, add more.

⭐ Blueberry Sauce

MAKES 1¼ TO 1½ CUPS SAUCE

▶ NO NUTS • NO SOY • NO SUGAR • NO WHEAT

This is used in the cake above, as well as in the icing to decorate it (which follows). This sauce is also good to serve with the Lemon and Blueberry Biscuits (page 83), and is great over ice cream, hot desserts, oatmeal, and as a sneaky snack, in fact, wherever you'd like a little fruity goodness.

4 cups frozen or fresh blueberries
¼ cup water
¼ cup agave nectar

1. Combine all the ingredients in a medium saucepan and heat over medium to high heat, then boil, stirring occasionally, until thick and syrupy and the volume has reduced by half (about 20 minutes after the berries have started to boil).

2. Let cool to room temperature and blend until smooth. Store the sauce in a covered container in the fridge until required. Return any refrigerated sauce to room temperature prior to using.

⭐ Blueberry Cream

MAKES ENOUGH CREAM FOR ONE 9-INCH LAYER CAKE

▶ NO NUTS • NO WHEAT

I wanted a creamlike filling to balance the richness of this cake, but I wanted it to hold some shape, too, a little like fruity whipped cream. I didn't want to have to break out the agar. I think this works quite well.

One of my tasters referred to this as "Atomic Cream" because of the super-vibrant color.

½ cup Blueberry Sauce (preceding recipe)
¼ cup soy creamer (see page 16)
1½ tablespoons tapioca starch

6 ounces tofu, firm silken (vacuum-packed, half of a 12-ounce package)
⅓ cup confectioners' sugar

1. In a small saucepan, combine the sauce, creamer, and tapioca and stir until the tapioca is fully dissolved.

2. Stir almost constantly over medium heat for 15 minutes, until the sauce has thickened and become very goopy (technical term!) and gel-like. Do not let the mixture boil. If you taste the mixture, at the beginning you'll find it quite chalky; at the end, the chalky taste will have cooked out—that's how you know it is done.

3. Combine the thickened sauce in a blender with the remaining ingredients and blend until smooth. Scrape down the sides of the blender as required.

4. Refrigerate in a covered container for at least an hour prior to using, to allow everything to combine and thicken, and store in the fridge.

Spiced Raisin Breakfast Cake

MAKES 12 LARGE OR 16 SMALL PIECES

▶ **NO SOY • NO SUGAR**

I'm being a bit cheeky calling this a breakfast cake, but the thing is, it could be! Sweetened without refined sugar and with very little oil, this cake is perfectly moist, well spiced, and just a little sweet, with a really crumbly topping that would make any breakfast fun. When I say crumbly, I mean crumbly, so have napkins ready when you eat it!

1¼ cups almond milk
1½ teaspoons apple cider vinegar

2¼ cups all-purpose flour
¼ cup unsweetened shredded coconut
2½ teaspoons baking powder
¾ teaspoon baking soda
½ teaspoon ground cardamom
½ teaspoon ground cinnamon
½ teaspoon ground nutmeg
½ teaspoon ground ginger
½ teaspoon ancho chile powder
½ teaspoon salt

½ cup raisins

¾ cup Date Paste (page 250)
2 tablespoons canola oil

2 tablespoons agave nectar
1 teaspoon vanilla extract
1 recipe Raisin Crumble Topping (recipe follows) (see Notes)

1. Preheat the oven to 375°F and line an 8-inch square cake (brownie) pan with parchment paper.

2. In a medium bowl, combine the almond milk and vinegar, and set aside for 5 minutes to curdle.

3. In a large bowl, whisk together the flour, coconut, baking powder, baking soda, spices, and salt. Toss in the raisins.

4. Add the date paste, oil, agave nectar, and vanilla to the soy milk mixture and stir to combine.

5. Form a well in the dry ingredients, then add the wet, mixing to just combine.

6. Spoon the batter into the prepared pan, sprinkle evenly with the topping, and gently press the topping into the batter.

7. Bake for 25 to 30 minutes, until golden, with edges lightly pulling from edges of pan, and a toothpick comes out clean.

8. Remove from the oven and let cool in pan for 10 minutes, then lift out using the parchment paper and transfer to a wire rack and let cool completely.

9. Once completely cool, slice into twelve or sixteen equal pieces, depending on how large you want them.

★ Raisin Crumble Topping

MAKES ENOUGH TOPPING FOR ONE CAKE

▶ **NO SOY • NO SUGAR**

½ cup all-purpose flour
¼ cup unsweetened shredded coconut
¼ cup vegan panko (see Notes)
½ teaspoon baking powder
¼ teaspoon salt

¼ cup raisins

1 tablespoon almond milk
1 tablespoon canola oil
1 tablespoon agave nectar

1. In a large bowl, use a fork to whisk together the flour, coconut, panko, baking powder, and salt, then stir in the raisins.

2. Form a well in the center of the dry ingredients and mix in the milk, oil and agave nectar.

3. The mixture will look crumbly and lumpy. Use as directed.

NOTES:

❖ If you'd prefer to make this without the crumble topping, go right ahead; who am I to try and stop you!

❖ Panko is a Japanese type of bread crumb that stays crisp during baking. Available in most supermarkets, health food stores, and Asian food stores, it is not hard to find.

Sticky Toffee Pudding Cake

MAKES 16 SERVING-SIZE PIECES

▶ **NO NUTS**

Based on the ever-popular Sticky Toffee Pudding, this cake is not for everyday. It is a sweet, rich, and heavy dessert, a treat for the middle of winter. It is equally at home hot or cold, and either plain or with custard, vanilla ice cream, or Crazy Whip Topping (page 249).

Make the Date Paste in advance, if you like (it's a good thing to have in the fridge, actually); just allow it to come to room temperature before adding in to the mixture.

1 cup soy milk
1 teaspoon apple cider vinegar

2 cups all-purpose flour
2 teaspoons baking powder
½ teaspoon salt
½ teaspoon baking soda

⅔ cup dark brown sugar, packed
½ cup vegan margarine

1 tablespoon blackstrap molasses
2 teaspoons vanilla extract

1 cup Date Paste (page 250)
¼ cup soy creamer (see page 16)

SAUCE
2 tablespoons vegan margarine
2 tablespoons brown sugar, packed
2 tablespoons granulated sugar
1½ tablespoons soy milk or creamer

1. Preheat the oven to 375°F and line an 8-inch square cake (brownie) pan with parchment paper.

2. Combine the soy milk with the vinegar in a small bowl and set aside for 5 minutes to curdle.

3. Sift together the flour, baking powder, salt, and baking soda, into a bowl.

4. In a large bowl, cream the margarine and brown sugar until fluffy (a whisk is handy for this).

5. Add the blackstrap molasses and vanilla, and mix well.

6. Add the soy milk mixture, the date paste, and the soy creamer, whisking well to combine.

7. Add the sifted dry ingredients and stir to combine.

8. Spoon the mixture into the prepared pan and bake for 35 to 40 minutes, until a toothpick comes out clean.

9. While the cake is baking, prepare the sauce by combining all its ingredients in a small saucepan over medium heat and stirring until dissolved together. Bring to a boil, lower the heat to medium-low, and boil, stirring occasionally, for 10 to 12 minutes, until reduced to half its original volume and thickened. Keep warm over low heat until required.

10. Once the cake is baked, remove from the oven and keep in the pan. Using the pointed end of a chopstick, poke holes in the cake about 1 inch apart, most of the way through. Spoon the warm sauce over the warm cake, encouraging it to go down the holes you made by guiding the sauce with the back of the spoon. If some remains on the top and hardens as a glaze, that is nice, too.

11. Leave in the pan until completely cool. Lift out using the parchment lining once cool and slice into sixteen equal pieces.

Tropical Banana Cake with Coconut Ice Icing ▢

SERVES 10 TO 12

▶ **NO NUTS**

A tropical taste party is going on right now, and you're invited! This is an easy cake that is sure to please anyone with a desire to taste the tropics. I've iced it with Coconut Ice Icing, but you can use whatever you wish.

3 cups all-purpose flour
¼ cup cornstarch

3½ teaspoons baking powder
¼ teaspoon salt

1 frozen banana, cut into chunks (about 1 cup) (see Note)
½ cup rice milk
½ cup mango nectar
½ cup canned pineapple, with juice (not drained)
1 teaspoon ground chia seeds
1 teaspoon vanilla extract

1 cup granulated sugar
½ cup vegan margarine, at room temperature
¼ cup canola oil
1 or 2 recipes Coconut Ice Icing, depending on how much icing you like! (recipe follows) (optional)

1. Preheat the oven to 375°F and prepare two 9-inch round layer cake pans by lining the bottoms with parchment paper, then spraying with nonstick cooking spray.

2. Sift together the dry ingredients (from flour through salt), into a medium bowl.

3. In another bowl, blend together the frozen banana, milk, mango nectar, pineapple and juice, chia seeds, and vanilla until very creamy and smooth. Let stand until required.

4. In a large bowl, cream together the sugar, margarine, and oil until soft, light, and fluffy.

5. Add the banana mixture and whisk to combine. It will look curdled, but that is fine.

6. Add the dry ingredients and mix to just combine.

7. Divide the batter evenly between the two pans, using a measuring cup and a "one for you, one for other you" method.

8. Bake for 20 to 25 minutes, until the top is light golden, with edges browned and pulling away from the sides of the pan, and a toothpick comes out clean.

9. Remove from the oven and let cool for 15 minutes in the pans, before inverting onto a wire rack to let cool completely.

10. Once completely cool, sandwich the two layers together with the Coconut Ice Icing, and ice the top and sides of the cake, if desired.

NOTE:

❖ Freeze any excess ripe bananas you may have, already peeled and cut into 1-inch chunks, in little plastic bags, for ease of access for such recipes as this, and for smoothies.

• •

★ Coconut Ice Icing

MAKES ENOUGH ICING FOR ONE CAKE, ABOUT 1½ CUPS

▶ NO NUTS • NO WHEAT

This is great stuff! Try to stop eating it out of the bowl. It's specifically for this cake, but would go just about anywhere you'd like a hit of coconut.

2 tablespoons canned coconut milk or soy creamer (see page 16)

2 tablespoons vegan margarine

2 tablespoons coconut oil, at room temperature

½ teaspoon coconut extract

¼ teaspoon salt

1¼ cups confectioners' sugar

¼ cup coconut milk powder (see Note)

½ cup shredded coconut

1. In a medium bowl, cream together the coconut milk, margarine, coconut oil, extract, and salt until thick and smooth. Using a whisk makes this easy.

2. Sift the confectioners' sugar and milk powder directly into the bowl, add the coconut, and mix until combined.

NOTE:

❖ Coconut milk powder is available from Asian grocery stores and many supermarkets. If you have trouble finding this, or can't find a brand that doesn't contain milk ingredients, substitute soy milk powder instead. One of my testers, SS, who lives in Finland, couldn't find coconut (or soy) milk powder anywhere. She had good results by grinding unsweetened shredded coconut to a heavy flour consistency in her spice grinder and substituted that instead. Thanks for the hint!

Remember...

Vanilla Bean Cupcakes 📷

▶ **NO NUTS**

Simply flavored and perfect for any occasion, these seem ever so much fancier with the addition of the vanilla bean as well as vanilla extract. Ice the finished cupcakes with Buttercream, More or Less (page 249), for a decadent cupcake, or just a little Drizzle Icing (page 251), for a perfect, simple, elegant vanilla treat.

If vanilla beans aren't convenient, substitute a teaspoon of vanilla paste or add an extra teaspoon of vanilla extract. The flavor won't be as intense with extract only, and you won't get the pretty flecks in the cupcake.

1 vanilla bean (see Note)
1 cup granulated sugar

1½ cups + 2 tablespoons soy milk

2½ cups all-purpose flour
2½ teaspoons baking powder
½ teaspoon salt

2 teaspoons vanilla extract
⅓ cup canola oil

1. Preheat the oven to 375°F and line twelve or eighteen cups of your muffin pan with cupcake liners, as desired. (If not using some of the cups, fill them halfway with water so the pan won't warp.)

2. Remove the bean from the sugar, if stored in it, (see Note) and scrape out the paste inside the pod into a small pan. Add the milk, sugar, and vanilla pod, then heat over medium-low heat, stirring frequently, for 5 to 7 minutes, until the sugar has completely dissolved. Do not boil. Remove from the heat and place the pan on a pot holder in the fridge to cool to room temperature, about 7 minutes. Remove the vanilla bean pod, squeezing out any paste left inside.

3. Sift together the flour, baking powder, and salt, into a large bowl.

4. Add the vanilla extract and oil to the milk mixture.

5. Make a well in the dry ingredients and add the wet ingredients, stirring to just combine and remove any large lumps.

6. Spoon into the prepared muffin pan. If using twelve cups, they will be full. Bake for 20 to 22 minutes, until a toothpick comes out clean. For more slightly smaller cupcakes, fill eighteen liners two-thirds of the way and bake for 18 to 20 minutes.

7. Remove from the oven and let cool in the pans for 5 minutes, then transfer to a wire rack to let cool completely.

NOTE:
❖ Unless you're making these immediately, a good idea is to place the vanilla bean and sugar in a sealable container. Seal and leave as long as possible to infuse the sugar with vanilla flavor. This step is optional.

Variation

Textured Vanilla Cupcakes
Replace ¼ cup of the flour with ground almonds, and use almond milk instead of soy milk, for a subtly textured and slightly almond-flavored cupcake.

Zebra Cake

SERVES 8 TO 10

▶ **NO NUTS**

This one is a bit of a gimmick. The cake part is based on the recipe for the Lamingtons (page 102), but presented in a fancy, looks-much-harder-than-it-actually-is sort of way. Just what you need to impress people, right?

Like a zebra, this cake is unique. It will come out with a different pattern each time you make it, which is part of the fun.

You can present this simply, lightly sprinkled with confectioners' sugar, or cut the cake in half and ice with your favorite icing. Either way, the top of the cake still shows off the pretty stripes you worked so hard to create.

1 cup + 2 tablespoons plain soy milk
1 cup granulated sugar
¼ cup canola oil
¼ cup water
1 tablespoon powdered egg replacer (for example, Ener-G)
½ teaspoon vanilla extract

1¼ cups all-purpose flour
¼ cup cornstarch
2 teaspoons baking powder
¾ teaspoon baking soda
½ teaspoon salt

2 tablespoons unsweetened cocoa powder
½ teaspoon chocolate extract, or more vanilla extract

2 tablespoons all-purpose flour
½ teaspoon vanilla extract or paste

1. Preheat the oven to 375°F and line a 9-inch round cake pan with parchment paper.

2. Blend the ingredients from soy milk through vanilla until really smooth and creamy. Scrape down the sides now and then.

3. Sift together the ingredients from flour through salt, into a large bowl. Add the liquid ingredients from your blender and fold until just combined.

4. Divide the mixture equally between two bowls. To one bowl, add the cocoa powder and chocolate extract; to the other, the extra flour and vanilla extract. Fold in the additions gently to just combine.

5. Using two equal containers, each with about ¼-cup volume (two measuring cups are great, but anything will work) and sprayed with nonstick spray, prepare the cake for baking.

6. Pour ¼ cup of the vanilla batter into the center of the pan. Don't spread it out.

7. Follow this with a measure of the chocolate batter poured into the center of the vanilla batter. The pressure of the new batter will make the vanilla batter spread out toward the side of the pan. Gently press the new batter down to encourage this spread, if yours is not moving enough by itself.

8. Repeat with vanilla batter, into the center of the chocolate you just poured. The batter will start to look like concentric rings (like tree rings) of alternating colors.

9. Continue with the batter pouring, alternating the two kinds, until all is used up. Jiggle the pan gently as required to spread the batter to the edges.

10. Bake 30 to 35 minutes, until golden, well risen, and a toothpick comes out clean.

11. Remove from the oven and let cool for 5 minutes in the pan, then let cool completely on a wire rack prior to icing or dusting.

NOTE:

❖ If you want more, narrower, rings, use a smaller amount of batter for each addition to the pan.

Cookies

THESE ARE THE most popular of all baked goods. Who doesn't love cookies? I think this is the case because cookies are:

* Preportioned. They are baked that way, and yes, you can stop at one!
* Usually small and not filling. You can have a cookie as a treat and not spoil your dinner (too much . . . and only if you do stop at one!).
* Sweet. This appeals to our basic taste preference.
* Often iced. This appeals to the desire for excess!
* Portable. Because they are small and often sturdy, cookies are an easy treat on the go; you can take them anywhere.
* Perfect for sharing. Small and easily transported, cookies are the perfect treat for giving to others.
* Filled with memories. The taste of a cookie you had as a child will send you spinning back in time.

For the home baker they are also super quick and easy. A batch of cookies can be mixed and baked in less than thirty minutes, if you're not planning on icing them. You can also take heart in the knowledge that because all the following great cookies are vegan, you and your loved ones can eat as much of the dough as you like, with fewer worries about *Salmonella*!

A few notes to make your cookies look their best and keep for as long as possible: Please make sure your cookies are completely cold prior to icing, to avoid an unattractive mess. Store them in a covered container, at room temperature, unless otherwise stated. They keep best in a container with an airtight lid, though if you find they start to get a little soggy, just put a crust of bread in the container with them. It will absorb any moisture and keep your cookies crisp. If your cookies are iced, try to keep in a single layer. If this is not possible, keep the layers separated with parchment paper.

You can freeze most cookies. If you wrap them in plastic wrap in pairs, all you need to do is take them out in the morning for lunches, for example; they'll be thawed by lunchtime. However, icing doesn't usually freeze well, so freeze uniced and then ice once thawed.

Car Tire Cookies 📷

▶ **NO NUTS**

One day after school, my kids were looking longingly at some other children eating those cookies that sandwich a marshmallow filling and are dipped in chocolate (no names but you know which I mean, right?), so I made my own version! One of my tasters said she could see the similarity to those other cookies (never having eaten one, I had to ask!).

These are soft, chocolaty cookies, with just a hint of cinnamon, encasing a sweet marshmallow-like filling, covered in rich Ganache-Style Chocolate.

COOKIES

1 cup + 2 tablespoons all-purpose flour

½ cup granulated sugar

¼ cup unsweetened Dutch-processed cocoa powder

1 teaspoon baking powder

¼ teaspoon ground cinnamon

¼ teaspoon salt

¼ cup vegan margarine

2 tablespoons vegan shortening

3 to 4 tablespoons soy milk

FILLING

½ recipe Buttercream, More or Less (page 249)

½ cup vegan marshmallows, chopped small, or ⅓ cup vegan marshmallow fluff (see Note)

COATING (OPTIONAL)

2 recipes Ganache-Style Chocolate (page 252), made with 2 tablespoons creamer for half-covered cookies, or 4 recipes for completely enrobed cookies

1. Sift together the ingredients from flour through salt, into a large bowl.

2. Using a pastry cutter (or two knives held together), cut in the margarine and shortening until the mixture resembles coarse bread crumbs.

3. Make a well in the center and add 3 tablespoons of the soy milk. Mix to form a stiff dough. If more liquid is required, add more soy milk by the teaspoon until the dough holds together when pressed.

4. Wrap the dough in plastic wrap, then chill in the fridge for 30 minutes for ease of rolling.

5. Preheat the oven to 400°F and line two baking sheets with parchment paper.

6. Remove the dough from fridge, then on a lightly floured board, roll to a thickness of about ⅛ inch.

7. Using a 2-inch-diameter cookie cutter, cut out the cookies, then place 1 inch apart on the prepared sheets. Reroll the scraps to make more cookies.

8. Bake for 6 to 8 minutes, until just puffed and lightly brown.

9. Remove from the oven and let cool on the baking sheets for 5 minutes, then let cool completely on a wire rack.

10. Once the cookies are completely cool, combine the marshmallows with the Buttercream, and mix well.

11. Spread about 2 teaspoons of filling onto the bottom of one cookie and sandwich together with the bottom of another cookie. Chill in the fridge for an hour if the cookie or filling seems too soft at this point.

12. If using the chocolate coating, hold the cookie sandwich by as small as area as possible, dip half in the ganache to coat, and place on a wire rack over a sheet of parchment paper (to catch the drips) to set; or completely cover in ganache (this is much messier!).

13. Place the coated cookie sandwiches on a baking sheet or large plate, and chill in the fridge for at least 30 minutes. Store in a covered container once set.

NOTE:

❖ The marshmallow fluff is much stickier than cut-up marshmallows, and will make the filling too soft if the same amount is used.

Variation

Coconut Crème Car Tire Cookies

If you don't have marshmallows, join two cookies together with the Creamy Coconut Icing (page 217), then coat with ganache as directed.

· ·

Cocoa Oatmeal Cookies with Cocoa Nibs

MAKES ABOUT 26 COOKIES

▶ **NO NUTS · NO SUGAR**

Cocoa nibs are one of those buzz products, a supposed superfood with antioxidants galore being super good for you! Team them up with another superfood (oats), sweeten without refined sugar, and you could even say these are healthy! That is, until you smother them in ganache!

The cookies themselves are soft, with an interesting texture from the cocoa nibs. They aren't overly sweet, but the ganache takes care of that.

1 cup quick-cooking or old-fashioned rolled oats (not instant)
1 teaspoon baking soda

¾ cup warmed soy milk, preferably chocolate flavored

⅓ cup canola oil
¼ cup agave nectar
¼ cup brown rice syrup
1 tablespoon ground flax seed
1 teaspoon vanilla extract

1 cup all-purpose flour
½ cup whole-wheat pastry flour
⅓ cup unsweetened cocoa powder
½ teaspoon salt
¼ teaspoon ground cinnamon

½ cup cocoa nibs (see Note)

1 recipe Ganache-Style Chocolate (page 252)

1. In a large bowl, combine the oats and baking soda, then stir in the warmed milk. Set aside for 5 minutes.

2. Add the oil, syrup, flax seed, and vanilla to the oat mixture and beat well for about a minute.

3. Sift together the ingredients from flour through cinnamon into this mixture and mix.

4. Fold in the cocoa nibs, then cover and chill for 15 minutes to make handling easier.

5. Preheat the oven to 375°F and line two baking sheets with parchment paper.

6. With dampened hands, scoop the dough into tablespoon-size balls, flatten between your hands to form disks 2 inches in diameter, and place 2 inches apart on the prepared sheets.

7. Bake for 10 to 12 minutes, until the bottoms are lightly browned and the tops are puffed, a little cracked, and soft.

8. Remove from the oven and let cool on the baking sheets for 5 minutes, then let cool completely on a wire rack.

9. Once completely cool, prepare the ganache and spread on each cookie, topping with cocoa nibs, if desired. Place on a large plate and cool in the fridge to set the ganache, and then store at room temperature in a covered container.

NOTE:

❖ If you'd prefer not to use cocoa nibs (they can be pricey) or you don't like their slight bitterness, replace half or all of the amount in the recipe with vegan chocolate chips, and just call these Chocolate-Oatmeal Cookies.

Coconut Cookies

MAKES ABOUT 24 COOKIES

▶ **NO NUTS • NO SOY**

My husband is mad for coconut. This cookie works on the layering idea of "more is more," and results in a delicate, very coconutty cookie that almost melts in your mouth.

2 tablespoons solid coconut oil

¾ cup granulated sugar
3 tablespoons vegan shortening

⅓ cup canned coconut milk
½ teaspoon coconut extract

1½ cups all-purpose flour
½ teaspoon baking soda
¼ teaspoon baking powder
¼ teaspoon salt

¾ cup unsweetened, shredded coconut

1 recipe Drizzle Icing (page 251) or Ganache-Style Chocolate (page 252) (optional)

1. Preheat your oven to 350°F and line two baking sheets with parchment paper.

2. If necessary, warm your coconut oil in the microwave on high in 10-second bursts until softened slightly and able to be mixed with no lumps. Add the shortening and sugar, then cream until light and fluffy.

3. Add the coconut milk and coconut extract, then mix well to combine. It may look a bit curdled at this point, but that is okay; just continue.

4. Sift together the flour, baking powder, baking soda, and salt into this mixture. Add the shredded coconut and stir everything together until soft dough is formed.

5. Using a tablespoon-size scoop, form the cookies and drop about 2 inches apart onto the baking sheets.

6. Bake for 10 to 12 minutes, until the undersides are just lightly browned and the cookies are puffy.

7. Remove from the oven and let cool on the baking sheets for 5 minutes, then let cool completely on a wire rack.

8. If desired, ice with thin Drizzle Icing or a little Ganache-Style Chocolate, for contrast.

Coconut and Oatmeal Cookies

MAKES ABOUT 12 LARGE OR 24 SMALL COOKIES

▶ **NO NUTS · NO SOY**

This is another recipe that I'm not calling by the name I knew it by while growing up. It's one you may not have come across before unless you're from New Zealand or Australia. The original was named for the brave ANZACs (Australia and New Zealand Army Corps) of World War I. ANZAC Biscuits (what we call cookies in New Zealand) were made from what was available at the time of postwar shortages. The method, while a little strange, is the one I remember using to make these as a kid.

As far as naming goes, the Australian government has very strict guidelines for using the name ANZAC to describe a type of cookie (i.e., biscuit) and to be so called, the recipe has to follow the "official" one. My version is an updated one, not traditional, and I don't want to get in trouble with the Australian government, so I changed the name. Rest assured that whatever they are called, they capture the taste and texture I remember.

1 teaspoon baking soda
¼ cup hot water

⅔ cup light brown sugar, packed
2 tablespoons canola oil
2 tablespoons agave nectar
1½ teaspoons blackstrap molasses
1 teaspoon ground flax seeds
½ teaspoon vanilla extract

¾ cup all-purpose flour

1½ cups quick-cooking or old-fashioned rolled oats (not instant)
½ cup unsweetened shredded coconut

1. Preheat the oven to 350°F and line two baking sheets with parchment paper.

2. In a large bowl, mix together the baking soda and water (it will get bubbly), and then add the ingredients from brown sugar through vanilla, whisking until smooth.

3. Sift in the flour, then add the coconut and oats and mix well. The dough will be thick and sticky.

4. For larger cookies, scoop with a ¼-cup measure, then with dampened hands, flatten to 2½ to 3 inches across and place 2 inches apart on the prepared baking sheets. Bake for 8 to 10 minutes, until lightly browned on the bottom.

5. For smaller cookies, use a generous, heaped tablespoon measure, then with dampened hands flatten to about 1½ inches across, place 1 inch apart on the baking sheet, and bake for 6 to 8 minutes.

6. Remove from the oven and let cool on the baking sheets for 5 minutes, then transfer to a wire rack and let cool completely.

Everything Cookies 📷

MAKES ABOUT 12 LARGE COOKIES

▶ **PEANUT ALERT!**

My testers requested a "Cowboy Cookie," which, I am led to believe, has everything and anything in it. So, here's a cookie with everything! Switch up the additions if you have a preference; they really are a "use what you have and what you like" cookie as far as the add-ins are concerned!

These are big cookies: big enough so you get a little of everything in each bite, and big enough for a cowboy-size appetite.

2 tablespoons vegan shortening

2 tablespoons canola oil

3 tablespoons light brown sugar, packed

3 tablespoons granulated sugar

3 tablespoons agave nectar

2 tablespoons smooth, natural peanut butter

1 tablespoon ground flax seeds

1 teaspoon vanilla extract

½ teaspoon baking soda

½ cup soy milk

1 cup all-purpose flour

1 cup whole-wheat pastry flour

1 teaspoon pie spice (see page 19)

½ teaspoon salt

¼ teaspoon ancho chile powder

½ cup quick-cooking or old-fashioned rolled oats (not instant)

2 tablespoons raisins

2 tablespoons dried cranberries

2 tablespoons vegan chocolate chips

2 tablespoons cocoa nibs or vegan white chocolate chips

2 tablespoons unsweetened shredded coconut

2 tablespoons sunflower or pumpkin seeds

2 tablespoons finely chopped walnuts or pecans

1 recipe Drizzle Icing (page 251) or Ganache-Style Chocolate (page 252) (optional)

1. Preheat the oven to 350°F and line two baking sheets with parchment.

2. In a large bowl, combine the shortening, oil, sugars, agave nectar, and peanut butter. Cream until smooth.

3. Add the ingredients from flax seeds through baking soda and mix well to combine.

4. Add the soy milk and beat well.

5. Sift in the ingredients from flour through chile powder, and mix well.

6. Add the remaining ingredients, then stir these in. The dough will be thick.

7. Using a ¼-cup measure sprayed with nonstick spray as required, scoop the dough and use dampened hands to form into balls and then flatten to 3 to 3½ inches in diameter (about palm size). Place 2 inches apart on the prepared baking sheets.

8. Bake for 12 to 15 minutes, until the bottoms are lightly browned.

9. Remove from the oven and let cool on the baking sheets for 5 minutes, then let cool completely on a wire rack.

10. Ice with thin Drizzle Icing or ganache, if desired.

Remember...

Gingered Chocolate Chip Cookies

MAKES ABOUT 30 COOKIES

▶ **NO NUTS**

This was invented at one of my daughter's playdates, where the attendees couldn't choose whether to make gingerbread cookies or chocolate chip cookies, so we made both at the same time, and everyone was happy.

These are flavored to a child's palate more than an adult's, so if you think you'd like more of a ginger hit, increase the ground ginger to 1½ teaspoons, or even more!

⅓ cup soy milk
1 tablespoon ground flax seed
½ teaspoon apple cider vinegar

1 cup granulated sugar
⅓ cup vegan margarine

1 teaspoon vanilla extract

1¾ cups unbleached all-purpose flour
½ teaspoon baking soda
½ teaspoon salt
1¼ teaspoons ground ginger
¼ teaspoon ground cinnamon

1 cup vegan chocolate chips

1. Preheat the oven to 375°F and line two baking sheets with parchment paper.

2. In a small bowl, combine the soy milk, flax seed, and vinegar. Set aside and allow to thicken.

3. In a large bowl, cream the sugar and margarine together until light and fluffy. Add the vanilla and mix well.

4. Add the soy milk mixture to the creamed mixture, and mix well.

5. Sift together the ingredients from flour through cinnamon directly into this bowl, add the chocolate chips, and stir to combine. The dough will be quite soft.

6. Scoop generous heaped tablespoons 2 inches apart onto the prepared baking sheets and bake for 10 to 12 minutes, until the cookies are puffy with lightly golden tops and lightly browned bottoms. They will deflate as they cool.

7. Remove from the oven and let cool on the baking sheets for 5 minutes, then transfer to a wire rack and let cool completely.

Variations

Super-Ginger Chip Cookies
For the ginger lover in your life! Add 2 tablespoons of finely chopped crystallized ginger with the chocolate chips.

Gingered Carob Chip Cookies
Replace the chocolate chips with vegan carob chips for a caffeine-free treat.

Green Tea Latte Cookies

MAKES ABOUT 20 COOKIES

▶ **NO NUTS** • **NO SOY** excluding icing

They sell them down at the coffee shop, those fancy green tea lattes or blended cold drinks topped with whipped cream. I took them as my inspiration and give you all the taste in a cookie! These are great for making little ice-cream sandwiches, too.

¼ cup vegan shortening

¼ cup + 3 tablespoons granulated sugar

⅓ cup rice milk

½ teaspoon vanilla extract

1¼ cups + 2 tablespoons all-purpose flour

1½ teaspoons matcha green tea powder
(see Note)

¼ teaspoon baking powder

¼ teaspoon salt

1 recipe Buttercream, More or Less (page
249)

1. Preheat the oven to 400°F and line two baking sheets with parchment paper.

2. In a large bowl, cream together the shortening and sugar, until light and fluffy, then add the milk and vanilla (it will look curdled) and mix well.

3. Sift together the ingredients from flour through salt directly into this bowl, and mix to form a soft, smooth dough. Cover and chill for 30 minutes, for ease of handling.

4. With dampened hands, scoop the dough into tablespoon-size balls, flatten between your hands to form disks 2 inches in diameter, and place 1 inch apart on the prepared sheets.

5. Bake for 8 to 10 minutes, until the bottoms are lightly browned.

6. Remove from the oven and let cool on the baking sheets for 5 minutes, then transfer to a wire rack and let cool completely.

7. Once completely cool, ice the tops of the cookies to produce a random, frothlike latte top, using the Buttercream.

NOTE:

❖ Matcha green tea powder is available in small cans from Asian grocery stores and well-stocked supermarkets or health food stores.

Variation

Green Tea Sandwich Cookies

Make the cookies slightly larger, a 2 ½- to 3-inch disk (as opposed to a 2-inch one), and using the back of a fork, gently press the tines into the cookie to leave a crosshatch (crisscross) design prior to baking. Once cool, ice two cookies together, leaving the crosshatches facing outward. Use 1 or 2 teaspoons of Buttercream, More or Less, made with a drop of vegan red food coloring and using rosewater instead of the extracts specified. These are perfect for an afternoon tea party.

Maple Crosshatch Cookies

MAKES ABOUT 20 COOKIES

▶ **NO SOY • NO SUGAR**

I wouldn't be a good Canadian resident if I didn't put this one in here. I wanted to use maple butter because I have heard it is wonderful and have seen bloggers rave about it. Once I saw the price, though, I couldn't justify the expense for just this recipe, so you'll have to make do with maple cookies flavored with a reduced syrup and maple extract instead.

Keep an eye on the time for these; go for the minimum time and check; they will become dry if you overbake them.

¾ cup pure maple syrup
¼ cup canola oil
1 tablespoon ground flax seeds
1 teaspoon maple extract
½ teaspoon vanilla extract

1½ cups all-purpose flour
⅓ cup cornmeal (see page 15)
½ teaspoon baking soda
½ teaspoon salt

2 tablespoons almond milk

1. Preheat the oven to 375°F and line two baking sheets with parchment paper.
2. In a small saucepan, bring the maple syrup to a boil, then lower the heat to medium-low and continue to boil, stirring frequently, for 10 minutes, until reduced to ½ cup. Transfer to a large bowl.
3. Add the oil, flax seeds, and extracts, and beat for about 2 minutes, until combined and thick.
4. Sift the flour, cornmeal, baking soda, and salt into the syrup mixture. Mix until a crumbly dough has formed.
5. Stir in the milk to form a stiff dough.
6. With dampened hands, scoop the dough into tablespoon-size balls, flatten between your hands to form disks 2 inches in diameter, and place 2 inches apart on the prepared sheets, then with the back of a fork press a crosshatch (crisscross) pattern into the top of each cookie.
7. Bake for 8 to 10 minutes, until the bottoms are lightly browned and the cookies look puffy and golden.
8. Remove from the oven and let cool on the baking sheets for 5 minutes, then transfer to a wire rack and let cool completely.

No-Bake Apricot Cookies

MAKES ABOUT 26 COOKIES

▶ **NO NUTS • NO SOY**

A fruity alternative for those among us who can't (or won't) turn on the oven to make traditional cookies. These are a little soft but still good, with or without the chocolate coating.

Goji berries are not always easy to find, and if you do find them they may be really expensive. Leave them out if you can't find them; the flavor dimension they add is really interesting, but the cookies are still good with apricots only.

An option is not to flatten the dough into cookie shapes but to leave as balls, call them truffles, and you have fruity petits fours to follow your meal!

½ cup roughly chopped dried apricots

2 tablespoons goji berries (optional) (see Notes)

1 cup water

3 cups vegan graham cracker crumbs (see Notes)

1 cup unsweetened shredded coconut

½ cup confectioners' sugar

½ cup vegan white chocolate chips (see Notes)

½ cup vegan white chocolate chips, melted (optional)

1. Line a small baking sheet with parchment paper.

2. In a small pan, over medium heat, combine the apricots, berries (if using), and water. Cover and bring to a boil, then lower the heat and simmer, covered, for 10 minutes, until soft. Remove from the heat and let cool to room temperature.

3. Using a handheld blender, potato masher, or fork, mash or puree the mixture until it is as smooth as you can make it or would like it, then transfer to a large mixing bowl. I like a little texture.

4. Add the cookie crumbs, confectioners' sugar, coconut, and chocolate chips to the bowl, and mix to combine everything. If the mixture seems too sticky, add more graham cracker crumbs by the tablespoonful. Remember that these will firm up a little in the fridge. The mixture should not be overly sticky.

5. With dampened hands, scoop the dough into tablespoon-size balls and flatten between your hands to form disks 2 inches in diameter. Place on the prepared baking sheet, then put the sheet into the freezer for 15 minutes, for the cookies to set hard if you plan to coat with melted chocolate. If you don't, then place directly in the fridge to set.

6. Dip half of each cookie into the melted chocolate (if using), or drizzle chocolate on top, and place on plate or small baking sheet to set in the fridge.

7. Once the chocolate is set, store the cookies in a covered container in the fridge.

NOTES:
- ❖ If not using goji berries, substitute an equal amount of roughly chopped dried apricots.
- ❖ Replace the graham cracker crumbs with vegan digestive biscuit crumbs or other plain vegan cookie crumbs, if you can't find vegan graham crackers where you live.
- ❖ If your white chocolate chips are button size rather than chip size, cut into quarters before using.

Variation

No-Bake Apricot Bar Cookies
Press the mixture into an 8-inch square cake (brownie) pan and chill in the freezer for 15 minutes prior to cutting into sixteen equal pieces. Drizzle with melted white chocolate, if desired, and store in a covered container in the fridge.

No-Bake Chocolate Truffle-Inspired Cookies 📷

MAKES ABOUT 20 COOKIES

▶ **NO NUTS**

My friend Karen says she can't bake. I don't believe her; she just hasn't tried all my recipes yet! In case I am wrong, and she really can't bake, I've made some no-baking-required cookies just for her.

I took some other no-bake cookies to preschool one day. One of the other mothers got ever so excited when she saw them, as she thought they were rum balls. No such luck, I'm afraid, but I promised to make something similar for her, and here we have them!

2 cups vegan graham cracker crumbs
(see Notes)

¼ cup vegan chocolate chips

¼ cup unsweetened Dutch-processed
cocoa powder, sifted if lumpy

2 tablespoons cocoa nibs (see Notes)

⅓ cup light brown sugar, packed

¼ cup vegan margarine

¼ cup vegan chocolate chips

2 tablespoons coconut oil

2 tablespoons ground flax seeds

2 tablespoons dark rum (see Notes)

2 tablespoons soy milk, if required

½ cup chocolate shavings, or other
topping, for garnish (see Notes)

1. Place the cookie crumbs, chocolate chips, cocoa powder, and cocoa nibs in a large bowl and mix together.

2. In a small pan, stirring constantly, combine the brown sugar, margarine, chocolate chips, and coconut oil over medium heat to melt the margarine, oil, and chocolate and dissolve the sugar. This will take only 3 to 5 minutes. Remove from the heat, add the flax seeds and rum, and beat well for about 30 seconds.

3. Pour into the crumb mixture and stir to coat everything. The mixture will look crumbly yet moist. Squeeze to form into tablespoon-size balls, adding soy milk by the teaspoonful if the mixture seems too dry. Roll in shaved chocolate or your desired topping, to coat.

4. Place on a small baking sheet or large plate and chill in the fridge for about an hour, until firm.

NOTES:

❖ Cocoa nibs can be pretty expensive, but they are so very good for you, full of antioxidants and the like, and they add a lovely slightly bitter crunch to the cookies. If you don't have cocoa nibs, add more vegan chocolate chips or some walnut pieces.

❖ If you want a nonalcoholic version, use your favorite nondairy milk.

❖ Replace the graham cracker crumbs with vegan digestive biscuit crumbs or other plain vegan cookie crumbs, if you can't find vegan graham crackers where you live.

❖ Make shaved chocolate by grating a vegan chocolate bar (freezing first is helpful!), if you don't want to buy the expensive already-shaved stuff.

❖ Instead of shaved chocolate, you could coat these cookies in confectioners' sugar, finely chopped nuts, turbinado sugar, shredded coconut, vegan mini chocolate chips, flax meal, or whatever takes your fancy!

Variations

No-Bake Carob Truffle-Inspired Cookies

Use vegan carob powder and carob chips in place of the cocoa powder and cocoa nibs.

No-Bake Truffle Bar Cookies

Press the mixture into an 8-inch square cake (brownie) pan and chill in the freezer for 15 minutes prior to cutting into sixteen equal pieces. Cover with Ganache-Style Chocolate (page 252), if desired, and store in a covered container in the fridge.

Oatmeal Raisin Cookies 📷

MAKES ABOUT 12 LARGE COOKIES

▶ **NO NUTS · NO SOY**

One of the all-time classic cookies, which every baking cookbook has some form of recipe for; mine is no exception! My cookies are big and soft, with a nice texture from the oats and bursts of sweetness from the raisins.

¾ **cup raisins**
½ **cup boiling water**

¼ **cup canola oil**
3 tablespoons light brown sugar, packed
3 tablespoons granulated sugar
2 tablespoons agave nectar
1 teaspoon ground chia seeds
1 teaspoon vanilla extract
½ **teaspoon baking soda**

1 cup all-purpose flour
1 teaspoon pie spice (see page 19)
½ **teaspoon salt**

2½ cups quick-cooking or old-fashioned rolled oats (not instant)

1 recipe Drizzle Icing (page 251) or Ganache-Style Chocolate (page 252) (optional)

1. Preheat the oven to 350°F and line two baking sheets with parchment paper.

2. In a small bowl, combine the raisins with the boiling water, cover, and set aside for 10 minutes to soak, to soften the raisins.

3. In a large bowl, combine the ingredients from canola oil through baking soda and beat with a fork until thick, 1 to 2 minutes. Add the raisins and their soaking water, beat again, and then set aside for 5 minutes

4. Sift in the ingredients from flour through salt, and mix well to combine.

5. Add the oats, then mix these in. The dough will be sticky and thick.

6. Using a ¼-cup measure sprayed with nonstick spray as required, scoop the dough and form into balls with dampened hands. use your hands to flatten to 3 to 3½ inches in diameter (about palm size), and place 2 inches apart on the baking sheets.

7. Bake for 10 to 12 minutes, until the bottoms are lightly browned.

8. Remove from the oven and let cool on the baking sheets for 5 minutes, then transfer to a wire rack and let cool completely.

9. Ice with thin Drizzle Icing, if desired. These cookies are so big, they look pretty when drizzled with two or more colors of icing, in a Jackson Pollock–esque way.

Orange Chocolate-Chip Cookies

MAKES ABOUT 20 COOKIES

▶ **NO NUTS**

Sometimes I make up recipes because my children request certain flavor combinations. This is one of them. Chewy and delicious, these are chocolate chip cookies, but with orange in them, as requested.

¾ cup granulated sugar

¼ cup canola oil

2 tablespoons plain soy milk

2 tablespoons orange juice

1 tablespoon ground flax seeds

1½ teaspoons orange zest (1 medium orange)

½ teaspoon vanilla extract

½ teaspoon vegan orange extract (see Note)

1½ cups all-purpose flour

½ teaspoon baking soda

¼ teaspoon salt

½ cup vegan chocolate chips

1 recipe Drizzle Icing (page 251), colored and flavored orange (optional)

1. Preheat the oven to 375°F and line 2 baking sheets with parchment paper.

2. In a large bowl, vigorously mix together the ingredients from sugar through orange extract until the mixture is smooth and glossy, about 2 minutes. Set aside for 5 minutes.

3. Sift together the flour, baking soda, and salt into the wet ingredients and mix to combine. Add the chocolate chips and mix well; your hands are good for this. The dough will be firm and will hold together well once pressed.

4. With dampened hands, scoop the dough into tablespoon-size balls, flatten between your hands to form disks 2 inches in diameter, and place 1½ inches apart on the prepared sheets.

5. Bake for 8 to 10 minutes, until the bottoms are lightly browned and the tops are puffy.

6. Remove from the oven and let cool on the baking sheets for 5 minutes, then let cool completely on a wire rack.

7. Ice with Drizzle Icing, if desired.

NOTE:

❖ One of my recipe testers suggested replacing the extracts with Grand Marnier (or any other orange flavored liqueur) for a grown-up cookie. Yum!

Variations

Orange Carob-Chip Cookies
Replace the chocolate chips with vegan carob chips for a caffeine-free treat.

Lemon Chocolate-Chip Cookies
Use lemon juice, zest, and extract for a lemony chocolate chip cookie.

Peanut Butter Cookies

MAKES ABOUT 26 COOKIES

▶ **NO SOY • PEANUT ALERT!**

My children don't like peanut butter. I know! I'd like them to, and thought I may be able to get them to try it, if it was presented to them in cookie form. No such luck, but nice try. Maybe these will be appreciated in your house!

Smooth peanut butter is easier for creaming, but there's no reason you can't use crunchy, if that's what you have or prefer.

¾ cup light brown sugar, packed
⅓ cup smooth natural peanut butter
¼ cup vegan shortening
1 tablespoon ground flax seeds

½ cup almond milk
1 teaspoon vanilla extract
¼ teaspoon almond extract

2 cups all-purpose flour
½ teaspoon baking soda
¼ teaspoon baking powder
½ teaspoon salt

¼ cup roughly chopped peanuts, toasted

1. Preheat your oven to 350°F and line two baking sheets with parchment paper.

2. In a large bowl, cream together the brown sugar, peanut butter, shortening, and flax seeds until well combined, thick, and smooth. This will not get light and fluffy.

3. Add the milk and extracts. Mix well to combine. It may look a bit curdled at this point, which is okay; just continue.

4. Sift in the flour, baking powder, baking soda, and salt. Add the chopped nuts and mix everything together until a soft, yet dense dough is formed.

5. With dampened hands, scoop the dough into tablespoon-size balls, flatten between your hands to form disks 2 inches in diameter, and place 2 inches apart on the prepared sheets, then using the tines of a fork, gently press a crosshatch (crisscross) pattern into the top of each cookie.

6. Bake for 8 to 10 minutes, until the undersides are just lightly browned and the cookies are puffy.

7. Remove from the oven and let cool on the baking sheets for 5 minutes, then let cool completely on a wire rack.

Variations

Peanut Butter Sandwich Cookies
Once completely cool, make these into huge sandwich cookies with the Peanut Buttercream (page 107), if you are a super peanut butter fan.

Peanut Butter and Chocolate Chip Cookies
Replace half of the chopped peanuts with vegan chocolate (or even vegan carob) chips.

Other Butter Cookies
Substitute any nut or seed butter of your choice, for a peanut butter–free cookie.

Pecan and Date Cookies 📷

MAKES ABOUT 16 COOKIES

▶ **NO SOY**

These are lovely, soft, not too sweet, nut-laden cookies. I really like the combination of the pecans with the dates, but if you aren't too keen on pecans, make one of the variations.

⅓ cup dark brown sugar, packed
¼ cup Date Paste (page 250)
¼ cup canola oil
2 tablespoons almond milk
1 teaspoon vanilla extract

1¼ cups all-purpose flour
¼ cup ground pecans (see Note)
½ teaspoon salt
½ teaspoon baking soda
½ teaspoon ground cinnamon
¼ teaspoon ground cardamom

¼ cup chopped pecans, toasted

16 pecan halves, for topping

1. In a large bowl, use a fork to whisk together the brown sugar, date paste, oil, milk, and vanilla until smooth.
2. Sift together the flour, salt, baking soda, and spices into the date mixture and mix to combine.
3. Stir in the toasted nuts.
4. Cover and chill the dough for 15 minutes.
5. Preheat the oven to 350°F and line two baking sheets with parchment paper.
6. With dampened hands, scoop the dough into tablespoon-size balls, flatten between your hands to form disks 2 inches in diameter, and place 2 inches apart on the prepared sheets. Press a pecan half into the top of each.
7. Bake for 10 to 12 minutes, until puffy and just browned at the edges.
8. Remove from the oven and let cool on the baking sheets for 5 minutes, then transfer to a wire rack and let cool completely. They will deflate slightly.

NOTE:

❖ Ground pecans may be found in the baking aisle of some supermarkets. If you are grinding your own, the result should be quite fine but not as fine as flour, with only a few larger pieces of nut. See (page 14) for instructions in greater detail.

Variations

Walnut and Date Cookies
Replace the ground, chopped, and whole pecans with walnuts.

Hazelnut and Date Cookies
Replace the ground, chopped, and whole pecans with hazelnuts.

Pinkalicious Cookies

MAKES ABOUT 16 COOKIES

▶ **NO NUTS**

The inspiration for these cookies is a children's book by Victoria Kahn and Elizabeth Kahn (HarperCollins, May 2006) called *Pinkalicious*, where a little girl eats too many pink cupcakes and turns pink. It's adorable and my girls loved it when they were a little younger. They also loved all things pink, and so loved these cookies!

These are big, pretty, chewy, yet moist, cookies with a hint of rose in both taste and looks. A much-requested favorite in my house.

¼ **cup soy milk**

½ **teaspoon apple cider vinegar**

5 **tablespoons vegan margarine, at room temperature**

¾ **cup granulated sugar**

1 **tablespoon agave nectar**

A few drops of vegan red food coloring

1½ **teaspoons of water with 3 drops of rose extract, or 1½ teaspoons rose water (see Notes)**

1½ **cups all-purpose flour**

¼ **teaspoon baking powder**

¼ **teaspoon baking soda**

¼ **teaspoon salt**

1 **recipe Drizzle Icing (page 251) (optional)**

1. Preheat the oven to 400°F and line two baking sheets with parchment paper.

2. In a small bowl, combine the milk and vinegar, and set aside for 5 minutes to curdle.

3. In a larger bowl, cream together the margarine and sugar, until light and fluffy. Add the agave nectar, food coloring, and rose extract mixture, and mix until well combined.

4. Sift together the flour, salt, baking powder, and baking soda into the creamed mixture and mix. Add the soy milk mixture and mix to form a soft dough.

5. Divide the dough into sixteen equal portions, roll into balls, flatten slightly between your hands, and place about 2 inches apart on the prepared baking sheets.

6. Bake for 8 to 10 minutes, until the bottoms are lightly browned and the cookies are puffy.

7. Remove from the oven and let cool on the baking sheets for 5 minutes, then transfer to a wire rack and let cool completely. The cookies will deflate a little as they cool.

8. Once cool, ice with lines of thin Drizzle Icing, left white or tinted pink, if desired.

9. When the icing is set, store in a covered container at room temperature.

NOTES:
- ❖ I have rose extract, and mix it with a little water prior to using, to ensure distribution through the dough. Rose extract is quite thick, and this helps to better control the flavor, as it is very strong. Alternatively, if you don't have rose extract, use rose water, which is easier to find. Check Middle Eastern or Asian grocery stores or gourmet markets.
- ❖ Ensure your red food coloring is vegan. Many varieties are made with cochineal, which comes from crushed-up beetles. There are, however, a number of plant-based alternatives available.

Plain Cookies 📷

MAKES ABOUT 20 COOKIES IF SLICED, AND ABOUT 36 IF ROLLED AND CUT (DEPENDING ON THE CUTTER SIZE)

▶ **NO NUTS** excluding variations

This is what my girls ask for when they don't want chocolate chip or any other cookie.

The recipe is really versatile and you can change it by switching the vanilla to a different extract, by adding food coloring, or by rolling the dough in chopped nuts or sugar prior to chilling. See the variations for a few ideas, and then let your imagination take off!

The dough, once prepared, can stay in the fridge for up to a week, as long as it is well wrapped.

3 tablespoons vegan margarine, at room temperature

3 tablespoons vegan shortening

½ cup granulated sugar

2 tablespoons agave nectar

1 teaspoon vanilla extract

1½ cups all-purpose flour

½ teaspoon baking powder

½ teaspoon baking soda

½ teaspoon salt

2 to 3 tablespoons soy milk

1 recipe Drizzle Icing (page 251) (optional)

Vegan sprinkles (optional)

1. In a large bowl, cream together the margarine, shortening, and sugar until light and fluffy. Add the agave nectar and vanilla and beat in.

2. Sift in the flour, baking powder, baking soda, and salt and mix until a crumbly stiff dough forms.

3. Add the milk a tablespoon at a time, to form a firm dough.

4. Shape the dough into a log 1½ to 2 inches in diameter, wrap firmly in plastic wrap, and place in the fridge to chill for at least an hour.

5. When ready to bake, preheat the oven to 375°F and line two baking sheets.

6. To bake sliced cookies, cut ½-inch thick slices off the log, or slice thicker as desired, place about 2 inches apart on the prepared baking sheets, and bake for 8 to 10 minutes, until the cookie bottoms are lightly browned.

7. To bake rolled-out cookies, roll out the log of dough to about ¼-inch thickness, and using shaped cookie cutters, cut out your cookies. Place these about 2 inches apart on the prepared baking sheets, and bake for 5 to 10 minutes, depending on the size of your cookies. Check smaller cookies at 5 minutes, and larger ones at 8 minutes. The cookies should be lightly browned, but not so much brown as golden.

8. Remove from the oven and let cool on the baking sheets for 5 minutes, then let cool completely on a wire rack.

9. Once completely cool, decorate with Drizzle Icing, either spread or drizzled on, and top with your choice of sprinkles. Just do what takes your fancy!

Variations

These are some fun ideas. Please don't limit yourself to these but use them as a launch pad to create your own unique cookie variations.

Candy Cane Cookies

Before chilling, slicing, and baking, mix 2 tablespoons of crushed candy canes into the dough and then roll the log in more crushed candy.

Checkerboard Cookies

Divide the dough in half and color (your choice) half, then shape each half into two long, thin, rectangular logs of dough. Make a square-shaped log by building it up with the colors alternating, press gently together and ensure the log is square; then chill, slice, and bake as directed.

Christmas Soy Nog Cookies

Add ¼ teaspoon of ground nutmeg with the flour, and ½ teaspoon of rum or brandy extract with the agave nectar and vanilla. Or use a nondairy nog instead of the soy milk, for another seasonally flavored cookie. Cut out into Christmas shapes and make your icing with a nondairy nog instead of water or soy milk.

Jammy Dodger Cookies

Make rolled and cut, circular plain cookies and form them into sandwich cookies with a little of your favorite jam. If you have a peekaboo-type cutter that lets some filling poke through, then cut half of the cookies with this for a cute look.

Kaleidoscope Cookies

Use plain dough, and shape into a square log. Before chilling, slicing, and baking, press each side of the square into a different colored sugar.

Lavender Cookies

Add 1 tablespoon of very finely chopped culinary lavender (see page 62) with the margarine and shortening. Before chilling, slicing, and baking, roll the log in purple colored sugar.

Lemon or Orange Slice Cookies

Make the dough using lemon or orange extract, not vanilla. Shape the cylindrical log thicker than usual, say, to 3½ to 4 inches in diameter. Before chilling, slicing, and baking, roll in yellow or orange sugar to look like the rind; then cut each disk in half to look like a lemon or orange slice. You can even mark segments.

Mint Cookies

Add 1 tablespoon of finely chopped fresh mint and ½ teaspoon of mint extract with the agave nectar and vanilla. Before chilling, slicing, and baking, roll the log in green colored sugar.

Nut-Coated Cookies

Before slicing and baking, roll the log in finely chopped nuts mixed with turbinado sugar for a pretty nutty cookie, with or without 2 tablespoons of finely chopped nuts added to the dough. Slice and bake as directed.

Swirl Cookies

Divide the dough in half, roll out one-half to about ½ inch thick, then color the other half of the dough any color you like and do the same. Place the colored dough on top of the plain dough, and starting from one end, roll up into a swirl to shape into a log, and chill. Slice and bake as usual, and you get a pretty swirl cookie.

Remember...

Princess Cookies

MAKES ABOUT 12 COOKIES

▶ **NO NUTS**

My elder daughter had a princess playdate at her friend's house one day and wanted cookies to take to share. She wanted them "sparkly like a crown with jewels" and this was the best I could come up with! The princesses liked them, so that's all that matters.

They are reminiscent of Snickerdoodles, my testers tell me. You'll have to take their word for it, as it is not a cookie I am familiar with!

2 tablespoons granulated sugar
2 tablespoons turbinado sugar
¼ teaspoon ground cinnamon

¼ cup water
¼ cup soy creamer (see page 16)
1 teaspoon finely ground chia seeds (see Note)

¼ cup canola oil
½ teaspoon vanilla extract

1½ cups all-purpose flour
¾ cup granulated sugar
½ teaspoon baking soda
¼ teaspoon salt
¼ teaspoon ground cinnamon

Extra turbinado sugar, for sprinkling (optional)

1. Preheat the oven to 375°F and prepare two baking sheets by lining with parchment paper.

2. In a small bowl, combine the sugars and cinnamon.

3. In a large bowl, combine the ground chia seeds with the water and creamer. Mix vigorously with a fork, and then set aside for 5 minutes.

4. Add the oil and vanilla to the chia mixture and whisk to combine.

5. Sift together the dry ingredients (from flour through cinnamon) into this bowl, and mix to form a firm yet sticky dough. If you find at this point that the dough is super sticky, add flour by the tablespoonful until more firm than sticky, before chilling.

6. Cover the bowl and chill for 20 to 30 minutes, to enable easier handling of the dough.

7. Shape scant ¼-cups of the dough into balls (about golf ball size) and roll each ball in the cinnamon mixture to get a good coating. Flatten into disks 2½ to 3 inches across and place 2 inches apart on the prepared baking sheets. Sprinkle the top of each cookie with a little more turbinado sugar, if desired.

8. Bake for 10 to 12 minutes, until the bottoms are lightly browned and the cookies are puffy.

9. Remove from the oven and let cool on the baking sheets for 5 minutes, then let cool completely on a wire rack.

NOTE:
❖ Chia seeds are commonly sold under the brand name Salba, and can be purchased ready ground. Otherwise, you can grind your own in a spice grinder.

Seed Cookies 📷

MAKES ABOUT 24 COOKIES

► **NO NUTS**

Sort of healthy, as they are loaded with seeds, and because of that, with protein, healthy fats, and zinc! Don't kid yourself too much, though; they're still cookies!

If you find blackstrap molasses too bitter for your taste, please use regular molasses. Again, this is one my kids request chocolate chips in. I haven't added them here, but if you'd like to, add 2 tablespoons with the seeds and raisins at the end.

¼ cup sunflower seeds, toasted
2 tablespoons sunflower or canola oil

1 cup all-purpose flour
⅓ cup whole-wheat pastry flour
1 tablespoon cornstarch
1 tablespoon ground flax seeds
½ teaspoon ground cinnamon
½ teaspoon salt
¼ teaspoon baking powder
¼ teaspoon baking soda

½ cup light brown sugar, packed
¼ cup vegan margarine
2 tablespoons vegan shortening
1 tablespoon blackstrap molasses

3 tablespoons soy milk
1 teaspoon vanilla extract

2 tablespoons hemp or sesame seeds
2 tablespoons pumpkin seeds
2 tablespoons sunflower seeds
2 tablespoons raisins

1 recipe Drizzle Icing (page 251) (optional)
Sunflower and pumpkin seeds, for garnish (optional)

1. Preheat the oven to 350°F and line 2 baking sheets with parchment paper.

2. In a mini food processor or spice grinder, grind the sunflower seeds to a fine meal, transfer to a small bowl, and mix with the oil to form a paste.

3. Sift together the ingredients from flour through baking soda into a medium bowl.

4. In a large bowl, cream together the shortening, brown sugar, and molasses until light and fluffy. Add the soy milk, vanilla, and seed paste, then mix to combine.

5. Add the dry ingredients to the creamed mixture and mix to form a soft dough. Mix in the seeds and raisins. Cover and chill for 15 minutes.

6. Once chilled, scoop into tablespoon-size balls, place 2 inches apart on the prepared baking sheets, and with the back of a measuring cup flatten the balls to 1½-inch disks.

7. Bake for 10 to 12 minutes, until the bottoms are lightly browned.

8. Remove from the oven and let cool on the baking sheets for 5 minutes, then transfer to a wire rack and let cool completely.

9. When completely cool, ice the center of the top of each cookie (so you can see the edges poking out) with Drizzle Icing and top with a few seeds, if desired.

Spelt Carob Cookies 📷

MAKES ABOUT 24 COOKIES

▶ **NO NUTS • NO WHEAT**

Carob gets no love. Until now.

If you don't have carob, substitute unsweetened Dutch-processed cocoa powder and vegan chocolate chips.

⅓ cup soy milk
½ teaspoon apple cider vinegar

¾ cup granulated sugar
3 tablespoons unsweetened applesauce
3 tablespoons canola oil
1 tablespoon ground flax seeds
½ teaspoon vanilla

2¼ cups spelt flour
2 tablespoons vegan carob powder
½ teaspoon baking powder
¼ teaspoon salt

¾ cup vegan carob chips (see Note)

1. Preheat the oven to 375°F and line two baking sheets with parchment paper.

2. Combine the soy milk and vinegar in a large bowl, and set aside for 5 minutes to curdle.

3. Add the sugar, applesauce, oil, flax seeds, and vanilla and beat well for a couple of minutes to combine and thicken slightly.

4. Sift together the dry ingredients (from flour through salt) into the wet mixture and mix to combine. Fold in the carob chips.

5. With dampened hands, scoop the dough into tablespoon-size balls, flatten between your hands to form disks 2 inches in diameter, and place 2 inches apart on the prepared sheets.

6. Bake for 10 to 12 minutes, until the bottoms are lightly golden and the cookies nicely puffed up.

7. Remove from the oven and let cool on the baking sheets for 5 minutes, then let cool completely on a wire rack.

NOTE:
❖ Double-check the ingredients of your carob chips, as many brands contain dairy.

Spelt Jam Thumbprint Cookies

MAKES ABOUT 24 COOKIES

▶ **NO NUTS • NO SOY • NO WHEAT**

Just as the title says, your favorite jam is baked into a cookie, with a cute thumbprint filled with more jam. Overload? Maybe, but it's your choice of jam. The cookie part of these isn't overly sweet; the idea when eating is to get a little of the jam filling with each bite, which makes them taste sweeter.

⅓ cup granulated sugar
2 tablespoons canola oil
2 tablespoons vegan shortening

⅓ cup rice milk
¼ cup of your favorite jam
1 tablespoon ground flax seeds
½ teaspoon vanilla extract

2½ cups spelt flour
2 tablespoons cornstarch
½ teaspoon salt
½ teaspoon baking soda

2 tablespoons jam, as above, for the thumbprints

Confectioners' sugar, for dusting

1. Preheat the oven to 375°F and line two baking sheets with parchment paper.

2. In a large bowl, cream together the granulated sugar, oil, and shortening until light and fluffy.

3. Whisk in the milk, jam, flax seeds, and vanilla extract for about 2 minutes to distribute the jam really well.

4. Sift in the flour, cornstarch, salt, and baking soda. Mix to form a firm dough.

5. Cover and chill for 10 to 15 minutes to enable easier handling.

6. With dampened hands, scoop the dough into tablespoon-size balls, flatten between your hands to form disks 2 inches in diameter, and place 2 inches apart on the prepared sheets.

7. Push the top of one thumb gently into the center of each cookie to form an indentation.

8. Bake for 7 minutes, then remove the baking sheet from the oven. If necessary, use the back of a ½-teaspoon measure to re-indent the center of each cookie. Scoop ½ teaspoon of jam into each indentation. Return to the oven to bake for a further 3 to 4 minutes; the cookies will be lightly browned underneath.

9. Remove from the oven and let cool on the baking sheets for 5 minutes, then let cool completely on wire racks.

10. Once completely cool, and just prior to serving, dust lightly with a little confectioners' sugar.

White Cookies

MAKES ABOUT 14 COOKIES

▶ **NO NUTS** excluding variation

These treats were the result of a desire to have a white cookie, to counteract the other colors I have, notably pink (Pinkalicious Cookies, page 132), brown (Cocoa Oatmeal Cookies with Cocoa Nibs, page 120), and green (Green Tea Latte Cookies, page 124). They are very rich, sweet, soft cookies, a complete dessert in themselves. Seriously, you only need one!

I don't think they need any extra decoration, but if you want to make them look extra pretty with Ganache-Style Chocolate or Drizzle Icing, then go ahead.

¼ **cup soy milk**
¼ **teaspoon ground chia seeds, or 1 teaspoon ground flax seeds (see Notes)**

¾ **cup granulated sugar**
3 **tablespoons vegan shortening**
2 **tablespoons vegan margarine**
½ **teaspoon vanilla extract**

1½ **cups all-purpose flour**
½ **teaspoon baking soda**
¼ **teaspoon salt**

¼ **cup vegan white chocolate chips (see Notes)**
¼ **cup vegan marshmallows, chopped small (see Notes)**

1 **recipe Ganache-Style Chocolate (page 252) or Drizzle Icing (page 251) (optional)**

1. Preheat the oven to 375°F and line two baking sheets with parchment paper.

2. In a small bowl, combine the soy milk and chia seeds. Set aside for 5 minutes.

3. In a large bowl, cream together the sugar, shortening, and margarine until light and fluffy. This may take a while, so give your arm a rest if needed, or use an electric mixer.

4. Add the soy milk mixture and vanilla, then mix well to combine. The mixture will look curdled at this point, but that is fine.

5. Sift together the flour, baking soda, and salt into this bowl, and mix to form soft dough.

6. Fold in the chocolate chips and marshmallows.

7. Cover and chill in the fridge for 15 to 20 minutes. This will make the dough easier to handle and less sticky.

8. Using a scant ¼-cup measure, scoop the dough (about golf ball size) onto the prepared sheets, about 2 inches apart. Using the bottom of a measuring cup, press the cookies into disks just under ½ inch thick.

9. Bake for 10 minutes, until the bottoms of the cookies are lightly browned and the tops barely colored.

10. Remove from the oven and let cool on the baking sheets for 5 minutes, then let cool completely on a wire a rack.

11. Decorate these with drizzles of ganache or icing, as desired.

12. When the icing is set, store in a covered container at room temperature.

NOTES:

❖ If you don't have chia seeds, substitute with ground flax seeds. The cookies will spread a little more, and may not look as white, but will still end up delicious.

❖ If you have button-size vegan white chocolate, not chip-size, cut into quarters to make the pieces more manageable.

❖ I use vegan mini marshmallows from Sweet & Sara, cut in half. I've found that if you're cutting up marshmallows, mini or standard size, using scissors sprayed with a little nonstick spray is the way to go!

Variation

Nutty White Cookies

If you don't have one or other of the white chocolate or marshmallows, or just don't feel like having them in your cookie today, substitute an equal amount of chopped macadamia nuts. Superb!

Whole-Wheat Rum Raisin Cookies

MAKES ABOUT 18 COOKIES

▶ NO NUTS • NO SOY • NO SUGAR

A soft, dense, wholesome, yummy, adult cookie with no added sugar, as it's sweetened with the raisins and is made with whole wheat. Feeling virtuous yet? There's enough rum for it to be noticed and provide a great flavor touch—just enough to spoil your virtue.

⅔ cup raisins
½ cup boiling water

1½ cups whole-wheat pastry flour
½ teaspoon salt
½ teaspoon baking soda

¼ cup raisins
¼ cup golden raisins

3 tablespoons canola oil
3 tablespoons rice milk
2 tablespoons ground flax seeds
2 tablespoons dark rum
½ teaspoon vanilla extract

½ teaspoon rum extract

1 recipe Drizzle Icing (page 251), made with rum extract (optional)

1. Preheat the oven to 375°F and line two baking sheets with parchment paper.

2. In a small bowl, combine the ⅔ cup of raisins (not the golden ones) and boiling water. Cover and set aside for 10 minutes to soften the raisins.

3. Sift together the flour, salt, and baking soda, into a large bowl, add the unsoaked raisins and golden raisins, and toss to coat.

4. In a blender or food processor, blend together the soaked raisins and their soaking water, and the oil, milk, flax seeds, rum, and extracts until smooth with no large lumps of raisin.

5. Pour the blended ingredients into the flour mixture and gently combine. The dough is thick but soft.

6. With dampened hands, scoop the dough into tablespoon-size balls, flatten between your hands to form disks 3 inches in diameter, and place 2 inches apart on the prepared sheets. Bake for 10 to 12 minutes, until the tops are puffed and the bottoms lightly browned.

7. Remove from the oven and let cool on the baking sheets for 5 minutes, then let cool completely on wire racks.

Variations

Child-Friendly Whole-Wheat Rum Raisin Cookies

Instead of the rum, add 2 tablespoons more soy milk. You'll still get some of the rum flavor from the extract.

Whole-Wheat Rum Raisin Chocolate Cookies

Replace 2 tablespoons of flour with unsweetened cocoa powder, increase the rum extract to ¾ teaspoon (to counteract the chocolate), and replace the golden raisins with vegan chocolate chips for a healthy, chocolaty version of this cookie.

Muffins

DID YOU KNOW that if you go to any online book retailer, Amazon.com, for example, and search for "muffins," you get over three thousand hits? (It's true, I've done it.) Many, many books have been written about muffins: low fat, sweet, savory, gluten free, from A to Z, you name it. And there are muffin books from all over the place. There must be a reason for all this popularity.

What we knew as a muffin in New Zealand, in the late '70s and early '80s, is now referred to as an English muffin (the crumpet-like kind). What the world now refers to as a muffin, we called American muffins. I think the change owes just as much (if not more) to the growing popularity of the baked good itself, rather than to the decline in popularity of the yeasted English muffin. People these days, in New Zealand and everywhere, have less time to spend on luxuries, including home baking, so the choice they make is to proceed with baking that gives the most delicious return in the smallest amount of time with the least amount of effort. Sorry, English muffin!

I think muffins are popular at least in part because they are:

* **Flexible:** More than with any other type of baked good, muffins lend themselves to a little bit of creativity. They are pretty robust, forgiving things, so once comfortable and more experienced, a home cook can make substitutions or variations to the recipes and not end up with a disaster. Good for the ego, that.

* **Worldly:** What can be put into muffins is limited only by the imagination.

* **Portable:** You can take them anywhere, without a special carrying case in most instances (some of the more fancy ones, maybe not), I often throw them into a resealable plastic bag (which is not the most elegant container, I know), when I'm taking them out and about.

* **Healthy:** You can make these good for you! You can add things, use healthier flour, replace the sugar and the fat, while still ending up with something delicious. As the ones that follow are vegan, they start out with an advantage over those "'traditional" muffins that contain eggs and dairy, in that they are cholesterol free and lower in fat from the get-go.

* **Delicious:** Muffins taste good! Sweet, chocolaty, fruity, spicy, salty, herby, savory, whatever they are, they are good! Why else would anyone make them at all, vegan or otherwise?

Muffins store well at room temperature: Cover them with a clean tea towel and they're good until tomorrow. If you're planning on keeping them longer, a covered container is the way to go. They freeze and thaw well, without texture issues, keeping in the freezer for up to 3 months.

As with biscuits, scones, and loaves, the batter for these really does need a gentle touch, so again—no electric mixers, please. As I've already said, where the recipe directs you to mix until just combined, it really does mean just. Small lumps in the batter are okay, as are small patches of unmixed-in flour.

Apricot and Cranberry Muffins

MAKES 12 MUFFINS

▶ NO NUTS • NO SUGAR • NO WHEAT

These tasty beauties are heavier than some of the other muffin recipes in this book because they contain a large amount of fruit and whole grain. They are a deliciously sweet start to the day, with no processed sugar.

You can use any fresh or frozen berry (for example, blueberries or raspberries) in place of the cranberries if you don't like those or need a little extra sweetness (cranberries can be tart)!

1 cup water
¾ cup dried apricots

1 cup soy milk
1 teaspoon apple cider vinegar

1⅔ cups spelt flour
½ cup quick-cooking or old-fashioned rolled oats (not instant)
2½ teaspoons baking powder
1 teaspoon baking soda
½ teaspoon salt
½ teaspoon ground cinnamon
¼ teaspoon ground allspice

¼ cup finely chopped dried apricots

3 tablespoons pure maple syrup

3 tablespoons cranberry juice
2 tablespoons canola oil
1 teaspoon vanilla extract

¾ cup fresh or frozen cranberries

1. In a small pan, soak the ¾ cup of apricots in the water for at least 1 hour. Bring to a boil and boil over medium heat for 10 minutes. Remove from the heat and let cool for 10 minutes. Mash with a fork or blend to a thick paste. Keep at room temperature until required. (If you have less than ¾ cup of apricot paste, add unsweetened applesauce to top up to the required quantity.)

2. Preheat the oven to 375°F and spray twelve cups of a muffin pan with nonstick spray. (If not using some of the cups, fill them halfway with water so the pan won't warp.)

3. In a small bowl, combine the soy milk and vinegar, and set aside for 5 minutes to curdle.

4. In a large bowl, whisk together the flour, oats, baking powder, baking soda, salt, and spices. Add the chopped apricots, break up to distribute evenly, and toss to coat with the flour.

5. Add the soy milk mixture, syrup, juice, oil, and vanilla to the apricot paste and stir to combine.

6. Pour the wet ingredients into the dry and just combine. Fold in the cranberries.

7. Spoon the mixture into the prepared pan. The cups will be full. Bake for 20 to 25 minutes, until a toothpick comes out clean.

8. Remove from the oven and let cool in the muffin pan for 5 minutes, then transfer to a wire rack to let cool completely.

Variation

Apricot and Dried Cranberry Muffins
If you find cranberries too tart when fresh, try dried, which tend to be sweeter. Use the same amount as for fresh.

Banana Walnut Muffins

MAKES 12 MUFFINS

Banana muffins are a standard and can be changed in so many ways. In this variation, the crunch of the walnuts contrasts with the smoothness of the banana and the creaminess of the yogurt. Use other nuts if you don't like walnuts, and leave them untoasted if time is not on your side—it's still good stuff.

The batter for these looks quite thick when mixed, but don't worry, the muffins bake well risen, lovely textured, and tender!

2 ripe bananas, well mashed

⅔ cup vegan yogurt

½ cup pure maple syrup

¼ cup canola oil

2 tablespoons blackstrap molasses (see Note)

1 teaspoon vanilla extract

2½ cups all-purpose flour

⅓ cup granulated sugar

¼ cup wheat germ

2 teaspoons baking powder

1 teaspoon ground cinnamon

½ teaspoon baking soda

¼ teaspoon salt

1 cup finely chopped walnuts, lightly toasted

1. Preheat the oven to 375°F and spray twelve cups of a muffin pan with nonstick spray. (If not using some of the cups, fill them halfway with water so the pan won't warp.)

2. In a large bowl, whisk together the yogurt, bananas, oil, molasses, syrup, and vanilla until smooth.

3. Sift together the dry ingredients into a separate bowl, add to the liquid ingredients, and mix to just combine.

4. Fold in the walnuts.

5. Spoon the mixture into the prepared pan. The cups will be full. Bake for 20 to 25 minutes, until a toothpick comes out clean.

6. Remove from the oven and let cool in the muffin pan for 5 minutes, then transfer to a wire rack to let cool completely.

NOTE:

❖ If you don't like the slightly bitter taste of blackstrap molasses, use whichever molasses you prefer.

Variations

Healthier Banana Walnut Muffins
Substitute whole-wheat pastry flour, or even whole-wheat flour for some or all of the all-purpose flour, for healthier though denser muffins.

Banana and Other Nut Muffins
Will be just as good, so feel free to substitute with your favorite nuts or what you have.

Banana, Nut, and Chocolate Chip Muffins

Replace half the walnuts with vegan chocolate chips, for an extra flavor dimension.

Banana, Nut, and Dried Fruit Muffins

Replace half the walnuts with raisins, dried currants, or your favorite dried fruit for a chewy burst of fruit.

Banana, Nut, and Coconut Muffins

Replace half the walnuts with lightly toasted shredded coconut, for my husband's favorite variation.

Banana and Blueberry Muffins

Replace all the walnuts with fresh or frozen blueberries, for my younger daughter's favorite variation.

Beet Chocolate Muffins

MAKES 12 MUFFINS

▶ NO NUTS • NO WHEAT

Believe me, if I hadn't told you there was beet in these, you would never have guessed. Serve these chocolaty and moist muffins and stump people with the "secret ingredient," knowing the treat you're giving them is good for them, too!

1 medium to large beet, peeled (about 8 ounces)

¾ cup rice milk
¼ cup canola oil
1 teaspoon vanilla extract

1¾ cups spelt flour

1 cup granulated sugar
⅓ cup unsweetened cocoa powder
3 tablespoons cornstarch
2½ teaspoons baking powder
½ teaspoon salt
½ teaspoon ground nutmeg

1. Using the fine grating side of your box grater, grate your beet into a small saucepan. Just about cover the grated beet with water and cook over medium heat, at a low boil, for about 15 minutes, until soft. Drain, reserving ¼ cup of the cooking water. Blend the beet and the reserved water to a smooth puree—you need 1 cup of puree. (If you end up with less, make up the difference with applesauce, and if you end up with more, save for some future use, such as in soup.)

2. Preheat the oven to 375°F and spray twelve cups of a muffin pan with nonstick spray. (If not using some of the cups, fill them halfway with water so the pan won't warp.)

3. Add the milk, oil, and vanilla to the beet puree and mix well.

4. Sift together the ingredients from flour through nutmeg, make a well in the dry mixture, and add the beet mixture. Stir gently to just combine.

5. Pour the batter into the prepared pan. Bake for 20 to 25 minutes, until a toothpick comes out clean.

6. Remove from the oven and let cool in the muffin pan for 5 minutes, then transfer to a wire rack to let cool completely.

Blackberry and Apple Crumble Muffins

MAKES 12 MUFFINS

▶ **NO NUTS • NO SOY**

There are some trails near our house that are a delight to walk in late summer, not just for the shade they provide on a hot day. Along the path are plenty of wild blackberry bushes, loaded with ripe juicy fruits. We love to take a walk with a big container and see how many we get; this muffin recipe is a perfect way to use them up!

The apple is from the applesauce, which also helps with keeping these moist—no oil in this recipe!

1½ cups spelt flour

1 cup all-purpose flour

2 teaspoons baking powder

½ teaspoon baking soda

½ teaspoon salt

½ teaspoon ground cinnamon

⅛ teaspoon ground cloves

1 cup rice milk

⅔ cup granulated sugar

½ cup unsweetened applesauce

1 tablespoon freshly squeezed lemon juice (½ medium lemon)

1 teaspoon vanilla extract

1 cup blackberries, halved if very large (see Notes)

CRUMBLE TOPPING

⅓ cup quick-cooking or old-fashioned rolled oats (not instant)

3 tablespoons granulated sugar

2 tablespoons canola oil

2 tablespoons vegan panko or bread crumbs (see Notes)

1 tablespoon agave nectar

¼ teaspoon ground cinnamon

1. Preheat the oven to 375°F and spray twelve cups of a muffin pan with nonstick spray. (If not using some of the cups, fill them halfway with water so the pan won't warp.) Sift together the dry ingredients (from flour through cloves), into a large bowl.

2. In another bowl, mix together the milk, sugar, applesauce, lemon juice, and vanilla.

3. Add the liquid ingredients to the dry and mix to just combine. Fold in the blackberries.

4. In a small bowl, mix the topping ingredients until well combined. Keep to one side until required.

5. Spoon the muffin batter into the prepared pan. The cups will be full. Evenly distribute the topping among the muffins and lightly press into the top of each muffin.

6. Bake for 18 to 22 minutes, until a toothpick comes out clean.

7. Remove from the oven and let cool in the muffin pan for 5 minutes, then transfer to a wire rack to let cool completely.

NOTES:

❖ Use store-bought blackberries, cut in half if they are huge, if you don't have access to a wild bush, but I find the lack of uniformity you get with wild berries makes them that much better.

❖ If picking wild blackberries, please don't pick from roadsides, or from where they are likely to have been sprayed by city workers; and needless to say, wash very well, watching for bugs!

❖ Panko is a Japanese type of bread crumb that stays crisp during baking. Available in most supermarkets, health food stores, and Asian food stores, it is not hard to find.

Bran and Germ Muffins

MAKES 12 MUFFINS

▶ **NO NUTS • NO SOY**

Packed with whole-wheat goodness, and then some more added for good measure! These muffins are a quintessential breakfast food.

¾ cup whole-wheat flour
1½ cups whole-wheat pastry flour
⅔ cup granulated sugar
½ cup wheat bran
½ cup wheat germ
1 tablespoon baking powder
½ teaspoon baking soda
½ teaspoon salt
½ teaspoon ground cinnamon

1½ cups rice milk
¼ cup unsweetened applesauce
¼ cup canola oil
1 teaspoon vanilla extract

2 tablespoons wheat germ

1. Preheat the oven to 375°F and spray twelve cups of a muffin pan with nonstick spray. (If not using some of the cups, fill them halfway with water so the pan won't warp.)

2. In a large bowl, whisk together the ingredients from flour through cinnamon.

3. In a small bowl, whisk together the ingredients from milk, applesauce, oil, and vanilla.

4. Make a well in the center of the dry ingredients and add the liquids. Mix to just combine.

5. Spoon the mixture into the prepared pan. The cups will be full. Sprinkle the top of each with a little wheat germ. Bake for 20 to 25 minutes, until a toothpick comes out clean.

6. Remove from the oven and let cool in the muffin pan for 5 minutes, then transfer to a wire rack to let cool completely.

Variations

Raisin and Bran Muffins
Add ⅓ cup of raisins (either as they are or after soaking in boiling water for 10 minutes, then draining) after mixing in the liquid ingredients. Alternatively, add your favorite dried fruit, such as apricots, dates, or apples, cut up if larger.

Nut and Bran Muffins
Add ⅓ cup of your choice of nuts in place of the raisins.

Berry and Bran Muffins
Add ⅓ cup of fresh or frozen berries in place of the raisins.

Chocolate Chip and Bran Muffins
I personally don't think chocolate chips are good here, but go right ahead if you want to toss in ⅓ cup.

Remember...

Caribbean-Inspired Muffins

▶ **NO NUTS**

Fancy a trip to a land bathed in sunshine? I can't get you on a cruise ship, but you'll feel like you are on one if you close your eyes as you enjoy these muffins; with just a little help from your imagination, of course.

1 cup mango nectar

½ cup soy milk

½ cup light brown sugar, packed

¼ cup canned crushed pineapple in juice

2 tablespoons light rum (see Notes)

½ teaspoon coconut extract

½ teaspoon vanilla extract

2½ cups spelt flour

¼ cup granulated sugar

2 teaspoons baking powder

1 teaspoon baking soda

½ teaspoon salt

¼ teaspoon ground allspice

¼ cup finely chopped crystallized ginger

½ cup unsweetened, shredded coconut, toasting optional (see Notes)

1. Preheat the oven to 375°F and spray twelve cups of a muffin pan with nonstick spray. (If not using some of the cups, fill them halfway with water so the pan won't warp.)

2. In a bowl, whisk the ingredients from mango nectar through vanilla until well combined.

3. Sift together the dry ingredients (from flour through allspice), into a large bowl. Add the crystallized ginger and coconut, then toss lightly to coat with the flour mixture.

4. Add the wet ingredients to the dry and mix to just combine.

5. Spoon the mixture into the prepared pan. The cups will be full. Bake for 20 to 25 minutes, until a toothpick comes out clean.

6. Remove from the oven and let cool in the muffin pan for 5 minutes, then transfer to a wire rack to let cool completely.

NOTES:

❖ If you'd prefer these to be alcohol free, use apple juice in place of the rum.

❖ I like these with toasted coconut, but some of my testers preferred them with the coconut untoasted. I'll leave the choice up to you.

Carrot and Pistachio Muffins

This is my variation on the usual carrot and "insert nut here" recipe you see wherever there are muffin recipes. The cardamom in these adds a lovely flavor and goes really well with the pistachios.

I bought my nuts ready toasted, but do it yourself (see instructions on page 21) if you'd prefer or if you can't find toasted pistachios.

½ cup all-purpose flour

½ cup whole-wheat flour

1 cup whole-wheat pastry flour

2½ teaspoons baking powder

½ teaspoon salt

¼ teaspoon ground nutmeg

¼ teaspoon ground cardamom

¾ cup shelled pistachios, chopped roughly and toasted

½ cup soy milk

½ cup light brown sugar, packed

¼ cup + 2 tablespoons apple juice

¼ cup soy creamer (see page 16)

¼ cup canola oil

2 tablespoons pure maple syrup

1¼ cups finely grated carrot (about 3 medium carrots), tightly packed

12 to 36 shelled pistachios, for garnish

1. Preheat the oven to 375°F and spray twelve cups of a muffin pan with nonstick spray. (If not using some of the cups, fill them halfway with water so the pan won't warp.)

2. Sift together flour, baking powder, salt, and spices into a large bowl. Add pistachios and toss to combine.

3. In another large bowl, whisk together the milk, creamer, juice, oil, brown sugar, and syrup, then stir in the grated carrot till well mixed.

4. Pour the carrot mixture into the dry ingredients, and mix to just combine.

5. Spoon the mixture into the prepared muffin pan. The cups will be full. Top each muffin with a pistachio (or two or three, as you prefer). Bake for 20 to 25 minutes, until a toothpick comes out clean.

6. Remove from the oven and let cool in the muffin pan for 5 minutes, then transfer to a wire rack to let cool completely.

NOTES:

❖ Try to get unsalted and undyed pistachios. If you can't, the recipe will work, but please leave out the salt.

Variations

Carrot and Walnut Muffins

Substitute another nut if you don't like pistachios. For this option, use walnuts, change the cardamom to ground cinnamon, top with a walnut half, and you're away.

Carrot and Raisin Muffins

Replace some or all of the nuts with raisins—½ cup is a good quantity—that have been soaked in boiling water for 15 minutes, then drained. Instead of the cardamom, use allspice.

Remember...

Corny Corn Bread Muffins

MAKES 12 MUFFINS

▶ **NO NUTS • NO SUGAR**

Not having grown up in the Southern United States, I have no cultural reference for, or childhood memories of, corn bread muffins. In fact the first time I was given a batch as a thank-you from a friend, I think I struggled through one and threw the rest away. I just didn't get it. I persevered, and with this recipe I have something that I'd quite happily eat alongside a bowl of chili, for brunch, with a salad, or as a snack by itself. I think you get the picture.

¾ cup plain soy milk
1 teaspoon apple cider vinegar

1 cup all-purpose flour
½ cup + 2 tablespoons yellow corn flour
½ cup cornmeal (see page 15)
2 tablespoons cornstarch
1 tablespoon baking powder
1 teaspoon baking soda
1¼ teaspoons salt
¼ teaspoon freshly ground black pepper

1½ cups canned creamed corn (see Note)
2 tablespoons agave nectar
2 tablespoons brown rice syrup

1. Preheat the oven to 400°F and spray twelve cups of a muffin pan with nonstick spray. (If not using some of the cups, fill them halfway with water so the pan won't warp.)

2. In a medium bowl, mix the soy milk with the vinegar, and set aside for 5 minutes to curdle.

3. In a large bowl, whisk together the ingredients from flour through salt.

4. Add the creamed corn, agave nectar, and brown rice syrup to the soy milk mixture and whisk until relatively smooth (you may still have corn lumps).

5. Make a well in the dry ingredients, add the wet, and mix until combined.

6. Spoon the mixture into the prepared pan. The cups will be full. Bake for 18 to 20 minutes, until well risen, golden brown and firm to the touch. Test, but be aware that the creamed corn may stick to your toothpick, so use the visual clues, too.

7. Remove from the oven and let cool in the muffin pan for 5 minutes, then transfer to a wire rack to let cool completely.

NOTE:

❖ If you have trouble finding canned creamed corn, then make your own! Using a blender or food processor, blend 1½ cups of of canned corn kernels, with the liquid they come in, until creamy. It won't be exactly the same, but it will still work!

Variation

Spicy Corny Corn Bread Muffins
If you like your corn bread with a little kick, add either a finely chopped jalapeño pepper or ½ teaspoon of chile flakes (or both) with the corn.

Double Almond Muffins

MAKES 12 MUFFINS

▶ **NO SOY**

Have you noticed that the personal beauty/bath product people would have you believe that you need to wash body and hair, deodorize, and perfume yourself all with the same fragrance to get the aromatic result they're aiming for? You can't just spray the perfume on and be done with it! This muffin buys into their logic: layer upon layer of almond goodness.

¾ cup whole-wheat pastry flour
¾ cup all-purpose flour
¾ cup ground almonds (see Note)
⅔ cup granulated sugar
2½ teaspoons baking powder
1 teaspoon baking soda
½ teaspoon salt
½ teaspoon ground nutmeg

½ cup almonds, chopped and toasted lightly

1 cup plain almond milk
¼ cup unsweetened applesauce
2 tablespoons sweet almond or canola oil
1 teaspoon almond extract

½ cup flaked almonds

1. Preheat the oven to 375°F and spray twelve cups of a muffin pan with nonstick spray. (If not using some of the cups, fill them halfway with water so the pan won't warp.)

2. In a large bowl, whisk together the ingredients from flour through nutmeg. Stir in the toasted almond pieces.

3. In another bowl, whisk together the milk, applesauce, oil, and almond extract until well combined.

4. Pour the liquid ingredients into the dry and mix to just combine.

5. Spoon the mixture into the prepared pan. The cups will be full. Top each muffin with ½ tablespoon of flaked almonds. Bake for 18 to 22 minutes, until a toothpick comes out clean.

6. Remove from the oven and let cool in the muffin pan for 5 minutes, then transfer to a wire rack to let cool completely.

NOTE:
❖ Ground almonds are also known as almond meal and almond flour (see page 14).

Remember...

Earl Grey Tea Muffins

MAKES 12 MUFFINS

▶ **NO NUTS**

My husband starts each day with a cup or two of Earl Grey tea. Now he can have his tea and eat it, too!

These muffins need a light hand. I know I say it all the time, but I found (as did my testers) that these are inclined to be a little gummy if at all overmixed, so please, mix just to combine.

1 cup boiling water
4 Earl Grey tea bags (see Note)

2¼ cups all-purpose flour
1 cup whole-wheat pastry flour
¾ cup granulated sugar
1 tablespoon baking powder
2 Earl Grey tea bags, contents only (about 2 teaspoons of tea)
½ teaspoon salt

1 cup soy milk
¼ cup canola oil
1 teaspoon orange zest
½ teaspoon vanilla extract
¼ teaspoon orange extract

1. In a cup, add the four tea bags to the boiling water. Cover the cup and steep, covered, for 15 minutes, then uncovered until room temperature. Squeeze out and remove the tea bags. You can speed up this process by placing the tea in the fridge for about 15 minutes once uncovered.

2. Preheat the oven to 375°F and spray twelve cups of a muffin pan with nonstick spray. (If not using some of the cups, fill them halfway with water so the pan won't warp.)

3. Sift together the dry ingredients (from flour through salt), into a large bowl.

4. In another large bowl, whisk together the cool tea, soy milk, oil, zest, and extracts.

5. Add the wet ingredients to the dry and gently mix to just combine.

6. Spoon the mixture into the prepared pan. The cups will be full. Bake for 18 to 22 minutes, until a toothpick comes out clean.

7. Remove from the oven and let cool in the muffin pan for 5 minutes, then transfer to a wire rack to let cool completely.

NOTE:

❖ If you're a super tea fan, and feel you'd like more of a tea taste to these, add an extra teabag, or two, in the steeping process, and ensure you wring out the teabags when removing, to get all the tannin-filled taste!

Variations

Masala Chai (Spiced Tea) Muffins
Replace the Earl Grey with bags of a regular black tea and add the following spices with the dry ingredients:

1½ teaspoons ground cardamom
1½ teaspoons ground cinnamon
¾ teaspoon ground ginger
¼ teaspoon ground cloves
¼ teaspoon freshly ground black pepper
¼ teaspoon ground allspice

Orange Pekoe Muffins
Not an Earl Grey fan? Change the tea to one you do like (Orange Pekoe, for example) and proceed with the recipe. Replace the orange zest and extract with lemon zest and extract, to have your tea muffin flavored subtly citrusy.

"Father's Day" Coconut and Blueberry Muffins

MAKES 12 MUFFINS

▶ **NO NUTS**

Two of my husband's favorite flavors are coconut and blueberry, so last Father's Day, for breakfast, I surprised him with this muffin that combined both. Needless to say, he loved them, and I hope you will, too.

If the dad in your life likes coconut but has other favorites, too, see the suggested variations. If your dad isn't a coconut fan, choose any muffin recipe in this book you think he'll like and just call it his "Father's Day" muffin.

½ cup shredded, unsweetened coconut

1¼ cups soy milk
1 teaspoon apple cider vinegar

¾ cup whole-wheat pastry flour
1 cup + 2 tablespoons all-purpose flour
¾ cup granulated sugar
2 tablespoons cornstarch
2½ teaspoons baking powder
½ teaspoon baking soda
½ teaspoon salt

¼ cup coconut chunks, chopped to about the size of corn kernels (see Note)

⅓ cup unsweetened applesauce
1 teaspoon coconut extract
1 teaspoon vanilla extract

⅔ cup fresh or frozen blueberries (try to get the little wild ones)

1. Preheat the oven to 375°F and spray twelve cups of a muffin pan with nonstick spray. (If not using some of the cups, fill them halfway with water so the pan won't warp.)

2. In a small saucepan, over medium heat, toast the coconut until a light golden color, stirring often for about 5 minutes. Remove from the heat and set aside.

3. In a medium bowl, whisk together the soy milk and vinegar, and set aside for 5 minutes to curdle.

4. In a large bowl, whisk together the ingredients from flour through salt and the toasted coconut. Add the coconut chunks and toss in the flour mixture.

5. Whisk the applesauce and extracts into the soy milk mixture, then add the liquid ingredients to the dry. Mix until just combined. Fold in the blueberries.

6. Spoon the mixture into the prepared pan. The cups will be full. Bake for 20 to 22 minutes, until a toothpick comes out clean.

7. Remove from the oven and let cool in the muffin pan for 5 minutes, then transfer to a wire rack to let cool completely.

NOTE:

❖ I found the coconut chunks at my local health food store. They were unsweetened chunks about ½ inch across. If you can't find them, just leave them out, or use one of the variations below; it'll work just the same but won't be quite as coconutty.

Variations

Coconut and Chocolate Blueberry Muffins

Replace the coconut chunks with vegan semisweet or white (or a combination of) chocolate chips.

(continued on next page)

> **Super-Blueberry and Coconut Muffins**
> Instead of the coconut chunks, use dried blueberries for a super-blueberry version.
>
> **Your Dad's Berry and Coconut Muffins**
> Change the berries to your father's favorite, raspberries, cranberries, or even chopped-up fresh peaches to make a coconut and "other fruit" muffin.

Good Morning Muffins

MAKES 12 MUFFINS

Full of oats, fruit, and nuts, this is a lovely, tasty, yet filling breakfast muffin. Have a batch in the freezer to zap in the microwave on those mornings when you're rushing out the door but need a healthy start to the day.

The top is a little crustier than you may be expecting in a muffin, but the texture inside is perfect.

1 tablespoon ground flax seeds
3 tablespoons pineapple juice (from the drained pineapple below)

1 cup spelt flour
½ cup all-purpose flour
½ cup granulated sugar
2 tablespoons cornstarch
1 tablespoon baking powder
1 teaspoon ground cinnamon
½ teaspoon baking soda
½ teaspoon salt

1 cup quick-cooking or old-fashioned rolled oats (not instant)
½ cup raisins
¼ cup finely chopped pecans

1 cup soy milk
¾ cup crushed pineapple, drained (liquid used above) (see Note)
⅓ cup canola oil
2 teaspoons vanilla extract

12 pecan halves

1. Preheat the oven to 375°F and spray twelve cups of a muffin pan with nonstick spray. (If not using some of the cups, fill them halfway with water so the pan won't warp.)

2. In a medium bowl, combine the flax seeds and pineapple juice. Set aside for 5 minutes.

3. Sift together the dry ingredients (from flour through salt) into a large bowl. Add the oats, raisins, and pecans, and stir to mix.

4. Add the pineapple, soy milk, oil, and vanilla to the flax mixture and stir well.

5. Pour wet ingredients into dry and mix to just combine.

6. Spoon the mixture into the prepared pan. The cups will be full. Top each with a pecan half. Bake for 20 to 25 minutes, until a toothpick comes out clean.

7. Remove from the oven and let cool in the muffin pan for 5 minutes, then transfer to a wire rack to let cool completely.

NOTE:
❖ Drain the pineapple to remove excess juice only; you want it still moist, but not sopping wet. Also, I used a 14-ounce (400 g) can and had pineapple left over, perfect for use in the Carrot and Pineapple Scones (page 77).

"It's All Good" Bran Muffins

MAKES 12 MUFFINS

▶ **NO NUTS**

"Breakfast cereal in your muffin?" I hear you ask. It actually works well, and all that bran helps keep you regular. These are dense, hearty, and filling muffins that are nicely sweet without being overly so.

Use any flavored yogurt. I've made them with both plain and strawberry. The flavor of the muffin will change slightly but it won't affect the outcome of the recipe.

I like these without any of the optional extras, but others in my family prefer the additions. It's up to you; try them all ways.

1 cup bran cereal (such as All-Bran), not the flaked kind
1 cup boiling water

1 cup soy milk
1 tablespoon apple cider vinegar

½ cup granulated sugar
¼ cup vegan yogurt
¼ cup canola oil
1 teaspoon vanilla extract

¾ cup whole-wheat pastry flour
¾ cup all-purpose flour
2 teaspoons baking powder
1 teaspoon baking soda
1 teaspoon ground cinnamon

1 cup bran cereal (same kind as above)
⅓ cup optional extras (see Note)

1. Preheat the oven to 375°F and spray twelve cups of a muffin pan with nonstick spray. (If not using some of the cups, fill them halfway with water so the pan won't warp.)

2. In a small bowl, combine the first cup of the bran cereal with the water, and set aside for 5 minutes until thick and the liquid is absorbed.

3. In another larger bowl, combine the soy milk and vinegar, and set aside for 5 minutes to curdle.

4. Add the sugar, yogurt, oil, and vanilla to the soy milk mixture and mix well. Add the soaked bran cereal and stir.

5. Sift the flour, baking powder, baking soda, and cinnamon into the bowl and mix well.

6. Add the unsoaked bran cereal and any extras and mix to just combine.

7. Spoon the mixture into the prepared pan. The cups will be full. Bake for 28 to 32 minutes, until a toothpick comes out clean.

8. Remove from the oven and let cool in the muffin pan for 5 minutes, then transfer to a wire rack to let cool completely.

NOTE:
❖ Your optional extras could be any of the following, so experiment and create your own variations, or don't add anything, if you prefer:
+ Dried fruit, such as cranberries, blueberries, raisins, chopped apricots, or dates
+ Nuts: any kind, in pieces or chopped
+ Seeds: possibly sunflower, pumpkin, or hemp
+ Vegan chocolate or carob chips

Parsnip and Orange Muffins

MAKES 12 MUFFINS

▶ **NO NUTS • NO SOY**

This combination sounds strange, I know, but these are really good. The parsnip adds sweetness that is offset, a little, by the sharpness of the orange. You'd never know there was parsnip in there if I hadn't told you.

You could make the parsnip puree in advance and store in the fridge until required. If you have leftover puree, it's good as baby food, or added to a lentil or root vegetable soup.

**2 cups peeled and coarsely grated
parsnips (about 14 ounces total)
(see Note)**

Applesauce, if required (see directions)

¾ cup orange juice

½ cup rice milk

1 teaspoon orange or vanilla extract

⅓ cup canola oil

¼ cup rice milk

**1 tablespoon orange zest
(1 medium orange)**

1½ cups all-purpose flour

¾ cup whole-wheat pastry flour

¾ cup granulated sugar

2 tablespoons cornstarch

2½ teaspoons baking powder

½ teaspoon salt

½ teaspoon pie spice (see page 19)

1. In a small saucepan, just cover the grated parsnip with water; bring to a boil, and cook, covered, at a simmer for 15 minutes, until soft. Drain. Blend the parsnips, orange juice, ½ cup of rice milk, and orange extract to a smooth puree. Measure out 1½ cups into a small bowl. If you have less than this, make up the difference with unsweetened applesauce.

2. Preheat the oven to 375°F and spray twelve cups of a muffin pan with nonstick spray. These muffins have a tendency to stick. (If not using some of the cups, fill them halfway with water so the pan won't warp.)

3. Sift together the dry ingredients (from flour through pie spice), into a bowl, and make a well in the center.

4. Mix the oil, ¼ cup of rice milk, and zest with the puree. Pour this mixture into the well in the dry ingredients and mix until just combined.

5. Spoon the mixture into the prepared pan. The cups will be full. Bake for 22 to 25 minutes, until a toothpick comes out clean.

6. Remove from the oven and let cool in the muffin pan for 5 minutes, then transfer to a wire rack to let cool completely.

NOTE:

❖ I use the whole parsnip for this; as it is being grated, then cooked, there is no issue with woodiness or hardness. One of my testers used a mandoline (a very sharp slicing utensil) to slice the parsnip into fine julienne, and that worked well, too.

Pomegranate and Caramelized Pecan Muffins

MAKES 12 MUFFINS

▶ **NO SOY**

Pomegranates are a real food symbol of Christmas, and these muffins make a great festive breakfast, served with seeds from the fresh fruit sprinkled on top. Or serve plain as a treat at any time of the year.

Just a warning, so you know and don't curse me, these aren't a huge muffin top–creating muffin; they stay quite compact, though the texture and taste are lovely.

1 cup all-purpose flour
½ cup whole-wheat pastry flour
½ cup ground pecans (see Notes)
2½ teaspoons baking powder
1 teaspoon baking soda
½ teaspoon ground cinnamon
½ teaspoon salt

½ cup + 1 tablespoon almond milk
½ cup pomegranate juice
¼ cup canola oil
3 tablespoons light brown sugar, packed
3 tablespoons granulated sugar
2 tablespoons pomegranate molasses (see Notes)

1 recipe Caramelized Pecans (recipe follows)

1. Preheat the oven to 375°F and spray twelve cups of a muffin pan with nonstick spray. (If not using some of the cups, fill them halfway with water so the pan won't warp.)

2. In a large bowl, whisk together the ingredients from flour through salt.

3. In another bowl, mix together the milk, juice, oil, sugars, and pomegranate molasses.

4. Add the liquid ingredients to the dry and mix to just combine. Fold in the caramelized pecans.

5. Spoon the mixture into the prepared pan. The cups will be full. Bake for 20 to 25 minutes, until a toothpick comes out clean.

6. Remove from the oven and let cool in the muffin pan for 5 minutes, then transfer to a wire rack to let cool completely.

Caramelized Pecans

MAKES ¾ CUP PECANS

▶ **NO SOY · NO WHEAT**

These nuts are super more-ish. You may find yourself needing to make a double batch, just to ensure there are enough left to make it into the muffin batter!

¾ cup chopped pecans
⅓ cup light brown sugar, packed

1. Line a baking sheet with parchment paper.

2. In a small saucepan, toast the pecans over medium heat for 5 minutes, until just lightly colored.

3. Remove the nuts from the pan and transfer to a small bowl.

4. Using the same pan, heat the brown sugar over medium-high heat, stirring constantly, until melted.

5. Remove from the heat, add the nuts, and continue stirring until the nuts are well coated.

6. Pour the mixture onto the prepared sheet and allow to cool. Once cool, after about 10 minutes break into small pieces and use as directed.

NOTES:

❖ If you can't find pomegranate molasses, some of my testers had great results making their own. Lane wrote, "I took 4 cups of pomegranate juice, ½ cup of sugar, 1 tablespoon of lemon juice, and boiled it until it reduced to about 1 cup and was nice and thick."

❖ Ground pecans may be found in the baking aisle of some supermarkets. If you are grinding your own, the result should be quite fine but not as fine as flour, with only a few larger pieces of nut. See (page 14) for instructions in greater detail.

Poppy Seed and Raspberry Muffins

MAKES 12 MUFFINS

▶ **NO NUTS**

When raspberries are in season and not costing an arm and a leg, these muffins are divine (they're also pretty good the rest of the year, using frozen berries). The poppy seeds add an interesting crunch; and the berries, that sweet/tart burst of flavor that is reminiscent of summer.

½ cup soy milk
1 teaspoon apple cider vinegar

⅓ cup canola oil
¾ cup granulated sugar
1 teaspoon raspberry or vanilla extract
⅓ cup soy creamer (see page 16)

1 cup all-purpose flour
1 cup whole-wheat pastry flour
2 teaspoons baking powder
¼ teaspoon salt

¼ cup poppy seeds

1 cup fresh or frozen raspberries

1. Preheat the oven to 375°F and spray twelve cups of a muffin pan with nonstick spray. (If not using some of the cups, fill them halfway with water so the pan won't warp.)

2. In a large bowl, combine soy milk and vinegar, and set aside for 5 minutes to curdle.

3. Add the oil, sugar, extract, and creamer to the soy milk mixture and mix well.

4. Sift in the flour and baking powder. Add the poppy seeds and mix to just combine.

5. Reserve twelve raspberries, then fold the rest into the mixture.

6. Spoon the mixture into the prepared pan. The cups will be full. Place one of the reserved raspberries in the middle of each muffin and press lightly into the batter to hold in place. Bake for 25 to 30 minutes, until a toothpick comes out clean.

7. Remove from the oven and let cool in the muffin pan for 5 minutes, then transfer to a wire rack to let cool completely.

Pumpkin and Cranberry Muffins

MAKES 12 MUFFINS

▶ **NO NUTS**

Pumpkin at Thanksgiving is not just about pie, folks. This is a perfect muffin combination for a holiday brunch, bringing together flavors associated with the season. Not just for Thanksgiving, either—a perfect autumnal, or even wintery, muffin taste sensation.

1 cup all-purpose flour
⅓ cup whole-wheat pastry flour (see Notes)
3 tablespoons cornstarch
2 teaspoons baking powder
1 teaspoon pie spice (see page 19)
½ teaspoon ground cinnamon
½ teaspoon ground nutmeg
½ teaspoon salt
¼ teaspoon ground cloves

1 cup canned pumpkin puree (see Notes)

½ cup granulated sugar

½ cup soy milk

⅓ cup oil

2 tablespoons blackstrap molasses (see Notes)

1 teaspoon vanilla extract

½ cup dried cranberries, chopped if large

1. Preheat the oven to 375°F and spray twelve cups of a muffin pan with nonstick spray. (If not using some of the cups, fill them halfway with water so the pan won't warp.)

2. Sift together the dry ingredients (from flour through cloves), into a large bowl.

3. In another large bowl, gently mix together the puree, sugar, oil, soy milk, vanilla, and molasses until smooth and creamy.

4. Add the liquid ingredients to the dry and mix gently to just combine. Be gentle because overmixing the pumpkin will make your muffins gummy.

5. Fold in the cranberries, then spoon the mixture into the prepared pan. The cups will be full. Bake for 20 to 25 minutes, until a toothpick comes out clean and the tops are slightly browned.

6. Remove from the oven and let cool in the muffin pan for 5 minutes, then transfer to a wire rack to let cool completely.

NOTES:

❖ These are quite dense muffins; if you'd like them to be a little less so, use all-purpose flour instead of the whole-wheat pastry flour.

❖ Be sure you get pureed pumpkin. The only ingredient should be pumpkin, and the can should not be labeled "pumpkin pie filling."

❖ If you don't like the bitterness of or don't have blackstrap molasses, then regular molasses, or the one you have in the cupboard, is fine.

Variations

Pumpkin Raisin Muffins

For a less Thanksgiving-like but still very autumnal muffin, switch the dried cranberries to raisins.

Super-Cranberry Pumpkin Muffins

Reduce the quantity of dried cranberries to ¼ cup and add ½ cup of fresh or frozen cranberries.

Super-Chocolate Muffins

MAKES 12 MUFFINS

▶ NO NUTS • NO SOY

These are very chocolaty but definitely a muffin. They were originally requested by my sister Sonia, as a low-fat fix for chocolate cravings. They are not light like a cupcake, but dense and filling. They're not too sweet, either; a lot of the sweetening comes from the chocolate, as does all the fat in the recipe.

My younger daughter ate two while they were still warm out of the oven!

¾ cup water

½ cup whole, seedless prunes

1¼ cups all-purpose flour

¾ cup whole-wheat pastry flour

¼ cup unsweetened cocoa powder

2½ teaspoons baking powder

1 teaspoon baking soda

½ teaspoon salt

½ cup vegan chocolate chips

½ cup rice milk

½ cup granulated sugar

¼ **cup unsweetened cocoa powder**

¼ **cup pure maple syrup**

1 teaspoon vanilla extract

½ **cup vegan chocolate chips (optional)**

1 recipe Ganache-Style Chocolate (page 252) (optional)

1. In a small saucepan, soak the prunes in the water for 1 hour. Then bring to a boil and boil for 10 minutes, adding water by the tablespoonful, if required, to prevent the mixture from sticking. Remove from the heat and let cool for 10 minutes. Blend, or mash with a fork, to a thick paste. Hold at room temperature until required. (If you have less than ½ cup of paste, add unsweetened applesauce to top up to the required quantity.)

2. Preheat the oven to 375°F and spray twelve cups of a muffin pan with nonstick spray. (If not using some of the cups, fill them halfway with water so the pan won't warp.)

3. Sift together the dry ingredients (from flour through salt), into a large bowl.

4. Combine the first ½ cup of chocolate chips, rice milk, sugar, the second (¼-cup) measure of cocoa powder, the maple syrup, and the vanilla in the top of a double boiler (or a heatproof bowl that fits over a saucepan), heat, and stir until melted and smooth. Add the prune mixture and stir to combine.

5. Work fast from now, as the chocolate will harden quickly once taken from the double boiler. Pour the chocolate mixture into the dry ingredients and mix to combine. Fold in the second ½ cup of chocolate chips (if using).

6. Spoon the mixture into the prepared pan. The cups will be full. Bake for 22 to 26 minutes, until a toothpick comes out clean.

7. Remove from the oven and let cool in the muffin pan for 5 minutes. If you want them to be even more chocolaty (though less low-fat), cover the tops with Ganache-Style Chocolate!

Variations

Super-Chocolate-Nibbed Muffins
Use cocoa nibs instead of the chocolate chips, or go half and half with them, for a crunchy chocolate change. Still super, only different.

Super-Carob Muffins
Replace the cocoa powder and chocolate chips with vegan carob powder and carob chips for a truly decadent carob-laced treat.

• •

Zucchini and Currant Muffins

MAKES 12 MUFFINS

▶ **NO NUTS • NO WHEAT**

At the end of summer you'll often find zucchini coming out of your ears! Though not literally, of course. This is a tasty, healthy, wheat-free way to use them up. Bake these for your friends, your office, your partner's office, your children's school; everyone will be pleased to have them!

½ **cup dried currants**
Boiling water

1¼ **cups soy milk**
1 teaspoon apple cider vinegar

2¼ **cups spelt flour**
¼ **cup cornstarch**

1 tablespoon baking powder

½ teaspoon baking soda

½ teaspoon salt

¾ teaspoon ground cinnamon

¼ teaspoon ground allspice

½ cup light brown sugar, packed

¼ cup canola oil

1 tablespoon blackstrap molasses

1 tablespoon agave nectar

½ teaspoon vanilla extract

2 cups grated zucchini (about 1 large zucchini)

1. Preheat the oven to 375°F and spray twelve cups of a muffin pan with nonstick spray. (If not using some of the cups, fill them halfway with water so the pan won't warp.)

2. In a small bowl, cover the currants with boiling water. Cover and set aside for 15 minutes. Drain, and discard the soaking water.

3. In a medium bowl, mix the soy milk with the vinegar, and set aside for 5 minutes to curdle.

4. Sift together the dry ingredients (from flour through allspice) into a large bowl.

5. Add the oil, brown sugar, molasses, agave nectar, and vanilla to the soy milk mixture and whisk together.

6. Add the wet ingredients to the dry and stir to just combine. Fold in the zucchini and drained currants.

7. Spoon the mixture into the prepared pan. The cups will be full. Bake for 22 to 26 minutes, until a toothpick comes out clean.

8. Remove from the oven and let cool in the muffin pan for 5 minutes, then transfer to a wire rack to let cool completely.

Variations

Just Zucchini Muffins

Leave out the currants and increase the cinnamon to 1 teaspoon.

Zucchini and Walnut Muffins

Leave out the currants and fold in ½ cup of walnut pieces with the zucchini. Or keep the currants and add the walnut pieces; the muffins can handle it, if you can.

Zucchini and Chocolate Chip Muffins

Leave out the currants and replace 1 tablespoon of the flour with 1 tablespoon of unsweetened cocoa powder. Fold in ½ cup of vegan chocolate chips with the zucchini.

Pies, Tarts, and Handheld Pastries

I DID SOME SEARCHING online to define the terminology and came to the conclusion that the main difference between a tart and a pie is that a tart is never enclosed with a top crust. A tart is usually sweet, may be large or small, and is baked in a flat pan with corrugated straight sides. A pie, however, may be open faced, totally enclosed, or something in between; it may be sweet or savory; and it is usually baked in a pan with flat sloping sides.

For the purposes of naming recipes in this book, you'll find that if something is baked in an 11-inch loose-bottomed tart pan, it's a tart. If it's baked in a 9-inch pie plate, it's a pie. As a general rule of thumb, that is, as you'll find some can be made in either!

You may be wondering why I've included this section, seeing that for some people, pies (especially the crusts) are neither quick nor easy! I'm here to change that, first, by creating a selection of recipes that will suit all levels of pie-making expertise from beginner to more experienced; and second, by giving you permission to not bake your own pie crust.

That's right, you read that correctly: You have permission to not bake your own crust and to not feel guilty about it. We're all about quick and easy here!

Most supermarkets stock brands of premade (often frozen) pie crusts that are vegan; you have to read the ingredients, and maybe even check with the companies, to be sure, but there are options out there. Store-bought crusts may not taste as great as homemade but, in a pinch or when you need really quick and easy, they are a lifesaver.

Another really quick and easy option is frozen, premade, store-brought vegan puff pastry. Again, check the ingredients. Sure, you have to actually roll it out, but it's made for you! It'll work (the companies that make it will pretty much guarantee that), so you no longer have an excuse for not making pies! (Also, if you already have a favorite pie crust recipe, use that with my filling recipes; it's all cool.)

I've included a few simple crust recipes, with variations, and indicated which pie I feel they would specifically suit, if you feel the need to make the crust or just want to be able to say, "I made it all myself." When you are making your own crust, it's easiest if you chill the dough, then roll out the chilled dough, on a sheet of parchment paper, to be larger than your inverted pie plate or tart pan by about an inch or so. You can then place pie plate/tart pan upside down over pastry, and using the parchment to hold it, flip the plate and pastry over so pastry is in the pie plate/tart pan. You can then crimp and trim the dough to fit the pie plate/ tart pan as needed. Alternatively, you can roll out the chilled pastry on a lightly floured board to less than ¼-inch thickness, and then roll the pastry around a lightly floured rolling pin and unroll it over the pie plate/tart pan.

In recipes where I say you need a "prepared pie crust," I mean pastry that has been placed in the pie plate/tart pan but has not been prebaked. I will specify "prebaked" in the ingredients list if that is required.

Hot pies are, obviously, best eaten straight out of the oven, but also reheat well. Please avoid the microwave except in a pie emergency, as this may make the pastry soggy. To reheat a whole pie, cover with tinfoil, place on a baking sheet, and heat at 350°F for about 15 minutes. For individual pieces, wrap in tinfoil and heat for only 10 minutes at the same temperature. If you aren't eating your pie immediately, allow it to cool completely before wrapping and storing in the fridge until needed.

Cold pies need chilling time to be at their best, so remember this when planning a menu. They need to be stored in the fridge. If held at room temperature for any length of time, such as when being sold or given away, be sure that you inform the recipient to chill them prior to serving.

Pies and tarts are great when served with toppings. Mix and match to see which suits your tastes best. I like custard, Crazy Whip Topping (page 249), and a good homemade (or store-bought) vegan vanilla ice cream!

In this section, I've also included items that aren't really pies or tarts but that use pastry as their base or are in some other way are pastry related. This is why you'll find Cinnamon Straws (page 179) and Vanilla Crème Puffs (page 186) in this section, rather than in any other.

FIRST THE CRUSTS . . .

For the following pie crust recipes I have used the term *pie plate* to mean the receptacle for your crust, be it a pie plate or tart pan or other pan.

Each recipe makes enough pastry for one pie crust, with varying amounts of dough scraps, depending on how thinly the dough is rolled. Ideas for using these trimmings are given following this section (page 172). If making a two-crusted pie (a bottom and a top), a double amount of the recipe you'll need.

Coconut Pie Crust

MAKES ONE SINGLE 9-INCH PIE CRUST

▶ **NO NUTS • NO SOY**

This is for the Lime Coconut Tart (page 181) or any pie that needs a little more coconut!

2 cups all-purpose flour
½ teaspoon salt

¼ cup granulated sugar
¼ cup unsweetened, shredded coconut

⅓ cup vegan shortening

¼ cup frozen, then grated, coconut oil (see Note)

7 to 9 tablespoons ice water

1. If baking, preheat the oven to 400°F and spray a pie plate with nonstick cooking spray.

2. Sift together the flour and salt into a large bowl. Stir in the sugar and coconut.

3. Using a pastry cutter (or two knives held together), cut in the shortening. Stir in the frozen coconut oil.

4. Add 7 tablespoons of the iced water and mix to combine. If the dough is not firm and holding together, then add water by the tablespoonful and mix until it is.

5. Roll out the dough on a sheet of parchment paper or a clean, lightly floured surface larger by 1 to 2 inches than your upside-down pie plate. The rolled-out dough should be less than ¼ inch thick. Place the pie plate upside-down over the pastry. Using the parchment to hold them together, flip the plate and pastry over so the pastry is in the pie plate.

Alternatively, wrap the rolled dough around your rolling pin, then unroll over the pie plate.

6. Press the pastry into place, crimp the edges with your fingers, and trim away any scraps.

7. Poke all over the bottom of the pie crust with a fork, and if prebaking, bake for 10 to 12 minutes until lightly browned.

8. Remove from the oven and let cool prior to use.

NOTE:

❖ To freeze coconut oil, place some coconut oil in the freezer in a plastic container for a few hours to freeze. Once frozen, remove from the container, and holding the oil with a paper towel (to prevent you getting melting oil on your hands), quickly grate over a sheet of tinfoil, using the larger compartment on your box grater. Wrap in the tinfoil and return to the freezer until required.

· ·

Pecan Pie Crust

MAKES ONE SINGLE 9-INCH PIE CRUST

Specifically for the Coconut and Pecan Pie (page 176), but there's no reason you can't use this for whichever pie you fancy! It's also great with the Sticky Nut Pie (page 184), if you don't mind a little nut overload.

1½ cups + 2 tablespoons all-purpose flour
¼ cup ground pecans (see Note)
2 tablespoons finely chopped pecans
¼ teaspoon ground cinnamon
¼ teaspoon salt

¼ cup almond milk
¼ cup water
2 tablespoons canola oil
2 tablespoons pure maple syrup
¾ teaspoon vanilla extract

1. If using as a prebaked crust, preheat the oven to 375°F and spray a 9-inch pie plate with nonstick spray.

2. In a large bowl, whisk together the ingredients from flour through salt.

3. In another bowl, whisk together the milk, water, oil, syrup, and extracts.

4. Add the wet ingredients to the dry and mix to form a soft dough. You may need to use your hands to knead slightly.

5. Roll out on a lightly floured board or a piece of parchment paper, as this mixture does stick a little, until larger by about 1 inch all around than your pie plate. The rolled-out dough will be less than ¼ inch thick. Place the pie plate upside down over the pastry. Using the parchment to hold them together, flip the plate and pastry over so the pastry is in the pie plate. Alternatively, wrap the rolled dough around your rolling pin, then unroll over the pie plate.

6. Press the pastry into place, crimp the edges with your fingers, and trim away any scraps.

7. Bake for 15 to 20 minutes, until lightly browned and just firm.

8. Remove from the oven and let cool while preparing the filling.

NOTE:

❖ Ground pecans may be found in the baking aisle of some supermarkets. If you are grinding your own, the result should be quite fine but not as fine as flour, with only a few larger pieces of nut. See page 14 for instructions in greater detail.

Variations

Almond Pie Crust
Swap ground almonds for the ground pecans and chopped almonds for the chopped pecans.

Hazelnut Pie Crust

As with Almond Pie Crust, but use ground and chopped hazelnuts.

Seeded Pie Crust

Use your choice of roughly chopped seeds in place of the ground and chopped pecans; add 2 tablespoons of flour.

Plain Pie Crust

MAKES ONE SINGLE 9-INCH PIE CRUST

▶ **NO NUTS • NO SOY**

This is a standard recipe that gives a lovely crust. It's not hard; you just have to be a little organized about getting your water and shortening chilled and your coconut oil prepared.

2 cups all-purpose flour

2 tablespoons granulated sugar

½ teaspoon salt

⅓ cup cold vegan shortening

¼ cup frozen and grated coconut oil (see Notes)

6 to 9 tablespoons ice water

1. If baking immediately after making, preheat the oven to 375°F and lightly spray a pie plate with nonstick spray.

2. Sift together the flour, sugar, and salt into a large bowl.

3. Using a pastry cutter (or two knives held together) cut in the shortening until the mixture resembles lumpy bread crumbs. Stir in the frozen coconut oil flakes with a fork.

4. Add 6 tablespoons of water and mix to form a loose dough. When ready, the dough will hold together when pressed, while there will be some loose bits that you will need to press in. If the dough is too dry, add the rest of the water 1 tablespoonful at a time until it reaches a firmer consistency.

5. Gather the dough and press into a ball. If not using immediately, wrap in plastic wrap and chill until ready to use, at least 1 hour.

6. Once chilled, roll out on a lightly floured board or a piece of parchment paper, as this mixture does stick a little, until about 1 inch larger all around than your pie plate.

7. Place the pie plate upside down over the pastry. Using the parchment to hold them together, flip the plate and pastry over so the pastry is in the pie plate. Alternatively, wrap the rolled dough around your rolling pin, then unroll over the pie plate.

8. Press the pastry into place, crimp the edges with your fingers, and trim away any scraps.

9. Poke the bottom of the pie crust all over with a fork. If prebaking, bake for 10 to 12 minutes, until lightly browned, if to be used in a baked pie; or for 13 to 15 minutes, until more golden, if for a chilled pie.

10. Remove from the oven and let cool prior to use.

NOTES:

❖ To freeze coconut oil, place some coconut oil in the freezer in a plastic container for a few hours to freeze. Once frozen, remove from the container, and holding the oil with a paper towel (to prevent you from getting melting oil on your hands), quickly grate over a sheet of tinfoil, using the larger compartment on your box grater. Wrap in the tinfoil and return to the freezer until required.

❖ If you have no prefrozen coconut oil and are in a rush, you can substitute nonfrozen coconut oil, or even shortening in equal amounts, though I really do prefer the result when made this way.

Variations

Spiced Plain Pie Crust

Add the following with the flour:

½ teaspoon ground cinnamon

½ teaspoon ground nutmeg

½ teaspoon salt

¼ teaspoon ground cloves

Savory Plain Pie Crust

Reduce the sugar to 2 teaspoons and increase the salt to 1 teaspoon, if you're making pastry for a savory pie and you want a less sweet base.

Spelt Pie Crust

Replace the all-purpose flour with 2¼ cups of spelt flour, add 2 tablespoons of cornstarch with the flour, and reduce the sugar to 1 tablespoon only. Continue with the recipe as directed.

Savory Cornmeal Pie Crust

MAKES ONE SINGLE 9-INCH PIE CRUST

▶ NO NUTS • NO SOY • NO SUGAR • NO WHEAT

This is the savory alternative to the Sweet Cornmeal Pie Crust (page 171). This crust is also gluten free, a bonus to its great taste.

As this recipe makes a very generous amount of dough, one of my testers, when making this crust, rolled the leftover dough out again, cut it with cookie cutters, and made crackers! He said he'd make the dough again just to make crackers, so there's a tip for you! Thanks, John. (See Notes.)

2 tablespoons ground flax seeds
¼ cup water

¼ cup canola oil

½ cup cornmeal (see page 15)
½ cup rice flour
½ cup millet flour
½ cup yellow corn flour
3 tablespoons cornstarch
1 teaspoon salt

½ cup water, plus additional if required

1. In a large bowl, combine the flax seeds and water. Set aside for 5 minutes, then add the oil. Whisk for 1 to 2 minutes, until thick.

2. Sift the cornmeal, flour, cornstarch, and salt into the flax mixture and mix until a thick, crumbly dough is formed.

3. Add the water and mix until the dough forms a firm ball when pressed together. If you need more water for the dough to hold together, add by the tablespoonful.

4. Knead the dough gently to form a large ball, wrap in plastic wrap, and chill in the fridge for at least 30 minutes prior to using.

5. If prebaking, spray a pie plate with non-stick cooking spray and preheat the oven to 375°F. (See Notes.)

6. Roll out the dough on a piece of parchment paper (this dough sticks, so this is the easiest way!), until larger by about 2 inches all around than your pie plate. Place the pie plate upside down over the pastry. Using the parchment to hold them together, flip the plate and pastry over so the pastry is in the pie plate. Alternatively, wrap the rolled dough around your rolling pin, then unroll over the pie plate.

7. Press the pastry into place, pressing any cracks together, crimp the edges with your forefingers and thumb, and trim away any scraps.

8. Poke the bottom of the pie crust all over with a fork; this one tends to puff up, so prick a lot.

9. If prebaking, bake for 10 to 12 minutes until lightly browned.

10. Remove from the oven and let cool prior to use.

NOTES:

❖ This crust is best prebaked only if using for a nonbaked filling. If using for a pie with a baked filling, prepare the crust in the pie plate, then fill and bake.

❖ To make those crackers, you need to roll out the dough thinly, ¼ inch thick or less, and cut with cookie cutters. Bake at 400°F for 8 to 10 minutes, depending on the size of the crackers, until golden brown.

Sweet Cornmeal Pie Crust

MAKES ONE SINGLE 9-INCH PIE CRUST

▶ **NO NUTS • NO SOY • NO WHEAT**

This crust doesn't suit every pie, but it comes pretty close. It has the added advantage of being gluten free (as is the savory version, page 170), so if the filling is gluten free, you can serve your GF friends pie! Hooray!

1 tablespoon ground flax seeds
2 tablespoons water

½ cup granulated sugar
¼ cup canola oil

½ cup cornmeal (see page 15)
⅓ cup rice flour

⅓ cup millet flour
⅓ cup yellow corn flour
2 tablespoons cornstarch
½ teaspoon salt

3 to 5 tablespoons water

1. In a large bowl, combine the flax seeds and water, and set aside for 5 minutes.

2. Add the sugar and oil. Whisk for 1 to 2 minutes, until thick.

3. Sift the cornmeal, flour, cornstarch, and salt into the flax mixture and mix until a thick, crumbly dough is formed.

4. Add water by the tablespoonful until the dough forms a firm ball when pressed together.

5. Knead the dough gently to form a large ball, wrap in plastic wrap, and chill in the fridge for at least 30 minutes prior to using.

6. If pre-baking, spray a pie plate with non-stick cooking spray and preheat the oven to 375°F. (See Note.)

7. Roll out dough on a piece of parchment paper (this dough sticks, so this is the easiest way!), until larger by about 2 inches all around than your pie plate. Place the pie plate upside down over the pastry. Using the parchment to hold them together, flip the plate and pastry over so the pastry is in the pie plate. Alternatively, wrap the rolled dough around your rolling pin, then unroll over the pie plate.

8. Press the pastry into place, pressing any cracks together, crimp the edges with your forefingers and thumb, and trim away any scraps.

9. Poke the bottom of the pie crust all over with a fork; this one tends to puff up, so prick a lot.

10. If prebaking, bake for 10 to 12 minutes until lightly browned.

11. Remove from the oven and let cool prior to use.

NOTE:

❖ This crust is best only prebaked if using for a nonbaked filling, such as the Creamy Dreamy Lemon Mousse Pie (page 177) or (You'll Never Guess What's in This) Chocolate Pie (page 174). If using for a pie with a baked filling, prepare the crust in the pie plate, then fill and bake.

LEFTOVER PIE CRUST DOUGH

What to do with the scraps of pastry you have left over when you've made your pie and trimmed the edges? Here are some ideas!

✷ Roll the pastry out to ¼-inch thickness or less, and using small, shaped cookie cutters, cut out decorations for the top of your pie. Brush the top crust of the pie with a little soy milk and place the decorations on top in an attractive pattern. Bake the pie as directed. This is fun to do with letters spelling out a name or a word. You could even spell out the filling, which would be helpful at a bake sale!!

✷ With the extra Savory Cornmeal Pie Crust (page 170), do what one of my testers did: turn it into Savory Cornmeal Crackers! Roll out the dough thinly, ¼ inch thick or less, cut with cookie cutters, and bake at 400°F for 8 to 10 minutes, depending on the size of the crackers, until golden brown. Thanks again for the idea, John.

✷ Currant Turnovers (page 178) are also great for using up leftover sweet pastry. Just follow the recipe, using the amounts of filling for the number of pastry circles you have, as specified by the directions.

Phyllo Pie Topper

More a concept than a real recipe, this is a nice way to add detail to a baked pie and use up leftover phyllo pastry.

4 sheets phyllo pastry
Melted vegan margarine
1 pie in need of a topping

1. Lay the phyllo sheets on a clean, slightly damp tea towel and cover with another.
2. One at a time, take a sheet of the pastry, cut it into quarters, and brush each piece with melted margarine.
3. Lay the quarters on top of each other, then cut the stack into quarters.
4. Take each pile, with four layers of pastry, and form it into a flower shape by pinching in the center and spreading the edges out like petals.
5. Cover the phyllo flower with a clean, slightly damp tea towel, to prevent drying.
6. Repeat until all the phyllo is used.
7. Remove the pie from the oven when 10 minutes of baking time are left.
8. Place the phyllo flowers decoratively on top of the pie filling, petals upward, return to the oven, and finish the last 10 minutes of baking. The phyllo will be golden brown.

Cheater's Cinnamon Straws

QUANTITY DEPENDS ON HOW MUCH PASTRY YOU HAVE

This recipe is specifically for leftover dough, which is why the quantities are a little vague. The results don't exactly match those you get with the from-scratch version (page 179), but it's pretty good in a pinch.

Leftover pastry
Ground cinnamon
Light brown sugar
Turbinado sugar
Soy milk, for brushing

1. Preheat the oven to 400°F and line a baking sheet with parchment paper.

2. Roll out the pastry to less than ¼ inch thick, as thin as it can go without tearing it.

3. Sprinkle half of the pastry with cinnamon, a little brown sugar, and a little turbinado sugar.

4. Fold the pastry in half, bringing non-sprinkled half over to cover the sprinkled half.

5. Roll dough lightly to compress the layers and ensure that the dough sticks together.

6. Sprinkle half again with cinnamon and the sugars.

7. Fold and roll lightly as before. Your dough will be about one-quarter the size of the original dough you rolled out, and about ½ inch thick.

8. Shape into a 10-inch wide rectangle that is as long as possible at this thickness.

9. Cut into 1-inch slices lengthwise. Twist this rope of dough, if desired, and place on the prepared baking sheet.

10. Bake for 15 to 20 minutes, until golden and risen, with the sugar melted.

11. Remove from the oven and let cool on the baking sheet for 5 minutes, then transfer to a wire rack to cool completely. Store in a closed container.

⭐ ## Cheater's "Cheesy" Straws

QUANTITY DEPENDS ON HOW MUCH PASTRY YOU HAVE

If you have leftover savory pastry, try this quick and easy cheater's recipe for cheese straws. Again the quantities are vague, because they depend on how much pastry you have. How many it makes, and how much of the ingredients you will need, depends on how much pastry you have, and how much you like nutritional yeast!

Leftover pastry
Nutritional yeast
Mustard powder
Paprika
Grated vegan cheese (optional)

1. Preheat the oven to 400°F and line a baking sheet with parchment paper.

2. Roll out the pastry to less than ¼ inch thick, as thin as it can go without tearing.

3. Sprinkle half of the pastry with nutritional yeast, a little mustard powder, and a little paprika. If using grated cheese, sprinkle on a little, too.

4. Fold the pastry in half, bringing the non-sprinkled half upward to cover the half that has been sprinkled.

5. Roll dough lightly to compress the layers and ensure that the dough sticks together.

6. Sprinkle half again with cinnamon and the sugars.

7. Fold and roll lightly as before. Your dough will be about one-quarter the size of the original dough you rolled out, and about ½ inch thick.

8. Shape into a 10-inch wide rectangle that is as long as possible at this thickness.

9. Cut into 1-inch slices lengthwise. Twist this rope of dough, if desired, and place on the prepared baking sheet. If desired, sprinkle with a little grated cheese.

10. Bake for 12 to 15 minutes, until golden and risen, with the cheese (if using), melted.

11. Remove from the oven and let cool on the baking sheet for 5 minutes, then transfer to a wire rack to cool completely. Store in a closed container.

(You'll Never Guess What's in This) Chocolate Pie

SERVES 10 TO 12

▶ **NO NUTS • NO SUGAR • NO WHEAT**
excluding crust

Any pie crust goes well with this one, even no crust at all, and just eating it like pudding! This is my children's favorite dessert treat, one they ask for by name. I don't mind making it for them, either; it's the only way I can get them to eat avocado! Shhhhh, don't tell them.

Please use the best-quality vegan chocolate you can buy for this; it really makes a difference.

About 2 cups soft, ripe avocado flesh (2 large or 3 smaller avocados)

One 12-ounce package tofu, firm silken (vacuum-packed)

2 tablespoons soy milk

1 tablespoon freshly squeezed lemon juice (½ medium lemon)

1 tablespoon pure maple syrup

2½ teaspoons vanilla extract

One 9-inch prebaked pie crust (Any of the crust recipes in this book are good here.)

2 cups vegan semisweet chocolate chips or chopped chocolate

1. In a blender or food processor, blend together the ingredients from avocado through vanilla until very smooth and lump free.

2. Melt the chocolate chips in either a double boiler or a microwave in 15 second bursts at high power, stirring after each burst of heat. When melted and smooth, add to the blender and blend into the avocado mixture.

3. Pour into the prepared pie crust, smooth the top, and chill overnight.

4. Decorate, if desired, with vegan chocolate chips, chocolate shavings, nuts, or fresh fruit; berries are particularly nice.

Variations

Chocolate Bottom Chocolate Pie
Spread a layer of Ganache-Style Chocolate (page 252) on your pie crust prior to filling.

(What's That Crunch in My) Chocolate Pie
Add ¼ cup of cocoa nibs to the mixture prior to pouring into the pie crust, for a slightly textured filling. You'll need to transfer everything to a bowl; mixing in the blender is not a good idea!

(You Won't Believe What's in This) Carob Pie
Use vegan carob chips instead of chocolate chips for a caffeine-free, yet still very decadent pie.

Bakewell Tart

SERVES 8 TO 10

▶ **NO WHEAT** excluding crust

One of the places where we lived, as kids growing up, had a huge almond tree in the backyard. It was ever so pretty with the blossoms in springtime, and later on in the year would drop enough nuts for us to fill big sacks (literally the size of small children) with almonds. Mum made this tart all the time to use them up; it was Dad's favorite dessert. He liked his with way more jam than I have allowed, so increase this to taste. This is lovely hot or cold.

1 prepared unbaked 9-inch pie crust, such as the Plain Pie Crust (page 169), or equivalent

¼ cup raspberry jam, or to taste

⅓ cup granulated sugar

¼ cup vegan margarine, at room temperature

One 12-ounce package tofu, firm silken (vacuum-packed)

½ teaspoon almond extract

1 cup ground almonds (see Notes)

¼ cup cornstarch, sifted if lumpy

1 cup flaked almonds

1 cup confectioners' sugar, sifted if lumpy

½ teaspoon almond extract

1½ tablespoons cold water

Flaked almonds, for garnish

1. Preheat the oven to 400°F and have your pie crust ready. Placing the pie plate on a baking sheet is handy in case of spills.

2. Spread the jam evenly on base of pie crust with the back of a spoon.

3. With a whisk or handheld beater, in a large bowl, cream the margarine and granulated sugar until light and fluffy.

4. Add the silken tofu and almond extract, whisk until well combined with no large lumps of tofu remaining.

5. Add the ground almonds and cornstarch, again whisk to fully combine.

6. Fold in the flaked almonds, then spoon into pie shell on top of the jam. Smooth the top as required.

7. Bake for 25 to 30 minutes, until starting to lightly brown. Remove from the oven and let cool while you mix the icing.

8. In a small bowl, mix together the confectioners' sugar, almond extract, and water to form a smooth paste.

9. Pour the icing mixture over the pie while still warm. Sprinkle the top with more flaked almonds.

10. Allow to cool in the pie plate if serving cold; if serving warm, let cool for 20 minutes prior to serving. Serve with fresh raspberries, if you have them.

NOTES:
❖ You can buy almonds preground, or grind your own in a blender or food processor until they have the consistency of heavy flour. Take care not to end up with nut butter!

❖ You may find ground almonds in the store sold as almond flour or almond meal; all are pretty much the same and work interchangeably.

Buttery Tarts

MAKES 12 INDIVIDUAL TARTS

▶ **NO NUTS • NO WHEAT** excluding crust

I've seen the original, nonvegan butter tarts in the bakery at our local supermarket, but never actually had one until I made my own! I had to Google a little to get an idea of what they were and contained. I think mine are creamier but less rich than the original, thanks to the addition of the tofu, but I found this was how I liked them best.

The extra layer of a baking sheet and parchment paper is necessary because these have a tendency to overflow!

12 unbaked mini tart shells, homemade using Plain Pie Crust (page 169) or store-bought

⅓ cup vegan margarine
⅓ cup dark brown sugar, packed
3 tablespoons brown rice syrup

2 tablespoons vegan margarine

⅓ cup (3 ½ ounces) tofu, firm silken (vacuum-packed)
½ teaspoon vanilla extract

¼ cup golden raisins (optional)

1. Preheat the oven to 375°F and place the tart shells on a parchment-lined baking sheet. (See Note.)

2. In a medium saucepan, combine the ⅓ cup of margarine, the brown sugar, and the syrup. Heat to melt, then bring to a boil. Cook at a boil, over medium heat, stirring frequently, for 6 minutes until thick. Be careful not to have the temperature too high or the sugar will burn.

3. Remove from the heat and beat in the 2 tablespoons of margarine with a wooden spoon.

4. Using a blender or food processor, blend together the tofu, vanilla, and hot margarine mixture until smooth, creamy, and well combined. Scrape down as required. Don't stress too much if the hot mixture forms little lumps of caramel; these will bake out in the oven. Take care when doing this step, as the mixture is hot!

5. If using the golden raisins, place 1 teaspoon of them in the bottom of each tart shell.

6. Pour the margarine mixture straight from your blender into each tart shell to about two-thirds full.

7. Bake for 15 to 18 minutes, until the pastry is browned and filling is very bubbly.

8. Remove from the oven and let cool on the baking sheet until firm and easily handled.

NOTE:

❖ If making homemade tart shells and using a muffin pan to make them in, spray the muffin pan cups and top with nonstick spray, and then place this pan onto a parchment-lined baking sheet.

• •

Coconut and Pecan Chocolate Pie

SERVES 10 TO 12

▶ **NO SOY • NO WHEAT** excluding crust

This is a lovely creamy, rich, and very moreish, pie with the added bonus of being soy free.

If you don't have a high-speed, superpowered blender, don't despair if you can't get your cashews ground completely silky smooth. The texture provided by the coconut and pecan pieces hides any small bits of the nuts that aren't totally creamy.

Garnishes are given, but are entirely optional as I really don't think this needs anything extra.

1½ cups raw cashews, soaked for at least 8 hours or overnight, then drained
¼ cup canned coconut milk
2 tablespoons cornstarch
2 tablespoons coconut milk powder (see Notes)

1½ cups vegan chocolate chips

¼ cup granulated sugar

¼ cup canned coconut milk

½ teaspoon vanilla extract

¼ teaspoon coconut extract

1 prebaked 9-inch pie crust (see Notes)

¼ cup finely chopped pecans

½ cup unsweetened, shredded coconut

1 recipe Ganache-Style Chocolate (page 252), toasted chopped pecans, or toasted coconut, for garnish (optional)

1. In a blender or food processor, pulse together the nuts, coconut milk, cornstarch, and coconut milk powder until thick and creamy. Scrape down the sides as required to ensure everything is well mixed and very smooth.

2. Using a medium bowl in a double boiler over medium-low heat, or in a microwave on high for 15-second bursts, stirring frequently, melt the chocolate chips, sugar, coconut milk, and extracts. Once melted with no lumps, add to the blender and blend until smooth.

3. Transfer to a large bowl and fold in the pecans and coconut prior to pouring into cooled pie shell. Smooth the top and refrigerate for at least an hour but preferably overnight, until the topping is firm.

4. Decorate, if desired, with Ganache-Style Chocolate, toasted nuts, or coconut.

NOTES:

❖ Coconut milk powder is available from Asian grocery stores and many supermarkets. Be sure to check the ingredients to make sure it is nondairy. If you have trouble finding this, or can't find a brand that doesn't contain milk ingredients, substitute soy milk powder instead. One of my testers, SS, who lives in Finland, couldn't find coconut (or soy) milk powder anywhere. She had good results from grinding unsweetened, shredded coconut to a heavy flour consistency, in her spice grinder, and substituted that instead. Thanks for the hint!

❖ The Pecan Pie Crust (page 168) is specifically for this recipe but you could also use the Plain Pie Crust (page 169), the Coconut Pie Crust (page 167), or a store-bought crust.

Creamy Dreamy Lemon Mousse Pie

SERVES 8 TO 10

▶ **NO NUTS • NO WHEAT** excluding crust

I needed help from my recipe testers to name this pie! I wasn't sure if the title I'd given it, Lemon Avocado Mousse Pie, was enticing enough. My husband suggested Green Lemon Pie, and while I can't use Grasshopper Pie (which is usually mint), one of the children kindly suggested Stink Bug Pie, the logic being it's a bug like a grasshopper and also green like one, too, not that the pie stinks. Then there was a rhyming option like Eenie Meenie Greenie Pie. In the end we went with the title you see above! (Thanks, Kim, for the suggestion.)

This is one of those ideas I had floating around in my head for ages, not sure if it would work, or would taste good if it did. In the end, boy, did it ever! Don't let the color put you off; this is smooth, creamy, and lemony!

This is also good with a scoop of Crazy Whip Topping (page 249), drizzled with a little Ganache-Style Chocolate (page 252), melted vegan white chocolate, or a commercial whipped-cream substitute such as Soyatoo!

¾ cup granulated sugar

½ cup water

¼ cup freshly squeezed lemon juice (2 medium lemons)

¾ teaspoon agar powder

6 ounces tofu, firm silken (vacuum-packed, half of a 12-ounce package)

1 large ripe avocado (about 6 ounces after pit and skin are removed)

¼ cup soy milk

1 tablespoon freshly squeezed lemon juice (½ medium lemon)

1 teaspoon vanilla extract

1 tablespoon lemon zest (1 medium lemon)

One 9-inch prebaked pie crust or Sweet Cornmeal Pie Crust (page 171)—your choice

1. In a medium saucepan, over medium heat, combine the sugar, water, lemon juice, and agar powder. Stir constantly until the sugar and agar are dissolved, then, stirring occasionally, bring to a boil. Remove from the heat.

2. In a blender or food processor, blend together the tofu, avocado, soy milk, lemon juice, and vanilla until smooth and creamy. Scrape down the sides as required.

3. Add the agar mixture (be careful; it is hot and you don't want it to splash!) and blend again until very smooth, creamy, and shiny looking. Scrape down the sides as required.

4. With a spatula, stir the lemon zest into the mixture while in the blender jar.

5. Pour into prepared pie shell, let cool to room temperature, then chill for at least 2 hours or preferably overnight, until firm.

6. Store covered in the fridge.

Variation

Creamy Dreamy Lime Mousse Pie
If the green-lemon combination is too much of a stretch for you, use lime juice and zest in place of the lemon. Then the pie will taste, as well as look, green.

Currant Turnovers

MAKES 14 TURNOVERS IF USING FULL AMOUNT OF PASTRY

▶ NO NUTS

We used to call these Currant Turnovers while growing up, and it wasn't until I was an adult that I found out they had a real name, "Eccles Cakes," for the little English town where they were invented! Simple, quick, and yummy, these are a nice way of using up any leftover pastry (see Note). Served warm or cold, they are nice with a dollop of Crazy Whip Topping (page 249).

1 recipe Plain Pie Crust Pastry (page 169—Spiced Variation is nice), or another pastry

2 tablespoons + 1 teaspoon vegan margarine (½ teaspoon per turnover)

¼ cup + 2 teaspoons dried currants (1 teaspoon per turnover)

¼ cup + 2 teaspoons golden raisins (1 teaspoon per turnover)

2 tablespoons + 1 teaspoon light brown sugar, packed (½ teaspoon per turnover)

¼ teaspoon pie spice (see page 19) (1 pinch per turnover)

Soy milk, for brushing (optional)

Granulated sugar, for sprinkling (optional)

1. Preheat the oven to 400°F and line two baking sheets with parchment paper.

2. Roll out the dough to less than a ¼-inch thickness and cut out fourteen circles with a 4½-inch pastry cutter. Reroll and cut again once only, if required, or the pastry will get too tough.

3. Place ½ teaspoon of margarine in the center of each circle.

4. Top the margarine with 1 teaspoon of currants, 1 teaspoon of golden raisins, ½ teaspoon of brown sugar, and a pinch of pie spice.

5. Fold the sides of the circle toward the center so they meet and overlap, pinch to seal, and squeeze the turnovers into a hockey puck or disk shape.

6. Turn over the pastry parcels (this is where they get their name) and place on the baking sheet about 1 inch apart.

7. Prick the top of each parcel with a fork twice, brush with a little soy milk, and sprinkle with granulated sugar, if desired.

8. Bake for 15 to 18 minutes until the pastry is golden.

9. Remove from the oven and let cool on the baking sheet for 5 minutes, then transfer to a wire rack and let cool completely.

NOTE:

❖ If using leftover pastry to make turnovers, just roll out your pastry scraps and cut out as directed. Count how many circles you have, use the amounts of filling given in the parentheses per circle of dough, then bake as directed. This works with any rolled-out pastry, including store-bought puff pastry.

From-Scratch Cinnamon Straws 📷

MAKES ABOUT 16 STRAWS

▶ **NO NUTS**

This is basically the plain pastry recipe with inclusions to make coffee shop–style cinnamon straws. Yummy! Better than a bought one!

There's a cheater's version, using leftover pastry (page 172), if even this is too much work.

2 cups all-purpose flour

⅓ cup turbinado sugar

2½ teaspoons ground cinnamon

½ teaspoon salt

½ teaspoon baking powder

¼ teaspoon ground nutmeg

¼ cup vegan shortening

¼ cup frozen and grated coconut oil (see Note)

5 to 8 tablespoons soy milk

About 2 tablespoons turbinado sugar, for sprinkling

About 1 teaspoon ground cinnamon, for sprinkling

Soy milk, for brushing (optional)

1. Preheat the oven to 375°F and line a baking sheet with parchment paper.

2. In a large bowl, whisk together the flour, turbinado sugar, cinnamon, salt, baking powder, and nutmeg.

3. Using a pastry cutter (or two knives held together), cut in the shortening until the

mixture resembles lumpy bread crumbs. Stir in the frozen coconut oil flakes with a fork.

4. Add 5 tablespoons of the milk and start to mix to form a loose dough. When ready, the dough will hold together when pressed; there will be some loose bits that you will need to press in. If too dry, add the rest of the milk 1 tablespoon at a time until the dough has a firmer consistency.

5. Gather the dough and press into a ball. Knead lightly to encourage it to hold together.

6. Roll out the dough into a 10 by 7-inch rectangle about ⅜ inch thick. Sprinkle with the cinnamon and turbinado sugar, pressing this into the dough.

7. Slice into sixteen ½- to ¾-inch wide, 7-inch long strips. Holding one end of each strip, twist from the other end, for a decorative effect.

8. Place each twisted strip on the baking sheet and brush with soy milk, if desired.

9. Bake for 12 to 15 minutes until the bottoms are golden and the straws are well risen.

10. Remove from the oven and let cool on the baking sheet for 5 minutes, then let cool completely on a wire rack.

NOTE:

❖ To freeze coconut oil, place some coconut oil in the freezer in a plastic container for a few hours to freeze. Once frozen, remove from the container, and holding the oil with a paper towel (to avoid getting melting oil on your hands), quickly grate over a sheet of tinfoil, using the larger compartment on your box grater. Wrap in the tinfoil and return to the freezer until required. If you are short on time, or would prefer not to do the freezing step for this, some of my testers had good results using room-temperature coconut oil and cutting it in with the shortening.

Individual Baklava

MAKES 24 INDIVIDUAL BAKLAVA

Completely nontraditional and pretty much made up, to be honest, these have all the sweet nuttiness of baklava, but are easier to eat. They are a little more time consuming and fiddly than making a big pan full, but don't be put off, they really are worth it. Don't be scared of the phyllo, either. It's not as hard to work with as you may think!

These can be eaten warm or cool, and are great served with vanilla ice cream, Crazy Whip Topping (page 249), or by themselves. To reheat, place on a baking sheet in a 250°F oven for 10 minutes, until the pastry is crisp again.

8 sheets phyllo pastry (thawed in the fridge, if frozen)

½ cup agave nectar
½ cup light brown sugar, packed
½ cup water
¼ cup brown rice syrup
¼ cup vegan margarine
2 teaspoons rose water, or 2 drops of rose extract (see Notes)

2 cups chopped pistachio nuts (see Notes)
1 cup chopped walnuts
½ cup bread crumbs
1 teaspoon ground cinnamon

¼ cup vegan margarine, melted

1. Preheat the oven to 400°F and line a baking sheet with parchment paper. Have one dry and three damp clean tea towels ready.

2. Take the thawed phyllo from the fridge, remove from its packaging, and cover with the dry tea towel, then a damp tea towel.

3. In a large saucepan, combine the agave nectar, brown sugar, water, syrup, margarine, and rose water. Bring to a boil, stirring frequently, until the margarine is melted, then boil, unstirred, over medium heat, for 5 minutes, until the mixture is slightly thickened. Remove a scant ¼ cup of this syrup and reserve for later.

4. Stir the nuts, bread crumbs, and cinnamon into the pan, containing the bulk of the syrup, to form a sticky filling.

5. To form the individual baklava, take a sheet of phyllo pastry, slice into thirds lengthwise, and brush with melted margarine. Place a scant 2 tablespoons of filling mixture in one corner of the strip.

6. Fold the phyllo strip into a triangle, starting by folding the corner containing the filling over on itself to start the triangle. Then fold over and over, maintaining the triangle, enclosing the filling.

7. Place the baklava on the prepared baking sheet and brush the top with melted margarine. Cover the baking sheet with a damp tea towel to prevent the pastry from drying out. I can fit all twenty-four on my large baking sheet if I place the triangles long sides together to make a square, and have three rows of the squares across the short side of the sheet, and six rows down.

8. Repeat until all the filling is used. Generously brush the completed baklava with the reserved syrup.

9. Bake for 10 to 12 minutes, until the pastry is golden. Be careful as it will go from golden to burned very quickly; keep an eye on it.

10. Remove from the oven and let cool on the sheet for 5 minutes, then transfer to a wire rack and let cool completely.

11. Once completely cool, store in a covered container at room temperature.

NOTES:
- ❖ If you don't have rose water or rose extract, substitute an equal amount of vanilla extract.
- ❖ Try to get raw pistachios, unsalted, unroasted, and undyed.

Variation

Fruited Baklava
Reduce the pistachios to 1 cup and add 1 cup of raisins or dried currants when you add the nuts.

· ·

Lime Coconut Tart

SERVES 8 TO 10

▶ **NO NUTS • NO WHEAT** excluding crust

This is divinely tropical, not too sweet and a little bit tart, and it will easily make you think you've woken up on a Caribbean Island.

To make the filling a little bit green, to look a little more "lime," add a few drops of vegan green food coloring in the blender with the tofu. I like it as it is.

One 12-ounce package tofu, firm silken (vacuum-packed)
⅔ cup granulated sugar
¼ cup plain or vanilla vegan yogurt
¼ cup coconut milk powder (see Note)
¼ cup cornstarch
1 teaspoon vanilla extract
½ teaspoon coconut extract
1½ to 2 tablespoons lime zest (3 medium limes)

6 tablespoons lime juice (3 medium limes)

1¼ cups unsweetened shredded coconut

1 prepared crust made in an 11-inch loose-bottomed tart pan, preferably, or a 9-inch pie plate. Coconut Pie Crust (page 167) is perfect here.

1 recipe Drizzle Icing (page 251), made with lime juice, not water, and tinted light green (optional)
Toasted coconut, for garnish (optional)
Lime zest strips, for garnish (optional)

1. Preheat the oven to 400°F.

2. In a blender or food processor, blend together the ingredients from tofu through lime juice until smooth and creamy, scraping down the sides a few times as required.

3. Transfer to a mixing bowl and stir in the coconut.

4. Pour into the prepared pie crust and level the top.

5. Bake for 15 minutes at 400°F, then lower the oven temperature to 350°F and bake for a further 30 to 35 minutes, until the top is just firm and set. If using a deeper 9-inch pie plate, you'll need to bake for the longer time. The edges will be firmer and drier looking.

6. Remove from the oven and let cool on a wire rack. Once completely cool, garnish, if desired, before serving, with Drizzle Icing randomly zigzagged on top, and sprinkled with a little toasted coconut and/or lime zest.

NOTE:

❖ Coconut milk powder is available from Asian grocery stores and many supermarkets. If you have trouble finding this, or can't find a brand that doesn't contain milk ingredients, substitute soy milk powder instead. One of my testers, SS, who lives in Finland, couldn't find coconut (or soy) milk powder anywhere. She had good results by grinding unsweetened shredded coconut to a heavy flour consistency in her spice grinder and substituted that instead. Thanks again for the hint!

• •

Raspberry Clafouti Tart

SERVES 8 TO 10

▶ **NO NUTS**

My brother, a very talented and experienced chef, will berate me for calling this clafouti. I shall take this space to explain, in my own defense, that it is not a clafouti but a tart inspired by clafouti. It doesn't contain cherries, after all!

This is a lovely dish, warm from the oven and dusted with a little confectioners' sugar, or cold as it is!

⅓ cup vegan margarine at room temperature
2 tablespoons canola oil
¾ cup granulated sugar

6 ounces tofu, firm silken (vacuum-packed, half of a 12-ounce package)
1 tablespoon freshly squeezed lemon juice (½ medium lemon)
1 teaspoon vanilla extract

1 cup all-purpose flour
2 tablespoons cornstarch
½ teaspoon salt
¼ teaspoon baking soda

1 cup fresh raspberries (see Note)

2 tablespoons granulated sugar

1. Preheat the oven to 375°F and line a baking sheet with parchment paper, in case of overspill, and place an 11-inch loose-bottomed tart pan on top, then spray the pan with nonstick spray.

2. In a large bowl, cream together the margarine, oil, and sugar until light and fluffy.

3. Using your blender, blend together the tofu, lemon juice, and vanilla until very smooth and creamy; scrape down the sides as required.

4. Pour the blended tofu mixture into the creamed mixture and combine. Sift in the flour, cornstarch, and salt and fold to combine. Pour the mixture into the tart pan and smooth the top.

5. Take care to leave a ½-inch margin around the edge, to become a "crust," and sprinkle the tart with the raspberries and then the sugar.

6. Bake for 30 to 35 minutes, until the tart is set, just firm to the touch, and browned around the edges.

7. Remove from the oven and let cool on a wire rack. Once cool, remove the sides from the pan, let cool completely on the rack, then store in the fridge.

NOTE:

❖ You can use frozen raspberries, but please thaw and drain prior to tossing with the sugar. The results aren't as spectacular, but the recipe will still work.

Variation

Blueberry Clafouti Tart
Replace the raspberries with blueberries!

Rhubarb and Strawberry Crumble-Top Pie

SERVES 8 TO 10

▶ **NO NUTS • NO SOY**

A great combination of flavors, sweet and tart at the same time, topped with a tasty crumble topping. You'll find that you're asking yourself, "Is it crumble?" "Is it pie?"—and the answer is, "It's both! And it's good!"

Fresh or frozen rhubarb and strawberries can be used in this recipe with good results, so it's not just for when they are in season.

FILLING
- **1¾ cups roughly chopped rhubarb (3 medium stalks)**
- **¾ cup granulated sugar**

- **2½ cups quartered strawberries**

- **3 tablespoons tapioca starch**
- **2 tablespoons water**
- **1 tablespoon freshly squeezed lemon juice (½ medium lemon)**

CRUMBLE TOPPING
- **⅓ cup all-purpose flour**
- **2 tablespoons quick-cooking or old-fashioned rolled oats (not instant)**
- **2 tablespoons vegan panko (see Note)**
- **1 tablespoon granulated sugar**
- **½ teaspoon baking powder**
- **¼ teaspoon salt**
- **⅛ teaspoon ground ginger**
- **Pinch of ground nutmeg**

- **2 tablespoons vegan shortening**

- **1 prepared 9-inch pie crust—the Plain Pie Crust (page 169), or your preference**

1. Preheat the oven to 375°F.

Prepare the filling

2. In a medium saucepan, combine the rhubarb and sugar. Bring to a boil, over medium heat, stirring frequently, then simmer, uncovered, stirring occasionally, for about 10 minutes, until fruit is cooked and syrupy.

3. Add the strawberries and cook in the same way for 10 more minutes, until softened. While the fruit is cooking . . .

Prepare the crumble topping

4. In a large bowl, whisk together the ingredients from flour through nutmeg.

5. Cut the shortening into the dry ingredients, then stir in with your hand to form a crumbly mixture.

Assemble

6. In a small cup or bowl, stir the tapioca, water, and lemon juice to become a slurry. Add to the fruit and stir to combine.

7. Pour the fruit mixture into the prepared pie crust. Smooth the top.

8. Evenly sprinkle the crumble topping on top of the fruit layer, and bake for 20 to 25 minutes, until the crumble is lightly browned.

9. Remove from the oven and let cool for 15 minutes prior to serving. If serving cold, let cool completely, then store covered in the fridge. The filling will firm up if kept refrigerated.

NOTE:

❖ Panko is a Japanese type of bread crumb that stays crisp during baking. Available in most supermarkets, health food stores, and Asian food stores, it is not hard to find.

Sticky Nut Pie 📷

SERVES 10 TO 12

▶ **NO WHEAT** excluding crust

This one is similar to a pecan pie but with random nuts. It is more in line with how I imagine pecan pie to be, as I have never had it! So not really like it at all, I suppose. Use whatever nuts you prefer and what you have on hand.

This is great served with Crazy Whip Topping (page 249) or vanilla ice cream, to take the edge off the sweetness a little.

2½ cups roughly chopped mixed nuts (see Note)

1 teaspoon pie spice (see page 19)
½ teaspoon salt
½ teaspoon ancho chile powder
Pinch of cayenne (optional)

½ cup light brown sugar, packed
¼ cup brown rice syrup
¼ cup hazelnut coffee syrup or agave nectar

2 tablespoons soy creamer (see page 16)
2 tablespoons vegan margarine

1 prebaked 9-inch pie crust, such as Plain Pie Crust (page 169) or Pecan Pie Crust (page 168)

1. In a large, deep-sided skillet, over medium heat, toast the nuts for 5 to 7 minutes, until lightly browned and aromatic. Add the salt and spices, and toast for 1 minute more.

2. Add the brown sugar, rice syrup, and syrup.

3. Heat the mixture until it comes to a boil. Lower the heat to low and simmer for 8 to 10 minutes, until thick, syrupy, and most of the liquid has evaporated.

4. Remove from the heat, add the creamer and margarine, and mix until the margarine is melted.

5. Pour the mixture into the prepared pie crust, smooth the top, and leave at room temperature for at least an hour until cool.

6. Chill for at least 1 hour (longer chilling is better for the texture), until ready to serve. When serving, for ease of slicing, use a knife that has been heated in hot water.

NOTE:

❖ Be random when chopping the nuts; the pie looks better if they are not uniform.

Variations

Chocolate-Infused Sticky Nut Pie
Replace ½ cup of the nuts with cocoa nibs, but don't toast them. Add with the creamer and margarine, for a different taste sensation.

Marshmallow Sticky Nut Pie
Stir ¼ cup of vegan mini marshmallows into the nuts just prior to spreading in the prepared crust.

- -

Sweet Potato Pie

SERVES 8 TO 10

▶ **NO NUTS • NO WHEAT** excluding crust

This is quite a simple chilled sweet potato pie, nothing fancy, good for after a gourmet meal where you want a little simple sweet something to finish it off. To jazz it up a little, serve with a scoop of Crazy Whip Topping (page 249).

I've used either orange-fleshed or white-fleshed sweet potatoes in this pie. They are subtly different but good; use whichever you prefer.

2 medium sweet potatoes

One 12-ounce package tofu, firm silken (vacuum-packed)

⅓ cup soy creamer (see page 16)

¼ cup light brown sugar, packed

3 tablespoons pure maple syrup

2½ tablespoons cornstarch

1 tablespoon blackstrap molasses

2½ teaspoons pie spice (see page 19)

1 teaspoon vanilla extract

¼ teaspoon ancho chile powder (see Notes)

¼ teaspoon salt

One 9-inch unbaked pie crust, such as Plain Pie Crust, spiced version (page 170), Pecan Pie Crust (page 168) or your preference

1. Preheat the oven to 400°F. Prick the sweet potatoes, place on a baking sheet lined with parchment paper, and bake for 1 hour, until soft. Remove from the oven, allow to cool, halve, remove the flesh and discard the skins, then roughly mash the flesh. You'll end up with about 2 cups of flesh. (I often do this the day before, if I'm using the oven for something else, to save time on the day.) (See Notes.)

2. Place the sweet potato flesh and all the other ingredients, except the pie crust, in a food processor and blend until very smooth, scraping down the sides as required. Spoon into the pie crust and smooth the top.

3. Bake at 400°F for 20 minutes, then lower the oven temperature to 350°F and continue to bake for a further 25 to 30 minutes, until the center of the top is just firm to the touch.

4. Remove from the oven and let cool to room temperature, and then refrigerate for at least 1 hour prior to serving.

NOTES:

❖ For a more traditional sweet potato pie taste, leave out the chile powder.

- If you're a microwave user, you can cook your sweet potatoes in the microwave instead of in the oven, to save time. Prick all over and bake on high until soft, checking after 10 minutes and adjusting the time from there.

Variation

Pumpkin Pie

Substitute 2 cups of mashed or pureed pure pumpkin, canned or home baked, for the sweet potato.

Vanilla Crème Puffs 📷

MAKES ABOUT 24 PUFFS

▶ NO NUTS

Fellow cookbook author (*American Vegan Kitchen*, Vegan Heritage Press, 2010) and blogger (www.veganappetite.com) Tamasin Noyes saw the call on my blog for bake sale idea requests and requested that I attempt cream puffs, having had no great success with them herself. Here's the result of numerous attempts and tweakings. She even agreed to be a guest tester for this one recipe! So, what do you think, Tami?

As an alternate filling, use a commercial whipped cream substitute, such as Soyatoo!

¼ cup + 2 tablespoons vegan margarine

1 cup water

1 cup all-purpose flour

¼ teaspoon salt

2 teaspoons finely ground chia seeds

¼ cup warm water

¼ cup (2½ ounces) tofu, firm silken (vacuum-packed)

¼ cup + 2 tablespoons water

2 tablespoons powdered egg replacer (such as Ener-G)

1 tablespoon cornstarch

2 teaspoons baking powder

½ teaspoon baking soda

1 recipe Vanilla Crème (recipe follows)

1 recipe Ganache-Style Chocolate (page 252)

Confectioners' sugar, for dusting (optional)

1. Preheat the oven to 425°F, ensure both oven racks are central, and line two baking sheets with parchment paper.

2. In a medium saucepan, bring the margarine and water to a full boil.

3. Remove from the heat, add the flour and salt, and using a wooden spoon, beat until thick and pulled away from the sides of the pot.

4. Let cool for a few minutes while you prepare the remaining ingredients.

5. In a small cup or bowl, combine the chia seeds and warm water. Set aside for 2 minutes.

6. In a blender or food processor, blend together the chia mixture, tofu, water, cornstarch, egg replacer, baking powder, and baking soda until thick and creamy. Scrape down the sides as necessary.

7. Add half of the blended mixture at a time to the floured mixture, and beat well between each addition, until it has pulled completely from the side of the pan. The mixture will look a little like very thick mashed potatoes but smoother and shinier, and will feel soft and pliable.

8. Measure out generous tablespoon-size balls of dough and place about 2 inches apart onto the prepared sheets.

9. Bake both pans at the same time, swapping positions in the oven after 10 minutes, for a total of 20 minutes, until golden.

10. Turn off oven, open the door partially, and allow the puffs to cool in the oven for 30 minutes.

11. After 30 minutes, remove from the oven, transfer to a wire rack, and let cool completely, prior to filling and coating.

12. To fill, place the vanilla crème in a piping bag fitted with a long, thin nozzle. With a small knife, poke a hole in the side of the pastry puff and fill with the vanilla crème. It will "puff" as it fills. Dip each filled crème puff into the chocolate ganache to partially coat, if desired, and place in the fridge to set.

13. Dust with confectioners' sugar prior to serving, and store in the fridge.

. . . .

★ Vanilla Crème

MAKES 1½ CUPS CRÈME

▶ **NO NUTS · NO WHEAT**

This custardlike filling is tasty enough to eat by itself. It makes a nice soft filling for cakes, goes well on pies, and is a good topping for sweet biscuits.

If you make this in advance and store it in the fridge, it will get quite firm and need rewhisking when you want to pipe into the crème puffs.

1 cup soy creamer (see page 16)
½ cup granulated sugar
¼ cup (2½ ounces) tofu, firm silken (vacuum-packed)
¼ cup canned coconut milk
3 tablespoons cornstarch

1 tablespoon vanilla extract
1 teaspoon vanilla paste (optional) (see Note)
¼ teaspoon agar powder

1. In a blender or food processor, blend all the ingredients until smooth and creamy. Scrape down the sides as required.

2. Transfer to a small saucepan and bring to a boil over medium heat, whisking constantly.

3. Boil for 2 minutes, still whisking, then remove from the heat.

4. Whisk every 5 minutes or so while the mixture cools to room temperature. It will be thick and will look lumpy (it isn't, it is just the agar setting), and the whisking helps it keep the creamy texture and prevent a skin forming.

5. Once cool, use wherever desired. Store leftovers in the fridge in a covered container.

NOTE:

❖ If you don't have access to vanilla paste, use the scrapings from half a vanilla bean instead, or just leave it out. Your crème won't have the pretty flecks in it but will still taste of vanilla.

. . . .

White Balsamic Fruit Tarts with Jam Glaze 📷

MAKES 12 INDIVIDUAL TARTS

▶ **NO NUTS · NO WHEAT** excluding crust

I remember reading about a recipe like this in a "foodie" magazine, I forget which one, a few years ago. The combination intrigued me so I made a note of it and then created my own vegan version.

I have included a number of versions to illustrate that you really can use any fruit you choose for the topping. Just use a matching jam for the glaze, or use apricot jam, which goes with almost everything!

These will keep for up to 24 hours in the fridge before the crust gets too soggy, but they are best made on the day they are to be consumed.

3 ounces tofu, firm silken (vacuum-packed, one quarter of a 12-ounce package)

2 tablespoons water

2 tablespoons soy creamer (see page 16)

1½ tablespoons cornstarch

½ teaspoon vanilla extract

¼ teaspoon agar powder

¼ cup white balsamic vinegar

¼ cup + 2 tablespoons granulated sugar

1 tablespoon vegan margarine

12 prebaked mini (about 3 inches across) tart shells, homemade using Plain Pie Crust (page 169), or store-bought

Your choice of stone fruit, for garnish (e.g., halved and pitted cherries, apricots, plums, or peaches), as required (roughly 1 cup)

1 recipe Jam Glaze (recipe follows), made with appropriately matching jam

1. Blend together the tofu, creamer, water, cornstarch, vanilla, and agar powder until smooth and creamy.

2. In a small saucepan, over medium-high heat, bring the vinegar to a boil and then boil, stirring occasionally, for 5 minutes, until reduced to half its original volume. The vinegar will darken as it reduces; this is normal.

3. Add the sugar and margarine and stir constantly until both are melted, about 3 minutes.

4. Add the tofu mixture and cook, stirring constantly, until the mixture comes to a boil and is very thick, 4 to 5 minutes.

5. Remove from the heat, let cool for 5 minutes, then spoon evenly into the prepared tart shells. They will be roughly ¾ full. If you like tarts with lots of fruit, you'll need to underfill these slightly to leave more space. (Any leftover filling is great to eat as firm custard!)

6. Arrange the fruit on top of the tarts as decoratively as possible and chill for at least 30 minutes, until the filling is set.

7. Spoon over, or brush with the Jam Glaze, then chill for at least 30 minutes until set.

8. Store covered in the fridge.

Variations

White Balsamic Berry Tarts
Instead of the stone fruit, use whatever berries you have or prefer, and use a jam to match; for example, raspberry, strawberry, blueberry, blackberry, or a berry mixture.

White Balsamic Tropical Tarts
Instead of the stone fruit, use whatever tropical or subtropical fruits you have or prefer; for example, sliced pineapple, melon, grapes, kiwifruit, or mango. Use a jam to match, such as pineapple preserves, or a neutral jam such as apricot.

Large White Balsamic Tart
Instead of using small tart cases, use an 11-inch loose-bottomed tart pan or a 9-inch pie plate, make a double

amount of filling, then fill and decorate with berries or fruit as described above. When made this way, the tart serves ten to twelve.

Jam Glaze

MAKES ABOUT ¼ CUP GLAZE

▶ **NO SOY • NO NUTS • NO WHEAT**

If using this to glaze the items in a recipe other than this one (and please do—it's a lovely glaze!), choose the flavor of jam that best complements the predominant flavor in the recipe you are making. This simple glaze adds shine to your finished baked items.

3 tablespoons jam
1½ tablespoons granulated sugar
1½ tablespoons water

1. Combine all the ingredients in a small saucepan, over medium-high heat, and bring to a boil, stirring constantly to melt everything.

2. Continue to boil, without stirring, for 2 minutes.

3. Remove from the heat and let cool for 5 minutes prior to spooning over the baked item or brushing on with a pastry brush, as required.

Yeasted Treats

AGAIN, YOU SAY, "I thought this was all about baking vegan goodies that are 'quick and easy'!" Well, yes, I say in my own defense, yeasted baking, while not quick, certainly is easy! That is, once you get over your fear of yeast. Yeast is vegan, it's not going to grow uncontrollably and take over your kitchen, and it's harder to kill than you fear! Sure, the recipes that ask you to roll fillings into dough, stuff it, or braid it can be fiddly, so start with the ones that don't ask you to do these things, until you get more confident. I include recipes for those!

A History of Yeasted Baking

Historically, the story of yeasted baking reads something like this, though I have simplified things:

First, there was unleavened bread: flour, and maybe fat, mixed with water or milk and heated on a flat surface or in an oven.

Then, no doubt by accident, dough that had been left sitting around was infected with wild yeast, which caused the dough to rise. This accident was cultivated and perfected, and the starters kept, as with modern sourdough starters.

Then the yeast itself was grown and kept to be transported place to place, initially as gray-colored blocks of live yeast; then, as technology improved, as dry yeast and quick-acting yeast, which has ascorbic acid added to speed rising.

In a nutshell, we've come to modern times!

A Quick FYI

The recipes that follow all call for either bread flour, which has higher gluten content than all-purpose flour, or an equal amount of all-purpose flour with 1 tablespoon of vital wheat gluten added per cup. The additional vital wheat gluten increases the gluten content of the all-purpose flour, so it acts more like bread flour. If you don't have either option, then make a note on your shopping list (you've remembered to make one already, right?), should you wish to try some yeast baking!

There's not really the space in each individual recipe to cover all this information every time, so here's a basic primer for you.

About Yeast

These days, most yeast you can buy for home baking is dried. You'll occasionally see wet yeast—it looks like a square of gray play dough—but only in specialized stores. For the purposes of this book, I have used standard, not quick-acting, dry yeast granules, available from the baking aisle of every good grocery store. The usual shelf life of dry yeast, once opened, is 6 months. Once opened, this yeast needs to be stored in the fridge. If the yeast is just over its "best before" date, it may still be active. Whatever its age, this type of yeast is usually guaranteed by the manufacturer to work every time, but it is still a good idea to check that the yeast is still active every time you use it. The process of this checking is called *proofing* or *proving* the yeast. Completing this proofing step will help you determine if the yeast is active enough to use.

TO PROOF YOUR YEAST

Combine the yeast called for in the recipe with a little sugar or other sweetener in lukewarm water. The warm water will activate the yeast and get it feeding on the sugar. Ideally, the water will be between 86°F (30°C) and 104°F (40°C). Test the temperature of the water as you would a baby's bottle, by dabbing a little on the inside of your wrist. It should feel neither hot nor cold. Stir these ingredients together and leave them for 5 to 10 minutes. In that time, the mixture should become bubbly and frothy, which indicates that the yeast is active. If the mixture doesn't froth at all, you need to buy new yeast.

Mixing in the Ingredients

Many recipes ask you to add some ingredients, then stir the dough one hundred times with a wooden spoon. This is just to ensure everything is mixed and to get the gluten and yeast working. It's a large number that will make you stir for a while! The mixed dough usually gets a chance to rest after this stirring, prior to kneading. This stage is called *making a sponge*.

Basic Kneading

Kneading is the process of creating a smooth texture in your dough, to give an even finish, rise, and crumb to your bread. You knead to activate the gluten (the protein in the wheat), which, when pummeled, becomes stretchy and elastic, allowing the yeast to lift the dough without tearing.

To knead, take your ball of dough, place it on a smooth, clean and lightly floured work surface. Your kitchen counter is ideal, as is a tabletop or large chopping board. Using your "smart" hand (if you are right-handed that would be your right), firmly press the heel of your hand into the ball of dough, rolling toward your fingers on the board to push the dough away from you slightly. Use your other hand to then turn the dough 90 degrees, and again press with your smart hand, then turn and repeat. After a few minutes of this, turn the dough ball onto its side, flatten a little, then continue to knead. Be as rough as you like— the harder you knead, the smoother your dough, and in the end, the better your bread.

Repeat all of these steps until the dough feels very smooth, supple, and elastic. When kneading, I like to use a knead-and-rest system. This consists of hard, continuous, full-on kneading for 3 minutes, followed by a period of 1 to 2 minutes' rest for both the dough and my hands. This is repeated until the dough has the desired feel and consistency, usually five repetitions or 15 minutes of active kneading. This does take longer, but the resting periods let the dough relax between the bursts of kneading, and I feel the dough stretches more that way. Alternatively, you can knead constantly for about 15 minutes, if you prefer and have the stamina!

If your dough feels too sticky at any point during the kneading process (this is usually more noticeable in the beginning), add flour by the scant handful (no measuring needed), and use your kneading motion to incorporate into the dough. The dough will get less sticky as you continue, but the amount you need to add, if any, varies by recipe, by batch of dough, and is influenced by such things as the temperature of your kitchen and the humidity of the day.

Raising the Dough

Once kneaded, your dough needs time and a warm place in which to rise. In my grandmother's (and even my mother's) day, every house had an "airing cupboard" attached to the hot water heater. This was where the towels and sheets were usually stored and aired. It was the perfect place to place a bowl of dough to rise. These days, not many houses have airing cupboards, so you'll need to find another spot to be your warm place.

I like to place the covered bowl of dough in the microwave. The heat generated by the "at work" yeast is trapped, creating an even warmer space to aid its working, without getting too hot. Another good place to use is your oven. If you preheat the oven to a low temperature—250°F is enough—and then turn it off, you can safely place your covered bowl in there for the dough to rise. You do have to remember to turn the heat off first! Alternatively, a warm spot on the counter in your kitchen, in the oven with just the light on, near to a radiator (or heat vent) when the heat is on, or in the sun on the living room table works well, too.

The dough is left in your warm place until it has roughly doubled in size, the time for which varies for each recipe and each batch of dough. Usually this process takes between 1 and 1½ hours, though sometimes longer for particularly heavy dough. That's the first rise. Depending on the recipe the dough is either shaped now, or after the second rise.

The second rise, if used, is quicker, as the dough is already stretched from the first rise. Between the first and the second rise, the dough is punched down (literally, punch it) and then kneaded gently for a few minutes to remove any excess gas generated by the yeast in the first rise. If necessary, a little flour is added, should the dough be too sticky.

After shaping, there is another, and final, rise. The number of rises varies with the recipe, loaf shape (where more stretch and leavening is needed, the dough often has more rises), and loaf density, as denser dough often has to have a third rise.

If at any time you need to slow the rising of the dough for any reason that requires you to leave immediately—an emergency at your child's school or with your companion animal, for example—then you can place the bowl containing the rising dough in the fridge. This slows the growth of the yeast; it puts it to sleep, if you will. The yeast will return to full action once removed from the fridge and warmed up. The length of time it takes to do this will depend on how long it has been on hold in the cooler conditions of the fridge.

Shaping the Dough

There are a number of ways your dough can be shaped prior to baking.

Loaves: You can make a loaf either free-form or by using a pan. If making a free-form loaf, just shape the risen dough on a lined baking sheet into either a circle or an oblong. The top is often scored with a cross, or with lines, to keep the top of the loaf from cracking as it rises in the oven. If using a pan, this needs to be oiled, to prevent the bread from sticking, then the dough is simply placed in the pan with any less perfect shaping hidden underneath.

Simple bread rolls: The dough is divided into an even number of balls, usually but not always twelve. Each portion is kneaded lightly and rolled into a ball, with any untidy shaping placed on the bottom. The rolls are either placed on a rimmed baking sheet, just apart for soft-sided rolls, so they will touch as they rise and are baked; or on a larger baking sheet, well apart, for crustier rolls, so the sides do not touch as the rolls bake.

Pinwheel type rolls: The dough is rolled and stretched to a desired thickness, using a rolling pin and your hands, usually ¼ to ½-inch thick, then a filling is placed on top. This is followed by the dough being rolled up, usually from the longest side into as tight a roll as possible. The individual rolls are sliced from this roll and placed cut side down in a rimmed baking sheet.

Braided bread: The dough is divided into three pieces and rolled into long strands. You secure three strands of dough together at one end by pinching and pressing the dough, then place on your work surface with the secured end away from you. To braid, take the right-hand strand of dough and place over the top of the middle strand, resting between this strand and the left-hand strand, essentially now becoming the middle strand. Then take the left-hand strand, place over the top of the middle strand (which began as the right-hand strand) between it and the (new) right-hand strand. Repeat, starting again from the right until you reach the end of all the strands. At the end, pinch and press the dough together to secure. Tuck the secured ends under the braid for neatness.

Once the dough is shaped, it needs time to rest, to stay in that shape, and this period is the final rise. This rise is usually only for 30 minutes. The dough will look puffy when it is ready to bake.

Bread dough can be made in advance as far as the final rise. After shaping, the bread can be covered and the final rise can be done, as a slow rise, in the fridge overnight. For fresh baked bread for breakfast, bring the dough back to room temperature while the oven heats for baking.

Baking the Bread

If you would like your finished bread to have a shiny top, prior to baking brush the surface lightly with a little soy milk, for a crisper finish, or with canola oil, for a softer crust.

Ensure the oven rack used for baking is in the center of your oven, and that your oven has been preheated to the right temperature before putting in your bread. The heat of the oven activates the yeast one final time, producing gases that leaven your bread, then the heat kills the yeast. The more supple the dough from the kneading, the better the bread will rise, hold its shape, and taste, once baked.

You will know when your bread is ready from the aroma, the look, and the sound of the loaf. The bread will smell divine; will look golden brown and well risen; and, if you lift the loaf from the pan and tap gently on its bottom, it will sound hollow. After it has been removed from the oven and the pan, you can choose to cool your loaf on a wire rack as it is, which will result in a firm crust. Alternatively, if you wrap it in a clean tea towel while it cools, which holds in some of the steam, that gives it a softer crust.

Storage

Yeasted breads store well at room temperature, though once sliced it is a good idea to cover the sliced end to prevent it from drying and becoming hard and less appetizing. They also freeze well, in case you feel the urge to bake a double batch to have more later. If the bread is usually eaten sliced, such as the Cinnamon Raisin Bread (for Toast) (page 197), you should slice prior to wrapping and freezing, then remove slices as required and toast straight from the freezer.

As stated, in all the recipes, I have given you the option of using bread flour or all-purpose flour plus vital wheat gluten. Bread flour is higher in gluten than all-purpose flour, and so is more suited to making the items in this section. However, I don't want you to run out and buy a big bag of something you may use only once, hence the option. See Ingredients for Baking (page 12) for more details.

A quick note about bread machines and dough hooks on mixers: I don't have either, and apart from seeing Mum use her bread machine last time I was in New Zealand, I have no experience in using them. However, some of my testers did use their bread machines or the dough hook attachments on their stand mixer to great effect when making the yeasted recipes, specifically for the kneading and rising of the dough. Feel free to do that, too, if it makes things easier for you. If you have a stand mixer with dough hook, or a bread machine, and you are comfortable (and experienced) in using it, then sort of ignore my directions and follow the ones you use for the mixer/machine!

Canadian Anniversary Bread

MAKES 2 BRAIDED LOAVES

▶ NO SOY • NO SUGAR

This bread was made to become a tradition for our family, marking the day we came to Canada from Scotland with a mixture of where we came from and where we came to. The bread contains walnuts and oats representing the United Kingdom, with maple syrup and pecans representing North America. It's not a sweet bread, but perfect for serving alongside dinner. Now part of our families' history, it could become part of yours.

1 cup boiling water
½ cup rice milk, room temperature
¼ cup pure maple syrup, room temperature

2 teaspoons dry yeast

1½ cups white bread flour, or 1½ cups all-purpose flour and plus 1½ tablespoons vital wheat gluten

1 cup oat flour (see Notes)
¼ cup quick-cooking or old-fashioned rolled oats (not instant)
2 tablespoons ground pecans (see Notes)
2 tablespoons ground walnuts (see Notes)
2 tablespoons vital wheat gluten
1 tablespoon freshly squeezed lemon juice (½ medium lemon)
1 tablespoon canola oil
1 teaspoon salt

1¼ cups white bread flour, or 1½ cups all-purpose flour and 1 tablespoon vital wheat gluten

Flour, for kneading
Canola oil, for greasing the bowl
Soy milk, for brushing (optional)

1. Mix the water, milk, and maple syrup in a large bowl. Check that the temperature is lukewarm (see page 193) and add the yeast, then set aside for 5 minutes to proof.

2. Add the ingredients from flour through salt. Stir briskly one hundred times or so, then set aside for 15 minutes.

3. Add the remaining flour and turn onto a floured board for kneading. The flour may not completely incorporate at first, but that is

fine; it will become part of the dough as you knead. Add more flour by the tablespoonful, as required, to ensure the dough is not sticky.

4. Knead for a total of about 15 minutes, until your dough is smooth and supple. You can do this in 3-minute bursts—that is, knead for 3 minutes, rest, and repeat—if you find kneading vigorously for the whole time too tiring.

5. Coat a large bowl with a thin film of oil, place the dough ball in the bowl, and turn the dough to coat it in oil. Cover the bowl and place in a warm place until the dough is doubled in size (about 1 hour).

6. Punch down the dough, knead for about 3 minutes to get it looking doughlike again, then return to the bowl, cover, and return it to your warm place for the second rise. It will take less time than before, 30 to 45 minutes, to double in size.

7. Remove the dough from the bowl. Knead lightly and then divide in half. Divide each half into three equal pieces, and roll each of these into a 14-inch long cigar-shaped log.

8. Secure three of the logs together at one end by pinching and pressing the dough, then place on your work surface with the secured end farthest from you. To braid, take the right-hand strand of dough and place over the top of the middle strand, resting between this strand and the left-hand strand, essentially now becoming the middle strand. Then take the left-hand strand, place over the top of the middle strand (which was the original right-hand strand) between it and the (now) right-hand strand. Repeat, starting again from the right, until you reach the end of all the strands.

9. At the end, again pinch and press the dough together to secure. Tuck the secured ends neatly under the braid. Repeat with the remaining three logs of dough. (See Notes.)

10. Line a large baking sheet with parchment paper and place the two braided loaves

at least 2 inches apart on it. Cover and allow to rise for 20 to 30 minutes, until well risen.

11. While the loaves are rising, preheat the oven to 375°F. Once the loaves have risen, brush with milk, if desired, and bake for 20 to 25 minutes, until golden brown. If you tap the bottoms lightly when you think they are done, they should sound hollow.

12. Remove from the oven and let cool on the sheet for 10 minutes, then transfer to a wire rack and let cool completely.

NOTES:

❖ Instead of buying oat flour for just this recipe, you can make your own at home by pulsing an equal amount of quick-cooking or old-fashioned rolled oats (not instant) in your food processor until they have a flourlike consistency.

❖ If you don't want to go to the trouble of braiding the bread, shape and rise in 9-inch loaf pans, or make free-form loaves (with scored tops) instead.

❖ Ground pecans and walnuts may be found in the baking aisle of some supermarkets. If you are grinding your own, the result should be quite fine but not as fine as flour, with only a few larger pieces of nut. See page 14 for instructions in greater detail.

Cinnamon Raisin Bread (for Toast)

MAKES ONE 9-INCH LOAF

▶ **NO NUTS • NO SOY**

Who doesn't love cinnamon toast, loaded with raisins, fresh from the toaster and dripping with margarine? Well, to get that breakfast treat, you need Cinnamon Raisin Bread, and that is what we have here. It's a basic recipe, but very cinnamony and packed with raisins.

1 cup hand-hot water (see Note)
½ cup rice milk, room temperature
1 teaspoon granulated sugar

2 teaspoons dry yeast

1 cup raisins

2 cups white bread flour, or 2 cups all-purpose flour and 2 tablespoons vital wheat gluten
3 tablespoons sugar
2 tablespoons ground cinnamon
1 tablespoon freshly squeezed lemon juice (½ medium lemon)
1 tablespoon canola oil
1 teaspoon salt
½ teaspoon ground nutmeg

1¼ cups white bread flour, or 1¼ cups all-purpose flour and 1 tablespoon vital wheat gluten

Flour, for kneading
Canola oil, for greasing the bowl
Rice milk, or canola oil, for brushing (optional)

1 recipe Sugar Glaze (page 252) (optional)

1. Mix the water, milk, and sugar in a large bowl. Check the temperature to ensure it is lukewarm (see page 193), then add the yeast, stir, and set aside for 5 minutes to proof.

2. Add the raisins, stir, and set aside for 5 minutes more.

3. Add the ingredients from flour through nutmeg. Stir briskly with a wooden spoon one hundred times or so, then set aside for at least 15 minutes.

4. Add the remaining flour and turn onto a floured board for kneading. The flour may not completely incorporate at first, but that is fine; it will become part of the dough as you knead. Add more flour by the tablespoonful as required to ensure the dough is not sticky.

5. Knead for a total of about 15 minutes, until your dough is smooth and supple. You can do this in 3-minute bursts—that is, knead for 3 minutes, rest, and repeat—if you find kneading vigorously for the whole time too tiring.

6. Coat the inside of a large bowl with a thin film of oil. Place the dough ball in the bowl, and turn to coat the dough in oil. Cover the bowl and place in a warm place until the dough has doubled in size (about 1½ hours).

7. Punch down the dough, knead for about 3 minutes to get it looking doughlike again, then return to the bowl, cover, and return it to your warm place for the second rise. This will take less time than before, about 1 hour, to double in size.

8. Remove the dough from the bowl. Knead lightly and then shape into a log. Place in a 9-inch loaf pan, cover, and allow to rise again. This will take about 30 minutes. Brush the top of your bread with soy milk or oil, if desired.

9. Preheat the oven to 375°F, during the last rise, then bake the loaf for 35 to 40 minutes, until aromatic, browned, and well risen. If you tap the bottom lightly when you think it is done, it should sound hollow.

10. Straight from the oven you can glaze the bread with a little Sugar Glaze, if desired. Remove from the oven and let cool in the pan for 5 minutes, then let cool completely on a wire rack.

NOTE:
❖ Hand-hot water is as hot as you can get it from your tap, as opposed to boiling from a kettle.

Coffee-Shop Fruit Swirl

MAKES 8 BUNS

▶ **NO NUTS • NO SOY**

There's an international chain of coffee shops that offers a yeasted fruit swirl loaded with fresh and dried cranberries and blueberries. I wanted to re-create this at home, so I did! This is softer and more spiced (or so I am told) than the one I used for inspiration, but it's only lightly yeasted, so needs a little more working.

1 cup warm water
1 teaspoon granulated sugar
1 teaspoon dry yeast

1½ cups white bread flour, or 1½ cups all-purpose flour and 1½ tablespoons vital wheat gluten
⅓ cup granulated sugar
2 tablespoons dried blueberries
2 tablespoons dried cranberries
2 tablespoons wheat germ
1 teaspoon salt
1½ teaspoons pie spice (see page 19)

1¼ cups white bread flour, or 1¼ cups all-purpose flour and 1 tablespoon vital wheat gluten

Flour, for kneading
Canola oil, for the bowl

3 tablespoons light brown sugar, packed
1 teaspoon pie spice

¼ cup fresh or thawed frozen blueberries
2 tablespoons fresh or thawed frozen cranberries

1 recipe Sugar Glaze (page 252) (optional)

1. In a large bowl, combine the water, granulated sugar, and yeast, stir, and set aside for 5 minutes to proof (see page 193).

2. Add the ingredients from white flour through pie spice, and then stir one hundred times with a wooden spoon to get it well mixed. Cover and set aside for 30 minutes.

3. Add the remaining flour and turn onto a floured board for kneading. The flour may not completely incorporate at first, but that is fine; it will become part of the dough as you knead. Add more flour by the tablespoonful, as required, to ensure the dough is not sticky.

4. Knead for about 15 minutes, until your dough is smooth and supple. You can do this in 3-minute bursts—that is, knead for 3 minutes, rest, and repeat—if you find kneading vigorously for the whole time too tiring.

5. Coat a large bowl with a thin film of oil, place the dough ball in the bowl, and turn the dough to coat it in oil. Cover the bowl and place in a warm place for 1½ hours. The dough will increase in volume by about half, but not as much as other breads.

6. Prepare a 7 by 11-inch brownie pan by lining with parchment paper.

7. Punch the dough in the bowl, then turn onto a lightly floured board and knead lightly for about 3 minutes. With a floured rolling pin and your hands, roll and stretch the dough to a ¼-inch thick square (as thinly as you can, anyway). It should be at least 16 inches square.

8. Sprinkle the brown sugar and pie spice over the dough, rubbing with your hand to spread it evenly.

9. Sprinkle the whole berries randomly over the dough. Roll the dough tightly into a pinwheel shape, starting with the side farthest from you and being careful not to disturb the berries too much.

10. Cut the rolled dough into eight 2-inch sections and place, cut side down, on the prepared pan. Cover and allow to rise for 45 to 60 minutes.

11. Preheat the oven to 375°F while the rolls are rising. Once they have risen, uncover and bake for 20 to 25 minutes, until golden.

12. Remove the pan from the oven. Pour the Sugar Glaze, if using, over the hot rolls and allow to cool on the pan.

Date Pinwheels

MAKES 12 BUNS

▶ NO NUTS • NO SUGAR

This sugar-free yeasted roll has naturally sweet date paste in the middle as filling, and also in the dough, along with a little agave nectar, to help it along. To make them extra healthy, replace half of the white bread flour with whole-wheat bread flour.

The easiest way to chop the dates is not to chop them at all but just snip into pieces with your kitchen shears.

1 cup hand-hot water

¼ cup Date Paste (page 250), room temperature

2 teaspoons dry yeast

2 cups white bread flour, or 2 cups all-purpose flour and 2 tablespoons vital wheat gluten

¼ cup agave nectar

1 teaspoon salt

¼ teaspoon ground nutmeg

¼ cup finely chopped dates

1 cup white bread flour, or 1 cup all-purpose flour and 1 tablespoon vital wheat gluten

Flour, for kneading

Canola oil, for the bowl

FILLING

¼ cup Date Paste (page 250)

2 tablespoons vegan margarine, at room temperature

2 tablespoons agave nectar

¼ cup dates, chopped roughly

GLAZE

2 tablespoons brown rice syrup

1 tablespoon agave nectar

1 tablespoon vegan margarine

1. In a large bowl, combine the hot water and date paste. Check the temperature of this mixture (see page 193), then add the yeast, stir, and set aside for 10 minutes to proof.

2. Add the ingredients from flour through nutmeg, then stir one hundred times with a wooden spoon to get it well mixed. Cover and set aside for 30 minutes.

3. Add the remaining flour and turn onto a floured board for kneading. The flour may not completely incorporate at first, but that is fine; it will become part of the dough as you

knead. Add more flour by the tablespoonful, as required, to ensure the dough is not sticky.

4. Knead for a total of about 15 minutes, until your dough is smooth and supple. You can do this in 3-minute bursts—that is, knead for 3 minutes, rest, and repeat—if you find kneading vigorously for the whole time too tiring.

5. Coat a large bowl with a thin film of oil, place the dough ball in the bowl, and turn the dough to coat it in oil. Cover the bowl and place in a warm place until the dough is doubled in size (1 to 1½ hours).

6. Prepare a 7 by 11-inch brownie pan by lining with parchment paper.

7. Combine the date paste, margarine, and agave nectar for the filling in a small bowl and mix well.

8. Punch down the dough, knead for about 3 minutes to get it looking doughlike again, then let it rest on your countertop for 10 minutes. With a floured rolling pin and your hands, roll and stretch the dough to form an 18 by 10-inch rectangle about ¼-inch thick (as thin as you can get it).

9. Position the rectangle with a long side toward you.

10. Spread the filling over the prepared dough, using the back of a spoon. Start with the long side farthest away from you and roll the dough tightly toward you, into a pinwheel shape, being careful to not squash out the filling. Press down on the dough log to seal the long edge of the pinwheel, and squeeze gently into an evenly cylindrical shape.

11. Carefully cut the rolled dough into twelve roughly 1½-inch sections; the filling will ooze out a little. Place, cut side down and just touching, on the prepared pan in four rows of three across. Cover and allow to rise for 20 to 25 minutes.

12. Preheat the oven to 375°F while rolls are rising.

13. Once the rolls have risen, uncover and bake for 20 to 25 minutes, until golden.

14. As the rolls are baking, prepare the glaze by combining all the ingredients in a small saucepan over medium-high heat and bringing to a boil, stirring frequently. Boil, still stirring frequently, for 2 minutes, then remove from the heat and let cool for 5 minutes.

15. Remove the rolls from the oven and drizzle with the prepared glaze. Let cool on the pan for 5 minutes, then lift out using the parchment liner and transfer to a wire rack and let cool completely.

Remember...

Fancy Almond Bread

MAKES TWO 14-INCH LOAVES

▶ **NO SOY**

Marzipan is one of my favorite confections, but I have to make it at home, as most commercial stuff has egg white in it. The marzipan I make is more suited for baking than eating out of hand, as is it not too sweet, which is fine by me, if it means I get to eat it in things like this! The bread is braided around the marzipan center, which is nice to bite into as you eat a slice.

This makes two big loaves, but don't worry—the bread freezes really well, so you can have one loaf now and one loaf ready for later.

¾ **cup boiling water**
¾ **cup almond milk**
1 teaspoon granulated sugar

2 teaspoons dry yeast

1½ cups white bread flour, or 1½ cups all-purpose flour and 1½ tablespoons vital wheat gluten
¾ **cup ground almonds**
¼ **cup granulated sugar**
1 tablespoon vital wheat gluten
1 tablespoon almond or canola oil
1 tablespoon freshly squeezed lemon juice (½ medium lemon)
1 teaspoon salt
¼ **teaspoon ground nutmeg**
¼ **teaspoon ground allspice**

2 cups white bread flour, or 1½ cups all-purpose flour and 1½ tablespoons vital wheat gluten

1 recipe Marzipan (page 102), at room temperature

Flour, for kneading
Canola oil, for the bowl

Almond milk or oil, for brushing (optional)

1 recipe Sugar Glaze (page 252), almond variation (optional)
Flaked almonds, for garnish (optional)

1. Combine the water, milk, and granulated sugar in a large bowl, check the temperature (see page 193), then add the yeast, stir, and set aside for 10 minutes to proof.

2. Sift in the ingredients from flour through allspice. Stir briskly one hundred times or so, then set aside for 30 minutes.

3. Add the remaining flour and turn onto a floured board for kneading. The flour may not completely incorporate at first, but that is fine; it will become part of the dough as you knead. Add more flour by the tablespoonful, as required, to ensure the dough is not sticky.

4. Knead for a total of about 15 minutes, until your dough is smooth and supple. You can do this in 3-minute bursts—that is, knead for 3 minutes, rest, and repeat—if you find kneading vigorously for the whole time too tiring.

5. Coat a large bowl with a thin film of oil, place the dough ball in the bowl, and turn the dough to coat it in oil. Cover the bowl and place in a warm place until the dough is doubled in size (about 1½ hours).

6. Punch down the dough, knead for about 3 minutes to get it looking doughlike again, then let rest on your countertop for 10 minutes. Divide the dough into two equal pieces and shape the loaves one at a time.

7. Using your hands, stretch and push the dough into a 10 by 14-inch rectangle about ½ inch thick. Have one of the short sides closest to you.

8. Divide the marzipan into two equal pieces and shape each piece into a strip about 13 inches long.

9. Place one marzipan strip lengthwise down the middle of one dough rectangle.

10. Using a sharp knife, cut the dough into 1-inch wide diagonal strips to each side down the length of the marzipan, leaving a ½-inch gap between the marzipan and where each cut starts.

11. Alternating strips from each side, braid the strips around the marzipan, taking care not to expose it and to cover the ends of the strips already braided. Once all the dough strips are braided over the marzipan core, secure the end with pressure and a little water.

12. Repeat with the remaining dough and marzipan.

13. Place the braided loaves on a parchment-lined baking sheet, cover, and allow to rise for about 30 minutes or so. Brush tops of the loaves with soy milk or oil, if desired.

14. Preheat the oven to 375°F during this final rise. Bake the loaves until golden brown, 22 to 27 minutes.

15. Remove from the oven and let cool on the sheet for 15 minutes, then transfer to a wire rack and let cool completely. Drizzle with Almond Sugar Glaze, and sprinkle with flaked almonds, if desired.

Garlic Flatbread

MAKES 2 FLATBREADS, EACH SERVING 8 TO 10

▶ NO NUTS • NO SOY

This one is garlicky, but it's also one where you can control the amount of garlic if you're a superfan, or a not-so-much-fan. Where you add the minced garlic to the top of the prepared bread, you can either go wild or be a little more restrained. I've taken the middle ground here.

The dough also makes a wonderful garlic-infused base for pizza. Try it!

I used a circular pizza pan, the kind with the holes in the bottom, as that is what I have. If you have a pizza stone, by all means use that, but if you have neither, use a large baking sheet and prick the dough with a fork a few times prior to adding the oil and garlic topping.

1¼ cups hot water

3 garlic cloves, minced

2 tablespoons granulated sugar

1 tablespoon olive oil

1 teaspoon salt

2 teaspoons dry yeast

2 cups white bread flour, or 2 cups all-purpose flour and 2 tablespoons vital wheat gluten

2 teaspoons garlic powder

1¼ cups white bread flour, or 1¼ cups all-purpose flour and 1 tablespoon vital wheat gluten

Flour, for kneading
Olive oil, for the bowl

Cornmeal

2 tablespoons olive oil (1 per flatbread)

4 garlic cloves, minced (2 per flatbread), or more if desired

2 pinches of salt (optional)

1. In a large bowl, mix together the water, garlic, granulated sugar, oil, and salt. Check the temperature (see page 193), add the yeast, and stir to combine. Set aside for 10 minutes to proof.

2. Add the 2 cups of flour and the garlic powder, stir one hundred times to mix well, then cover and set aside for 30 minutes.

3. Add the remaining flour and turn onto a floured board for kneading. The flour may not completely incorporate at first, but that is fine; it will become part of the dough as you knead. Add more flour by the tablespoonful, as required, to ensure the dough is not sticky.

4. Knead for a total of about 15 minutes, until your dough is smooth and supple. You can do this in 3-minute bursts—that is, knead for 3 minutes, rest, and repeat—if you find kneading vigorously for the whole time too tiring.

5. Coat a large bowl with a thin film of oil, place the dough ball in the bowl, and turn the dough to coat it in oil. Cover the bowl and place in a warm place until the dough is doubled in size (about 1 hour).

6. Punch down the dough, knead for about 3 minutes to get it looking doughlike again, then let rest on your countertop for 10 minutes.

7. As dough is resting, preheat the oven to 425°F and either spray two 13-inch pizza pans with nonstick spray or sprinkle them with a little cornmeal, to prevent sticking.

8. Divide the dough into two equal pieces. (See Note.)

9. Using a floured rolling pin and your hands, roll and stretch one ball of dough until it forms a 13-inch circle. Place on the prepared pan, then brush on 1 tablespoon of olive oil and sprinkle with two minced cloves of garlic and a pinch of salt, if using.

10. Bake for 12 to 15 minutes, until golden. Slice and serve while still hot.

11. Repeat the shaping and baking with the second piece of dough.

NOTE:

❖ If you are only making one flatbread, at this point place the second ball of dough in a small container or plastic bag and freeze. When you want to use it, thaw, knead, and allow to rest at room temperature until it no longer feels cool.

Variations

Basil Garlic Flatbread
Add 1 teaspoon of dried basil with the garlic powder and sprinkle with 2 tablespoons of shredded fresh basil when you add the minced garlic.

"Cheesy" Garlic Flatbread
Prior to baking, sprinkle with ¼ cup of your favorite shredded vegan cheese.

Hot Cross Buns 📷

MAKES 12 BUNS

▶ **NO NUTS**

What would Easter be without Hot Cross Buns? Please believe me when I tell you that homemade is best, by far. You have the option of changing the fruit in your buns for what you like, upping the spice if you are a cinnamon fiend, and that's not to mention the satisfaction of making them yourself. As a bonus, your house will smell divine for the rest of the day!

If it isn't Easter, or you don't celebrate this festival, then omit the piped crosses, for delicious fruit buns.

BUNS

1 cup boiling water
¾ cup raisins
½ cup golden raisins

¾ cup warm soy milk
1 tablespoon vegan margarine, room temperature
2 teaspoons dry yeast

1 teaspoon granulated sugar

2 cups white bread flour, or 2 cups all-purpose flour and 2 tablespoons vital wheat gluten

2 teaspoons granulated sugar

1 teaspoon ground cinnamon

1 teaspoon pie spice (see page 19)

1 teaspoon salt

½ teaspoon ground nutmeg

1 cup white bread flour, or 1 cup all-purpose flour and 1 tablespoon vital wheat gluten

¼ cup dried cranberries (see Note)

¼ cup dried blueberries (see Note)

Flour, for kneading

Canola oil, for the bowl

CROSSES

2 tablespoons water

2 tablespoons all-purpose flour

2 tablespoons confectioners' sugar

1 tablespoon cornstarch

GLAZE

2 tablespoons granulated sugar

1 tablespoon water

1. In a medium bowl, combine the raisins, golden raisins, and water. Set aside for 10 minutes, then drain, reserving ¾ cup of the soaking water, which should still be warm.

2. In a large bowl, combine the soy milk, raisin-soaking water, margarine, yeast, and granulated sugar, stir to combine and melt the margarine, then set aside for 10 minutes to proof (see page 193).

3. Add the 2 cups of flour, granulated sugar, and spices, then stir one hundred times with a wooden spoon to mix really well. Set aside for 10 minutes.

4. Add the remaining flour and turn onto a floured board for kneading. The flour may

not completely incorporate at first, but that is fine; it will become part of the dough as you knead. Add more flour by the tablespoonful, as required, to ensure the dough is not sticky.

5. Knead for a total of about 15 minutes, until your dough is smooth and supple. You can do this in 3-minute bursts—that is, knead for 3 minutes, rest, and repeat—if you find kneading vigorously for the whole time too tiring.

6. Coat a large bowl with a thin film of oil, place the dough ball in the bowl, and turn the dough to coat it in oil. Cover the bowl and place in a warm place until the dough is doubled in size (1 to 1½ hours).

7. Punch down the dough, knead for about 3 minutes to get it looking doughlike again. Return the dough to the bowl, re-cover, and return the dough to your warm place for a second rise. It will take less time than before, 30 to 45 minutes, to double in size.

8. Prepare a 9 by 13-inch baking (brownie) pan by lining with parchment paper during the second rise.

9. Once the dough has risen, remove it from the bowl, and on a lightly floured board knead for another 3 minutes, before dividing into twelve equal pieces. Roll each piece into a ball and place in the prepared pan. Cover as before and set aside for 20 to 25 minutes, for a final rise.

10. While the buns are rising, preheat the oven to 400°F and prepare the cross mixture by mixing all its ingredients together in a small bowl until smooth. Transfer to a piping bag fitted with a narrow, smooth tip.

11. Once buns have risen, pipe the top of each with a cross, then bake for 20 to 25 minutes until well risen and golden. While baking, prepare the glaze by mixing the granulated sugar and water together. Heat in a small saucepan or in a bowl in the microwave on high in 10 second bursts, until the sugar is dissolved. Keep warm until required.

12. Remove the buns from the oven. Glaze while still hot from the oven and let cool completely on the pan prior to serving, if you can make them last that long!

NOTE:

❖ If you'd prefer a more traditional taste to your Hot Cross Buns, use dried currants or more raisins in place of the dried blueberries and cranberries.

Lemon and Cranberry Bread-and-Butter Puddings

MAKES 12 INDIVIDUAL PUDDINGS

► NO NUTS

An individual portion of a tasty, zingy, variation on the traditionally English bread-and-butter pudding, sans butter, of course! Serve hot with ice cream or custard, or cold as you would a muffin.

1¾ cups soy milk

½ cup granulated sugar

½ cup (5 ounces) tofu, firm silken (vacuum-packed)

1 tablespoon freshly squeezed lemon juice (½ medium lemon)

½ teaspoon vanilla extract

½ teaspoon lemon extract

2 cups Plain Bread (page 208) cut into ½-inch cubes, carefully packed; or store-bought alternative (see Notes)

½ cup dried cranberries

1 tablespoon lemon zest (1 medium lemon)

1¼ cups all-purpose flour

2 tablespoons vegan custard powder (see Notes)

2 teaspoons baking powder

½ teaspoon baking soda

½ teaspoon salt

1. In a blender or food processor, blend together the soy milk, granulated sugar, tofu, lemon juice, and the extracts until smooth and creamy. Pour into a large bowl.

2. Add the bread cubes, cranberries, and lemon zest to the tofu mixture, toss to coat, and set aside for 15 minutes, for the bread to partially absorb the liquid.

3. Preheat the oven to 375°F and prepare a twelve-cup muffin pan by spraying with nonstick spray.

4. Sift the remaining ingredients into the bread mixture and stir to just combine.

5. Spoon the mixture into the prepared pan. The cups will be just full. Be sure to fill any unused cups with water, so the pan won't warp. Bake for 20 to 25 minutes, until risen, lightly browned, and a toothpick just comes out clean. A little residue on the toothpick is fine.

6. Remove from the oven and let cool in the pan for 5 minutes, then let cool completely on a wire rack.

NOTES:

❖ Substitute store-bought firm, white bread for homemade if you prefer. Ensure it is not a flimsy bread, as it will just become mush when soaked.

❖ Bird's Custard Powder is the most commonly available brand, and, at time of writing, is vegan, though, as always, check the ingredients.

❖ If you cannot find any vegan custard powder, replace each tablespoon of custard powder needed with 1 tablespoon of cornstarch, along with ⅛ teaspoon of vanilla extract for flavor, and a pinch of turmeric (about 1/16 teaspoon) for color.

Variations

Orange and Blueberry Bread-and-Butter Puddings

Replace the lemon juice, extract, and zest with orange juice, extract and zest, and replace the dried cranberries with dried blueberries.

Lime and Raisin Bread-and-Butter Puddings

Replace the juice and zest of the lemon with lime, and the dried fruit with raisins.

Large Lemon Cranberry Bread-and-Butter Pudding

Instead of baking the mixture in a muffin pan, spread in a layer in a lightly greased or parchment-lined 9 by 13-inch baking (brownie) pan and bake for the same length of time until browned.

. . . .

Pannetone-Inspired Christmas Bread

MAKES ONE 8-INCH LOAF

▶ NO SOY

I used to love sharing a big pannetone at Christmas when I lived in the United Kingdom. Someone would invariably bring one of these traditional Italian Christmas breads in to work, and we'd all devour it. Oh, fond memories. Now I can have my bread and eat it, too, with this loaf inspired by my Yuletide favorite!

1 cup almond milk, room temperature
½ cup boiling water

1 teaspoon granulated sugar

2 teaspoons dry yeast

¼ cup canola oil
1 tablespoon freshly squeezed lemon juice (½ medium lemon)
1½ tablespoons orange zest (1 medium orange)
1 tablespoon lemon zest (1 medium lemon)
1 teaspoon vanilla extract

1½ cups white bread flour, or 1½ cups all-purpose flour and 1½ tablespoons vital wheat gluten
1 cup ground almonds
¼ cup granulated sugar
¼ cup candied orange or mixed peel
2 tablespoons dried currants
1 tablespoon vital wheat gluten
1 teaspoon salt
½ teaspoon ground nutmeg

1¾ cups all-purpose flour

Flour, for kneading
Canola oil, for the bowl

Almond milk, for brushing (optional)

1. In a large bowl, combine the milk, water, and granulated sugar and stir to combine. Check the temperature (see page 193), add the yeast, then set aside for 10 minutes to proof.

2. Add the oil, lemon juice, zest, and vanilla and stir well.

3. Add the ingredients from flour through nutmeg, then stir one hundred times with a wooden spoon to mix really well. Cover and set aside for at least 30 minutes.

4. Add the remaining flour and turn onto a floured board for kneading. The flour may not completely incorporate at first, but that is fine; it will become part of the dough as you

knead. Add more flour by the tablespoonful, as required, to ensure the dough is not sticky.

5. Knead for a total of about 15 minutes, until your dough is smooth and supple. You can do this in 3-minute bursts—that is, knead for 3 minutes, rest, and repeat—if you find kneading vigorously for the whole time too tiring.

6. Coat a large bowl with a thin film of oil, place the dough ball in the bowl, and turn the dough to coat it in oil. Cover the bowl and place in a warm place until the dough is doubled in size (1 to 1½ hours).

7. Prepare an 8-inch springform cake pan by lining with parchment paper and then spraying with nonstick spray.

8. Punch down the dough, knead for about 3 minutes to get it looking doughlike again, then let rest on your countertop for 10 minutes.

9. Shape into a disk and place in the bottom of the prepared pan. Cover as before and set aside for 30 minutes for a final rise.

10. While the bread is rising, preheat the oven to 350°F. Brush the bread with almond milk, if desired, then bake for 45 to 50 minutes, until well risen and golden.

11. Remove from the oven and let cool in the pan for 10 minutes, then let cool completely on a wire rack.

12. Slice, as you would a cake, to serve.

. . . .

Plain Bread

MAKES ONE 9-INCH LOAF OR 12 ROLLS

▶ **NO NUTS**

This basic recipe can be made as is, for lovely soft rolls or loaves, or you can easily jazz up the recipe a little by using your imagination. Add any of the listed ingredients for the variations below, or those of your own devising, with the first addition of flour.

1 cup hand-hot water (see Note)
¼ cup soy milk
2 teaspoons dry yeast
1 teaspoon granulated sugar

2 cups white bread flour, or 2 cups all-purpose flour and 2 tablespoons vital wheat gluten
¼ cup wheat germ
1 tablespoon freshly squeezed lemon juice (½ medium lemon)
1 tablespoon canola oil
1 teaspoon salt

1 cup white bread flour, or 1 cup all-purpose flour and 1 tablespoon vital wheat gluten

Flour, for kneading
Canola oil, for the bowl

1. Mix the water, milk, sugar and yeast in a large bowl and set aside for 10 minutes to proof (see page 193).

2. Add the ingredients from flour through salt, stir briskly one hundred times, then set aside the mixture for 15 minutes.

3. Add the remaining flour and turn onto a floured board for kneading. The flour may not completely incorporate at first, but that is fine; it will become part of the dough as you knead. Add more flour by the tablespoonful, as required, to ensure the dough is not sticky.

4. Knead for a total of about 15 minutes, until your dough is smooth and supple. You can do this in 3-minute bursts—that is, knead for 3 minutes, rest, and repeat—if you find kneading vigorously for the whole time too tiring.

5. Coat a large bowl with a thin film of oil, place the dough ball in the bowl, and turn the dough to coat it in oil. Cover the bowl

and place in a warm place until the dough is doubled in size (about 1½ hours).

6. Punch down the dough, knead for about 3 minutes to get it looking doughlike again, then return to the bowl, cover, and return to your warm place for the second rise. This will take less time, about 1 hour, to double in size.

7. Remove the dough from the bowl. Knead lightly and then shape into twelve equal rolls or one large log. Place on a lightly greased baking sheet or in a lightly greased 9-inch loaf pan, cover, and allow to rise again. This final rising will be about 30 minutes.

8. Preheat the oven to 400°F while the bread is rising. Once the dough has risen, brush the top(s) with soy milk or oil, if desired.

9. Bake until the bread is golden brown, 20 to 25 minutes for buns and 35 to 40 minutes for a loaf. If you remove the loaf from the pan and lightly tap the bottom when you think it is done, it should sound hollow.

10. Remove from the oven and let cool on the sheet or pan for 5 minutes, then transfer to a wire rack and let cool completely.

NOTE:
❖ Hand-hot water is as hot as you can get it from your tap, as opposed to boiling from a kettle.

Variations

Again, add any of the additions with the first lot of flour. These are suggestions only, as you are only limited by your imagination and confidence.

Sweet Bread

Add ¼ cup granulated sugar plus up to ½ cup of any of the following:

+ Cocoa nibs and/or vegan chocolate chips with ½ teaspoon of ground cinnamon
+ Chopped dried apricots and goji berries with ½ teaspoon of ground nutmeg
+ Dried blueberries and cranberries with ½ teaspoon of pie spice (see page 19)

Savory Bread

Add ½ cup of any of the following:

+ Finely chopped sun-dried tomatoes with ¼ teaspoon of dried thyme and ¼ teaspoon of dried rosemary
+ Caramelized onions
+ Chopped roasted garlic cloves and a few ground peppercorns
+ Chopped black and green olives and ½ teaspoon of marjoram
+ Mixed seeds (e.g., sesame, poppy, hemp, sunflower, and pumpkin) and ½ teaspoon of oregano
+ Grated vegan cheese

Sourdough Bread

One of my testers, John, put 4 ounces of sourdough starter into the dough to give a little sourdough-type flavor. He said it worked perfectly!

Rosemary and Zucchini Focaccia

MAKES ONE 13-INCH LOAF

▶ **NO NUTS • NO SOY**

I love to put my own spin on things, and recipes are no exception! When there was a request for focaccia, I immediately started thinking of ways to make my focaccia unique.

I had a think about ingredients that had been used only once in the recipes I'd made so far. I also thought "Italian," to try to keep it a little authentic, and I came up with this beauty of a recipe!

1½ cups warm water
1 tablespoon granulated sugar

2 teaspoons dry yeast

2 cups white bread flour, or 2 cups all-purpose flour and 2 tablespoons vital wheat gluten
1½ cups grated zucchini, loosely packed (1 medium zucchini) (see Notes)
2 tablespoons olive oil
2 tablespoons fresh rosemary, chopped finely
1 teaspoon salt

2 cups white bread flour, or 2 cups all-purpose flour and 2 tablespoons vital wheat gluten

Flour, for kneading (see Notes)
Olive oil, for the bowl

Olive oil, for brushing
1½ tablespoons fresh rosemary, chopped finely
Pinch of coarse salt

1. Mix the water and granulated sugar in a large bowl, check the temperature (see page 193), then add the yeast, stir, and set aside for 10 minutes to proof.

2. Add the ingredients from flour through salt, stir briskly one hundred times, then set the mixture aside for 30 minutes.

3. Add the remaining flour and turn onto a floured board for kneading. The flour may not completely incorporate at first, but that is fine; it will become part of the dough as you knead. Add more flour by the tablespoonful, as required, to ensure the dough is not sticky.

4. Knead for a total of about 15 minutes, until your dough is smooth and supple. You can do this in 3-minute bursts—that is, knead for 3 minutes, rest, and repeat—if you find kneading vigorously for the whole time too tiring.

5. Coat a large bowl with a thin film of oil, place the dough ball in the bowl, and turn the dough to coat it in oil. Cover the bowl and place in a warm place until the dough is doubled in size (about 1 hour).

6. Prepare a 9 by 13-inch baking (brownie) pan by lining with parchment paper.

7. Punch down the dough, knead for about 3 minutes to get it looking doughlike again, and then shape into one large loaf shape of about the same dimensions as the pan. Place in the pan, cover, and allow to rise again for 30 minutes or so.

8. Preheat the oven to 400°F while the dough is rising, and once it has risen, make shallow indentations randomly in the top of your bread, using the back of a teaspoon measure sprayed with nonstick spray.

9. Brush the top of the bread with a generous amount of olive oil, making sure lots goes into the indentations, too. Sprinkle with the chopped rosemary and salt.

10. Bake until the bread is golden brown and firm to the tap, 25 to 30 minutes.

11. Remove from the oven and let cool in the pan for 10 minutes, then let cool completely on a wire rack.

NOTES:
❖ If your zucchini looks especially watery after grating, pat dry with paper towels to remove as much of the excess liquid as possible.
❖ This is one of those recipes where the amount of extra flour needed will be different every time it is made, depending on the moisture in the zucchini and its dimensions.

Variations

Black Olive and Zucchini Focaccia
Substitute an equal amount of finely chopped black olives for the rosemary.

Sun-Dried Tomato and Zucchini Focaccia
Substitute an equal amount of finely chopped reconstituted sun-dried tomatoes for the rosemary.

Roasted Garlic and Zucchini Focaccia
Substitute an equal amount of chopped roasted garlic (page 20) for the rosemary.

. . . .

Sally Lunns

MAKES 12 BUNS

▶ **NO NUTS**

You may know these by another name—"Sally Lunns" is the most common name I knew them by while growing up, but they are also called Boston Buns and Pink Currant Buns—or maybe you don't know them at all and are in for a treat. These are how I envisage the buns to be in the children's nursery rhyme: "Five Currant Buns in the baker's shop / Round and fat with sugar on the top."

If you're not a coconut fan, just use a thick Drizzle Icing (page 251) instead of the icing given here.

1 cup hand-hot water (see Notes)
½ cup soy creamer (see page 16), room temperature
1 teaspoon granulated sugar

2 teaspoons dry yeast

½ cup dried currants
2 cups white bread flour, or 2 cups all-purpose flour and 2 tablespoons vital wheat gluten
¼ cup granulated sugar
2 tablespoons canola oil
1 teaspoon salt
1 teaspoon pie spice (see page 19)

1½ cups white bread flour, or 1½ cups all-purpose flour and 1½ tablespoons vital wheat gluten

Flour, for kneading
Canola oil, for the bowl
Soy creamer or canola oil, for brushing (optional)

ICING
2½ cups confectioners' sugar
1 cup unsweetened shredded coconut
4½ tablespoons soy creamer (see page 16)
A few drops of vegan red food coloring

1. Mix the water, creamer, and granulated sugar in a large bowl, check the temperature (see page 193), then add the yeast and set aside for 5 minutes to proof.

2. Add the currants, stir, and set aside for 5 minutes more.

3. Add the ingredients from flour through pie spice, stir briskly with a wooden spoon one hundred times or so, then set aside for at least 15 minutes.

4. Add the remaining flour and turn onto a floured board for kneading. The flour may not completely incorporate at first, but that is fine; it will become part of the dough as you knead. Add more flour by the tablespoonful, as required, to ensure the dough is not sticky.

5. Knead for a total of about 15 minutes, until your dough is smooth and supple. You can do this in 3-minute bursts—that is, knead for 3 minutes, rest, and repeat—if you find kneading vigorously for the whole time too tiring.

6. Coat a large bowl with a thin film of oil, place the dough ball in the bowl, and turn the dough to coat it in oil. Cover the bowl and place in a warm place until the dough is doubled in size (about 1¼ hours).

7. Punch down the dough, knead for about 3 minutes to get it looking doughlike again, then return to the bowl, cover, and return to your warm place for the second rise. This will take less time, 45 to 50 minutes, to double in size.

8. Line a rimmed baking sheet with parchment paper. (See Notes.)

9. Remove the dough from the bowl. Knead lightly and shape into twelve equal buns. Place on the baking sheet, cover, and allow to rise again. This last rise will be about 30 minutes. Brush the top of your buns with soy creamer or oil, if desired.

10. While the buns are rising, preheat your oven to 400°F. Once they have risen, bake the buns for 18 to 22 minutes, until golden brown and well risen. If you tap the bottom of a bun lightly when you think it is done, it should sound hollow.

11. Remove from the oven and let cool on the sheet for 15 minutes, then transfer to a wire rack and let cool completely.

12. Once completely cool, make the icing by mixing all the icing ingredients together in a small bowl, then spread the icing generously on the top of each bun.

NOTES:
- ❖ Hand-hot water is as hot as you get from your tap, as opposed to boiling from a kettle.
- ❖ If your baking sheet is large and the buns do not touch, the sides will be firm and have a crust. If your baking sheet is smaller and the sides of the buns touch after rising, the sides will be soft and not have a crust. I prefer these buns with a side crust, but it is up to you.

- ❖ Ensure your red food coloring is vegan. Many varieties are made with cochineal, which comes from crushed-up beetles. There are, however, a number of plant-based alternatives available.

Savory Pinwheels

MAKES 15 BUNS

▶ **NO NUTS** excluding filling

One of my testers, Celia, suggested a savory pinwheel-type yeasted bun as an alternative to the sweet yeasted breads I was posting on my test site. I took it further and gave you four filling options! Feel free to invent your own fillings, or mix and match as you see fit.

Please note that all of the fillings can be prepared in advance and stored in the fridge until needed.

1 cup soy milk, room temperature
½ cup boiling water
1 tablespoon granulated sugar

2 teaspoons dry yeast

2 cups white bread flour, or 2 cups all-purpose flour and 2 tablespoons vital wheat gluten
1 tablespoon canola oil
1 teaspoon salt
½ teaspoon dried thyme
½ teaspoon onion powder
¼ teaspoon freshly ground black pepper

1½ cups white bread flour, or 1½ cups all-purpose flour and 1 tablespoon vital wheat gluten

Flour, for kneading

Canola oil, for the bowl

Filling of your choice (see options below, or create your own)

Vegan cheese, for sprinkling (optional)

1. In a large bowl, combine the soy milk, boiling water, and granulated sugar. Test temperature (see page 193), then add the yeast, stir, and set aside for 10 minutes to proof.

2. Add the ingredients from flour through spices, then stir one hundred times with a wooden spoon to get it well mixed. Cover and set aside for 30 minutes.

3. Add the remaining flour and turn onto a floured board for kneading. The flour may not completely incorporate at first, but that is fine; it will become part of the dough as you knead. Add more flour by the tablespoonful, as required, to ensure the dough is not sticky.

4. Knead for a total of about 15 minutes, until your dough is smooth and supple. You can do this in 3-minute bursts—that is, knead for 3 minutes, rest, and repeat—if you find kneading vigorously for the whole time too tiring.

5. Coat a large bowl with a thin film of oil, place the dough ball in the bowl, and turn the dough to coat it in oil. Cover the bowl and place in a warm place until the dough is doubled in size (about 1¼ hours).

6. Prepare the filling while the dough rises.

7. Prepare a 9 by 13-inch baking (brownie) pan by lining with parchment paper.

8. Punch down the dough, knead for about 3 minutes to get it looking doughlike again, then let rest on your countertop for 10 minutes. With a floured rolling pin and your hands, roll and stretch the dough to form a 22 by 11-inch rectangle about ¼ inch thick (get it as thin as you can).

9. Position the rectangle with a long side closest to you.

10. Spread the filling over the prepared dough. Start with the long side farthest away from you and roll the dough tightly into a pinwheel shape. Press down along the long edge of the dough log to seal it, and squeeze gently into a cylindrical shape. Brush with a little water or soy milk as required.

11. Cut the rolled dough into fifteen roughly 1½-inch sections and place, cut side down and ½ inch apart, on the prepared pan in five rows of three across. Cover and allow to rise for 20 to 25 minutes.

12. Preheat the oven to 375°F while the rolls are rising. Sprinkle with a little vegan cheese, if desired, just prior to baking.

13. Once risen, uncover and bake for 25 to 30 minutes, until golden.

14. Remove from the oven and let cool on pan for 10 minutes, then let cool completely on a wire rack.

. . . .

★ **Filling 1:**
Sun-Dried Tomato and Olive

Reminiscent of pizza, with full-on Italian-type flavor, this is one filling that you'd like to have more of!

½ cup sun-dried tomatoes
½ cup boiling water

½ cup black olives, chopped finely
¼ cup vegan margarine
2 tablespoons tomato paste
½ teaspoon dried basil
½ teaspoon salt
Freshly ground black pepper

1. In a small bowl, soak the sun-dried tomatoes in the water. Cover and set aside for 15 minutes, until soft. Drain, discard the liquid, and finely chop the tomatoes.

2. Combine the chopped tomatoes with the remaining ingredients in a small bowl, and mix well. Set aside until required.

. . . .

⭐ Filling 2: Pesto and Cheese

Summer in a bun! Pesto made with fresh basil is one of life's great treats. Pair with your favorite vegan cheese for a melty sensation.

⅔ **cup Basic Basil Pesto (page 236)**
¼ **cup grated vegan cheese**
2 **tablespoons vegan margarine**

1. Combine all the ingredients in a small bowl and set aside until required.

. . . .

⭐ Filling 3: Caramelized Onion and Roasted Garlic

Creamy and mild, roasted garlic combines with sweet caramelized onions in this sophisticated filling.

2 **tablespoons olive oil**
2 **medium onions, quartered and sliced thinly (about 1½ cups)**
2 **tablespoons light brown sugar, packed**

1 **head garlic, roasted, flesh squeezed out and mashed (see instructions, page 20)**

1. In a large skillet over medium heat, sauté the onion in the oil for 7 to 10 minutes, until soft and starting to brown. Add the brown sugar and cook for a further 5 minutes, to lightly caramelize. Add splashes of water if it sticks. The volume will reduce to about half.
2. Remove from the heat and add the mashed roasted garlic flesh. Mix well to

ensure everything is well combined, and set aside until required.

. . . .

⭐ Filling 4: Corny Refried Beans

Mexican inspired, this filling is a great way to use up those beans you have hiding in a container in the fridge!

1 **tablespoon olive oil**
1 **medium onion, chopped finely**
2 **garlic cloves, minced**
2 **teaspoons ground cumin**
1 **teaspoon dried oregano**
½ **teaspoon salt**

½ **teaspoon paprika**
Pinch of cayenne

1 **cup canned black beans, drained and rinsed**
¼ **cup water**

½ **cup fresh cilantro, chopped finely**
½ **cup corn kernels (see Note)**
2 **tablespoons vegan margarine**

1. In a large skillet over medium heat, sauté the onion and garlic in the oil for 5 minutes, until soft. Add the spices and sauté for 1 minute more.
2. Add the beans and water, mashing the beans with the back of a wooden spoon until falling apart. Cook for a further 2 minutes.
3. Remove from the heat and stir in the cilantro, corn, and margarine. Mix well to ensure everything is well combined, then set aside until required.

NOTE:
❖ If using frozen corn, thaw and drain; if using canned, it needs to be drained and rinsed.

Sticky Spice Buns 📷

MAKES 15 BUNS

▶ **NO NUTS**

These are my variation on cinnamon buns. I thought that, seeing everyone does them, they must be super popular, I'll have to include a recipe, but I wanted my recipe to stand out a little and be different. So I have made cardamom, not cinnamon, the dominant spice flavor in these buns, which are as sticky as any others you may have had.

These are good warm or cold, so don't feel you have to eat them all straight out of the oven, but you may not be able to help yourself.

1 cup soy milk, room temperature
½ cup boiling water
1 teaspoon granulated sugar

2 teaspoons dry yeast

2½ cups white bread flour, or 2½ cups all-purpose flour and 2½ tablespoons vital wheat gluten
¼ cup light brown sugar, packed
1 teaspoon salt
1 teaspoon ground cardamom
½ teaspoon ground ginger
½ teaspoon ground allspice
¼ teaspoon ground cinnamon
¼ teaspoon ground coriander
¼ teaspoon ancho chile powder

½ cup white bread flour, or ½ cup all-purpose flour and ½ tablespoon vital wheat gluten

Flour, for kneading
Canola oil, for the bowl

FILLING
¼ cup light brown sugar, packed
¼ cup granulated sugar
½ teaspoon ground cardamom
¼ teaspoon ground ginger
¼ teaspoon ground allspice
⅛ teaspoon ground cinnamon
⅛ teaspoon ground coriander
⅛ teaspoon ancho chile powder

3 tablespoons vegan margarine

1 recipe Sugar Glaze (page 252) (optional)

1. In a large bowl, combine the boiling water, soy milk, and granulated sugar. Check the temperature (see page 193), then add the yeast, stir, and set aside for 10 minutes to proof.

2. Add the ingredients from flour through ancho chile powder, then stir one hundred times with a wooden spoon to get it well mixed. Cover and set aside for 30 minutes.

3. Add the remaining flour and turn onto a floured board for kneading. The flour may not completely incorporate at first, but that is fine; it will become part of the dough as you knead. Add more flour by the tablespoonful, as required, to ensure the dough is not sticky.

4. Knead for a total of about 15 minutes, until your dough is smooth and supple. You can do this in 3-minute bursts—that is, knead for 3 minutes, rest, and repeat—if you find kneading vigorously for the whole time too tiring.

5. Coat a large bowl with a thin film of oil, place the dough ball in the bowl, and turn the dough to coat it in oil. Cover the bowl and place in a warm place. The dough will double in bulk in 45 to 60 minutes.

6. Prepare a 9 by 13-inch baking (brownie) pan by lining with parchment paper.

7. Combine the sugars and spices for the filling in a small bowl and mix well.

8. Punch down the dough, knead for about 3 minutes to get it looking doughlike again, then let rest on your countertop for 10 minutes. With a floured rolling pin and your hands, roll and stretch the dough to form a 22 by 10-inch rectangle about ¼ inch thick (get it as thin as you can, anyway).

9. Position the rectangle with a long side closest to you.

10. Spread the margarine over the prepared dough, using the back of a spoon, then sprinkle evenly with the spice mixture. To roll the dough, start with the long side farthest away from you (cut in half along this side to form two 11 by 10-inch rectangles and do in two parts, if you find this difficult), and roll the dough tightly into a pinwheel shape. Press down along the long edge of the dough log to seal it, and squeeze gently into a cylindrical shape.

11. Cut the rolled dough into fifteen roughly 1½-inch sections and place, cut side down and ½ inch apart, on the prepared sheet in five rows of three across. Cover and allow to rise for a second time, 20 to 25 minutes, to double in size.

12. Preheat the oven to 375°F while the rolls are rising.

13. Once the rolls have risen, uncover and bake for 25 to 30 minutes, until golden.

14. Remove from the oven. Pour the Sugar Glaze, if using, over the hot rolls and let cool on the pan.

Variation

Raisin Sticky Spice Buns
Add ¼ cup of raisins with the spices for the filling and sprinkle with the margarine prior to rolling.

Sweet Long Coconut Rolls with Creamy Coconut Icing

MAKES 8 ROLLS

▶ **NO NUTS**

Shaped like the "Long John Donut" at your local Tim Hortons (or other doughnut shop), these rolls are what I would expect to find a pirate enjoying any morning in the tropical sun, made with coconut harvested from a nearby island! Be warned: These are not doughnuts, just a soft, delectable, more-ish sweet bread roll!

Another word of warning: The icing is very addictive and you'll find yourself using it on everything!

¾ cup hot water
½ cup canned coconut milk, room temperature
1 teaspoon granulated sugar

2 teaspoons dry yeast

1½ cups white bread flour, or 1½ cups all-purpose flour and 1½ tablespoons vital wheat gluten
¼ cup unsweetened, shredded coconut
¼ cup granulated sugar
¼ cup chopped coconut chunks (optional) (see Note)
1 tablespoon coconut oil
1 tablespoon freshly squeezed lemon juice (½ medium lemon)
1 teaspoon salt
½ teaspoon ground nutmeg

1½ cups white bread flour, or 1½ cups all-purpose flour and 1½ tablespoons vital wheat gluten

Flour, for kneading

Canola oil, for the bowl

Soy milk or oil, for brushing (optional)

1 recipe Creamy Coconut Icing (recipe follows)

2 tablespoons toasted, shredded coconut, to garnish (optional)

1. Combine the water, milk, and granulated sugar in a large bowl, check the temperature (see page 193), add the yeast, stir, and set aside for 5 minutes to proof.

2. Stir in the ingredients from flour through nutmeg, and stir briskly one hundred times or so, then set aside for least 15 minutes.

3. Add the remaining flour and turn onto a floured board for kneading. The flour may not completely incorporate at first, but that is fine; it will become part of the dough as you knead. Add more flour by the tablespoonful, as required, to ensure the dough is not sticky.

4. Knead for a total of about 15 minutes, until your dough is smooth and supple. You can do this in 3-minute bursts—that is, knead for 3 minutes, rest, and repeat—if you find kneading vigorously for the whole time too tiring.

5. Coat a large bowl with a thin film of oil, place the dough ball in the bowl, and turn the dough to coat it in oil. Cover the bowl and place in a warm place until the dough is doubled in size (about 1½ hours).

6. Punch down the dough, knead for about 3 minutes to get it looking doughlike again, then return to the bowl, cover, and return to your warm place for the second rise. This will take less time, about 1 hour, to double in size.

7. While the dough is rising, line a baking sheet with parchment paper.

8. Remove the dough from the bowl. Knead lightly and then shape into eight equal rolls about 4½ inches long and 1½ inches in diameter. The easiest way to do this is to roll each between your palms until it reaches the desired size. Place on the prepared pan, cover, and allow to rise again. This final rise will take about 30 minutes. Brush the tops of your rolls with soy milk or oil, if desired.

9. Preheat the oven to 375°F during the final rise, then bake the rolls for 20 to 25 minutes, until golden brown. If you tap the bottom lightly when you think they are done, they should sound hollow.

10. Remove from the oven and let cool on the sheet for 10 minutes, then transfer to a wire rack and let cool completely.

11. Once the rolls are completely cool, spread the tops generously with the Creamy Coconut Icing and garnish with toasted coconut, if desired.

NOTE:

❖ I found the coconut chunks at my local health food store. They were unsweetened chunks about ½ inch across. if you can't find them, just leave them out or use an additional ¼ cup of unsweetened shredded coconut.

★ Creamy Coconut Icing

MAKES 1½ CUPS ICING

▶ **NO NUTS • NO SOY • NO WHEAT**

Although specifically made for these rolls, this icing is good enough to be used anywhere—anywhere you'd like a sweet, smooth, creamy, not-too-coconutty good taste, that is. Try it on cakes, cookies, and, of course, the rolls, and let me know what you think! Good, or what?

2 tablespoons vegan shortening
1 tablespoon coconut oil

1 cup confectioners' sugar

2 tablespoons canned coconut milk

½ teaspoon coconut extract

1. In a medium bowl, cream together the shortening and coconut oil until smooth and well combined.

2. Add the confectioners' sugar and mix until crumbly with no lumps of fat remaining.

3. Make a well in the sugar mixture, add the coconut milk and coconut extract, then mix until smooth.

· ·

Vanilla and Cinnamon Monkey Bread

MAKES 6 BUNS

▶ NO NUTS

I love the idea of monkey bread. It's all about sharing, being messy, and eating with your fingers! Yes, it does take a little more time to put together and make, but the result is so very worth it! My children especially love this—the one time they don't get told off for eating with their fingers.

½ cup soy milk

1 vanilla bean, halved along its length (see Note)

¼ cup warm water

2 teaspoons dry yeast

1 teaspoon granulated sugar

¼ cup granulated sugar

¼ cup vegan margarine, melted

¼ cup soy creamer (see page 16)

¼ cup (2½ ounces) tofu, firm silken (vacuum-packed)

2 teaspoons vanilla extract

1 teaspoon ground cinnamon

1 teaspoon salt

2 cups white bread flour, or 2 cups all-purpose flour and 2 tablespoons vital wheat gluten

1 cup white bread flour, or 1 cup all-purpose flour and 1 tablespoon vital wheat gluten

Flour, for kneading

Canola oil, for the bowl

TO ASSEMBLE

¼ cup vegan margarine, melted

1 teaspoon vanilla paste, or extract

¼ cup light brown sugar, packed

3 tablespoons granulated sugar

1 teaspoon ground cinnamon

1 recipe Sugar Glaze, made with vanilla paste or extract (page 252) (optional)

1. In a small saucepan, combine the soy milk and vanilla bean halves. Bring to a boil, then remove from the heat and set aside, covered, about 30 minutes, until lukewarm.

2. Once the milk mixture is lukewarm, squeeze out the contents of the vanilla bean pod into the milk and discard the empty pod.

3. In a large bowl, combine the soy milk mixture, water, yeast, and granulated sugar, and set aside for 5 minutes to proof (see page 193).

4. While the yeast is proofing, blend the ingredients from sugar through salt in a blender or food processor, until smooth and creamy. Add the blended mixture and the first 2 cups of flour to the yeast mixture and stir to combine. Cover and set aside at least 30 minutes.

5. Add the remaining flour and turn onto a floured board for kneading. The flour may not completely incorporate at first, but that is fine; it will become part of the dough as you knead. Add more flour by the tablespoonful, as required, to ensure the dough is not sticky.

6. Knead for a total of about 15 minutes, until your dough is smooth and supple. You can do this in 3-minute bursts—that is, knead for 3 minutes, rest, and repeat—if you find kneading vigorously for the whole time too tiring.

7. Coat a large bowl with a thin film of oil, place the dough ball in the bowl, and turn the dough to coat it in oil. Cover the bowl and place in a warm place until the dough is doubled in size (about 1 hour).

8. Punch down the dough, knead for about 3 minutes to get it looking doughlike again, then let rest on your countertop for 10 minutes.

9. Grease a six-cup maxi-muffin pan with a little vegan margarine or spray with non-stick spray.

10. Divide the dough into six equal pieces, one piece for each cup in the muffin pan. Further divide each of these into twelve smaller pieces. Roll these into balls, keeping each dozen balls together as a group.

11. To assemble, combine the melted margarine and vanilla in one small bowl and the sugars with the cinnamon in a second small bowl.

12. Dip the balls of dough into the margarine mixture, and then into the cinnamon mixture, then place each dozen into one of the cups in the muffin pan. This is a little random; not every ball has to be fully coated in the cinnamon mixture. The cups will be about three-quarters full.

13. Once all the balls are in the pans, press gently to remove any gaps, cover, and allow to rise for 20 to 25 minutes.

14. While the dough is rising, preheat the oven to 375°F.

15. Remove the cover from the risen dough and bake for 18 to 22 minutes, until golden.

16. Remove from the oven and let cool in pan for 10 minutes, then let cool completely on a wire rack. Glaze while warm, if desired.

NOTE:
❖ If you don't have a vanilla bean, substitute 1 teaspoon of vanilla paste or vanilla extract.

Variation

Large Vanilla and Cinnamon Monkey Bread

Instead of using maxi-muffin pans, place all the dough balls in a greased 10-inch Bundt cake pan, and once risen, bake for 35 to 40 minutes, until golden.

Walnut and Banana Cinnamon Rolls

MAKES 15 ROLLS

▶ **NO SOY • NO SUGAR** excluding glaze

I wanted to see if I could make a cinnamon roll that was sticky, sweet, and just plain delectable, yet without using processed sugar. I thought agave nectar and brown rice syrup would be good sweetening contenders, so I have made use of them in both the dough and filling. Without the optional glaze, they meet my goal!

I also wanted the rolls to be a slight variation on the whole cinnamon roll theme, so here we have a banana-infused nutty roll.

1 frozen banana, in chunks (see Notes)
½ cup agave nectar
¼ cup almond milk

½ cup boiling water
2 tablespoons vegan margarine, melted
2 teaspoons dry yeast

2 cups white bread flour, or 2 cups all-purpose flour and 2 tablespoons vital wheat gluten
½ cup ground walnuts (see Notes)
2 teaspoons ground cinnamon
1 teaspoon salt
1¼ cups white bread flour, or 1¼ cups all-purpose flour and 1 tablespoon vital wheat gluten

Flour, for kneading
Canola oil, for the bowl

FILLING
¼ cup finely chopped walnuts
4 teaspoons ground cinnamon

2 tablespoons agave nectar
1 tablespoon brown rice syrup
1 tablespoon vegan margarine

1 recipe Sugar Glaze (page 252) (optional) (see Notes)

1. In a blender or food processor, puree the frozen banana, agave nectar, and soy milk until smooth, creamy, and fluffy. Pour into a large bowl, then stir in the boiling water and melted margarine. Check the temperature (see page 193), add the yeast, stir, and set aside for 10 minutes to proof.

2. Add the ingredients from flour through salt, then stir one hundred times with a wooden spoon to get it well mixed. Cover and set aside for 30 minutes.

3. Add the remaining flour and turn onto a floured board for kneading. The flour may not completely incorporate at first, but that is fine; it will become part of the dough as you knead. Add more flour by the tablespoonful, as required, to ensure the dough is not sticky.

4. Knead for a total of about 15 minutes, until your dough is smooth and supple. You can do this in 3-minute bursts—that is, knead for 3 minutes, rest, and repeat—if you find kneading vigorously for the whole time too tiring.

5. Coat a large bowl with a thin film of oil, place the dough ball in the bowl, and turn the dough to coat it in oil. Cover the bowl and place in a warm place until the dough is doubled in size (about 1¼ hours).

6. Prepare a 9 by 13-inch baking (brownie) pan by lining with parchment paper.

7. In a small bowl, toss together the nuts and cinnamon for the filling.

8. In a small saucepan, combine the agave nectar, syrup, and margarine over medium heat, stir until melted together, and keep

warm until required.

9. Punch down the dough, knead for about 3 minutes to get it looking doughlike again, then let rest on your countertop for 10 minutes. With a floured rolling pin and your hands, roll and stretch the dough into a 22 by 10-inch rectangle, about ¼ inch thick (as thin as you can get it).

10. Position the dough with a long side toward you.

11. Spread three-quarters of the warm filling mixture over the prepared dough, sprinkle with all the cinnamon mixture. Starting with the long side farthest from you (cut in half and do in two pieces if you find this difficult), roll the dough tightly into a pinwheel shape, then press along the long edge of the pinwheel to seal and squeeze gently into a cylindrical shape.

12. Cut the rolled dough into about fifteen 1½-inch sections, then place cut side down on prepared pan. Brush the tops with the remaining syrup mixture from the filling. Cover and allow to rise for 20 to 25 minutes, until roughly doubled in size.

13. Preheat the oven to 375°F while the rolls are rising.

14. Once the rolls have risen, uncover and bake for 25 to 30 minutes, until golden.

15. Remove from the oven. Pour the Sugar Glaze, if using, over the hot rolls and let cool completely on the pan.

NOTES:

❖ Freeze any excess ripe bananas, already peeled and cut into 1-inch chunks, in little plastic bags for ease of access for recipes like this or for smoothies.

❖ Grind the walnuts in your food processor or spice grinder, a little at a time, until they reach the consistency of heavy flour.

❖ If you would like these to have a glaze but can't bring yourself to use one with refined sugar, use the glaze from the Date Pinwheels (page 200).

Variation

Other Nut and Banana Cinnamon Rolls
Use your favorite nut instead of the walnuts! These were made with pecans by one of my testers, with superb results.

Savory Goodies

Arugula and Pine Nut Muffins

Arugula Tart

Asparagus, Pine Nut, and
Roasted Garlic Quiche

Chile and Cilantro Corn
Bread 📷

Dinner Biscuits

From-Scratch "Cheesy" Straws

Irish-Inspired Soda Bread

Mini Cheese and Onion
Pasties

Mini Sausage Rolls

Oven Potato Farls

Pea, Tarragon, and Cream
Cheese Tart

Pesto Muffins

Roasted Garlic and
Peppercorn Crackers 📷

Savory "Cheesy" Biscuits

Savory Herbed Crackers

Spanikopita Loaf

Spicy Corn Biscotti

Spicy Spinach and Cream
Cheese Muffins

Sun-Dried Tomato, Olive, and
Sausage Pie

Tomato and Herb Biscotti

Upside-Down Olive, Sun-Dried
Tomato, and Red Pepper
"Cake"

SOMEONE HAD TO include savory goodies in a baking book! And that someone would be me! Not everyone has a sweet tooth, and those who don't would appreciate being able to share (or even be able to buy at a bake sale) creative, interesting and tasty baked goods as much as do those of us with "sweet teeth."

I've included all styles of savory items in the same chapter, to make it easier to find that little something when you've a hankering for a baked good but not for something sweet. The styles run the gauntlet from biscuits and scones, to savory cookies and muffins, to pies and tarts, so there is bound to be something in this chapter that takes your fancy.

These recipes are all great as a light lunch alongside soup and/or a salad, as well as eaten as snacks; some can even cope with being dinner. Many items in this section also add an interesting touch to main dishes. The flavored loaves, biscuits, and scones in particular make great dinner accompaniments.

For storage guidelines, and for other troubleshooting points, please refer to the information regarding the type of savory goodies you have made in the Storage section (page 41), or just contact me at http://veganyear.blogspot.com! A little extra help in looking after your savory baking is just as important in looking after your sweet treats.

Arugula and Pine Nut Muffins

MAKES 12 MUFFINS

▶ NO SOY • NO SUGAR • NO WHEAT

Arugula (a.k.a. rocket or roquette) is a sharp, peppery-flavored salad green. Spicy and a little bitter, it contrasts well to the smoothness of the toasted pine nuts and makes for a very interesting muffin.

2¾ cups + 2 tablespoons spelt flour
2½ teaspoons baking powder
1¼ teaspoons salt
½ teaspoon baking soda
½ teaspoon paprika
¼ teaspoon freshly ground black pepper
¼ teaspoon mustard powder

2 cups finely sliced arugula (see Notes)
½ cup toasted pine nuts

2 cups rice milk
¼ cup olive oil
2 tablespoons freshly squeezed lemon juice (1 medium lemon)
2 teaspoons lemon zest (1 medium lemon)

1. Preheat the oven to 375°F and prepare a twelve-cup muffin pan by spraying with non-stick spray.
2. Sift together the ingredients from flour through mustard powder, into a large bowl.
3. Add the sliced arugula and the toasted pine nuts, and use your fingers to separate and toss to coat.
4. Mix together the ingredients from milk through lemon zest in a small bowl, then add to the dry ingredients and mix to just combine.

5. Spoon the mixture into the prepared pan. The cups will be full. Bake for 18 to 22 minutes, until a toothpick comes out clean.
6. Remove from the oven and let cool in the pan for 5 minutes, then transfer to a wire rack and let cool completely.

NOTES:
- ❖ Finely chop the arugula first and pack it in the measuring cup when getting your 2 cups' worth. It's about 3 cups loosely packed, prior to chopping.
- ❖ Arugula varies in strength from batch to batch, depending on where and how it is grown. Taste-test yours prior to adding to the batter, and use less if it is very strong.

Variation

Baby Spinach and Pine Nut Muffins
Can't find arugula? Or is it too expensive? Substitute finely sliced baby spinach leaves for a subtle yet delicious change.

Arugula Tart

SERVES 6 TO 8

▶ NO SOY • NO SUGAR • NO WHEAT
excluding crust

This one's soy free, but still creamy, thick, and dreamy! The slightly bitter kick of the arugula contrasts really well with the rest of the filling.

When baking with chickpea flour, *don't* taste the dough prior to baking—the chickpea flavor makes it taste awful until it's been baked!

If you don't have an 11-inch loose-bottomed tart pan, use a 9-inch pie plate.

1 tablespoon olive oil

3 garlic cloves, minced

3 cups arugula, packed, rinsed

1 cup raw cashews, previously soaked
for 8 hours or overnight, drained and
rinsed

½ cup almond milk

¼ cup chickpea flour

2 tablespoons tapioca starch or
cornstarch

1 tablespoon nutritional yeast

½ teaspoon salt

½ teaspoon mustard powder

Freshly ground black pepper

1 unbaked pie crust, preferably made in
an 11-inch loose-bottomed tart pan,
or store-bought equivalent crust. The
Savory Cornmeal Pie Crust (page 170)
goes really well here.

1. Preheat the oven to 400°F.

2. In a large skillet over medium heat, sauté the garlic in the oil until aromatic (less than a minute). Add the arugula and sauté until just wilted, about 2 minutes; add a few splashes of water, if required. The volume will reduce to about a cupful. Remove from the heat.

3. Combine the ingredients from nuts through pepper in a blender or food processor and blend until very smooth and creamy. Scrape down the sides as required. Add the garlic and arugula to the blender and pulse once or twice to combine.

4. Scrape the filling into the prepared pie crust, smooth the top, and bake for 30 to 35 minutes, or until the filling is firm to a light touch and top is golden.

5. Remove from the oven and let cool for at least 15 minutes prior to serving either hot or cold.

Asparagus, Pine Nut, and Roasted Garlic Quiche

SERVES 6 TO 8

▶ **NO SUGAR** • **NO WHEAT** excluding crust

I adore asparagus. I make it into soup, grill it, eat it in salads and sandwiches, roast it, make stir-fries with it, and it's in this quiche! I hope you'll love it as much as I do.

I purposely made this a nutritional yeast–free quiche, but there is a variation that includes it, in case you couldn't consider having one without it! Again a 9-inch pie plate is fine if that is what you have.

1 bunch (about 1 pound) asparagus,
trimmed and blanched (see Notes)

1 teaspoon olive oil

½ medium onion, finely chopped, about
½ cup

½ cup cashews, previously soaked for
8 hours or overnight, drained and
rinsed

6 ounces tofu, extra-firm regular (water-
packed, half of a 12-ounce package)

1 head garlic, roasted and peeled (see
Notes)

2 tablespoons tapioca starch

1 teaspoon salt

¼ teaspoon mustard powder

Freshly ground black pepper

⅓ cup pine nuts, toasted (see Notes)

1 prebaked plain pie crust, such as the
Spelt Pie Crust Variation (page 170),
made in an 11-inch loose-bottomed
tart pan

1. Preheat the oven to 375°F.

2. Remove the tips (2-inch lengths) from the asparagus spears and reserve. Roughly chop the rest of the stems to ¼ inch across (about the size of pine nuts) and reserve.

3. In a medium skillet over medium heat, sauté the onion for 10 minutes, until it is very soft and translucent. Remove from the heat.

4. In a blender or food processor, blend the ingredients from cashews through pepper until very smooth. This mixture is very thick, so scrape down the sides often, as required. (See Notes.)

5. Transfer to a mixing bowl and stir in the toasted pine nuts, chopped asparagus stems, and sautéed onion.

6. Scrape the filling into the prepared crust, smooth until level, and decorate the top in an attractive pattern with the asparagus tips.

7. Bake for 30 to 35 minutes, until the filling is firm and golden. If using a 9-inch pie plate, bake for the longer time stated.

8. Remove from the oven and let cool in the pan for at least 15 minutes prior to serving. Serve hot or cold.

NOTES:

❖ To blanch asparagus, bring a large saucepan of water to a boil. Have ready a colander in a basin of very cold water. If the water is not very cold, add some ice cubes. Add the trimmed asparagus spears to the boiling water and bring back to a boil. As the water starts to boil, remove the asparagus, using tongs, and immediately place in the colander in the very cold water for 2 minutes to refresh and stop the cooking process. The asparagus will be cold and look bright green.

❖ To roast the garlic, preheat the oven to 400°F. Remove the loose papery skin from the outside of the garlic head, and slice off the top ¼ inch of the head, removing the tops of most of the cloves. Place the trimmed garlic on a square of tinfoil and drizzle a little olive oil over it. Wrap the garlic in the foil and roast for 20 to 25 minutes, until soft to the touch. Remove from the oven and let cool to make handling easier, then peel, reserving the roasted cloves.

❖ See the instructions for toasting nuts (page 21).

❖ If you need to add a little water to keep your mixture moving in the blender and to avoid any lumps, then by all means do so, by the tablespoonful. A little water (no more than 2 tablespoons) isn't going to impact the finished product.

Variation

"Cheesy" Asparagus, Pine Nut, and Roasted Garlic Quiche

Add 2 tablespoons of nutritional yeast with the tofu mixture, if you are a fan of it, and sprinkle the top with grated vegan cheese prior to baking.

Chile and Cilantro Corn Bread 📷

MAKES 16 PIECES

▶ **NO NUTS • NO SUGAR**

This isn't too spicy. Roasting the pepper and garlic gives them a mellowness that works really well with the corn flavors and the fresh taste of the cilantro. Slices of this are nice to munch on while you're waiting for your dinner to barbecue. I really like it.

The chile flakes are optional, so you can control the heat; I know everyone has different preferences. If you like food to be super hot, leave the seeds in the pepper!

1 serrano chile pepper, halved, seeds removed

6 garlic cloves, unpeeled

¾ cup canned creamed corn (see Note)

¾ cup (8 ounces) tofu, firm silken (vacuum-packed, two thirds of a 12-ounce package)

⅓ cup fresh cilantro, lightly packed

¼ cup water or vegan vegetable broth

2 tablespoons olive oil

1 tablespoon agave nectar

1 cup all-purpose flour

½ cup cornmeal (see Note and page 15)

¼ cup yellow corn flour

1 tablespoon baking powder

1 teaspoon baking soda

1 teaspoon salt

½ teaspoon ground coriander

½ teaspoon ground cumin

½ teaspoon freshly ground black pepper

¼ teaspoon chile flakes (optional)

¼ cup finely chopped red onion

1. Preheat the oven to 375°F and line a baking sheet with parchment paper; also line an 8-inch square cake (brownie) pan.

2. Place the serrano pepper (cut side down) and garlic cloves on the prepared baking sheet and bake for 20 minutes, until the garlic is soft and the pepper skin is lightly browned. Remove from the oven and allow to cool; once cool, peel the garlic.

3. Place the ingredients from pepper through agave nectar in a blender or food processor, and process until smooth and creamy.

4. Sift together the dry ingredients (from flour through chile flakes [if using]), into a large bowl. Toss in the onion to coat with the flour.

5. Add the blended mixture to the dry and mix to just combine. Pour into the prepared 8-inch square pan and bake for 25 to 30 minutes, until a toothpick comes out clean.

6. Remove from the oven. After 10 minutes' cooling in the pan, lift out using the parchment paper lining and transfer to a wire rack. Serve warm or cold.

NOTE:

❖ If you have trouble finding canned creamed corn, then make your own! Using a blender or food processor, blend an equal amount of canned corn kernels with the liquid they come in until creamy. It won't be exactly the same, but it will still work!

Dinner Biscuits

MAKES 6 TO 8 BISCUITS

▶ NO NUTS • NO SOY

A simple, plain biscuit, good for eating alongside dinner, be it soup, salad, stew, chili, or whatever. I've added a little interest with the caraway, but if you don't like the unique flavor of these seeds, leave them out.

As always when baking with chickpea flour, *don't* taste the dough prior to baking—the chickpea flavor makes it taste awful until it's been baked!

1 cup + 1 tablespoon all-purpose flour

½ cup whole-wheat pastry flour

2 tablespoons chickpea flour

2 teaspoons baking powder

1 teaspoon granulated sugar

½ teaspoon salt

½ teaspoon mustard powder

¼ teaspoon caraway seeds (optional)

3 tablespoons frozen, grated coconut oil (see Note)

¾ cup rice milk

1. Preheat the oven to 425°F and line a baking sheet with parchment paper.

2. Sift together the ingredients from flour through caraway seeds, into a large bowl.

3. Stir in the coconut oil, then add the milk. Stir with a fork to form a sticky, thick dough.

4. Turn onto a floured board and pat into a 1-inch thick circle. Using a 2½-inch cookie cutter, cut out the biscuits, gently reshaping and recutting any leftover dough.

5. Transfer the biscuits to the prepared sheet and bake for 10 to 12 minutes, until well risen, lightly golden, and the bottoms are browned.

6. Remove from the oven and let cool on the sheet for 5 minutes, then let cool completely on a serving plate or wire rack.

NOTE:
❖ To freeze coconut oil, place some coconut oil in the freezer in a plastic container for a few hours to freeze. Once frozen, remove from the container, and holding the oil with a paper towel (to avoid getting melting oil on your hands), quickly grate over a sheet of tinfoil, using the larger compartment on your box grater. Wrap in the tinfoil and return to the freezer until required. If you don't have frozen coconut oil grated and in your freezer, and are in a hurry, you can use room-temperature oil and cut in as you would shortening, if you must.

From-Scratch "Cheesy" Straws

MAKES ABOUT 16 STRAWS

▶ **NO NUTS**

I remember Mum making cheese straws when I was little. She often made them the cheater's way (page 173), but occasionally would make them specifically from scratch, like this recipe.

You can leave the grated cheese out if you like, but you will need to add an extra 2 tablespoons of grated frozen coconut oil. When the cheese melts, as it bakes it acts as a fat. An extra tablespoon of nutritional yeast for a replacement burst of cheesiness wouldn't hurt, either.

2 cups all-purpose flour
2 tablespoons nutritional yeast
2 teaspoons granulated sugar
1 teaspoon salt
½ teaspoon baking powder
½ teaspoon mustard powder
½ teaspoon paprika
Freshly ground black pepper

¼ cup vegan shortening

¼ cup frozen and grated coconut oil (see Note)
¼ cup grated vegan cheese (see above)

½ cup + 2 tablespoons soy milk

Soy milk, for brushing, if desired

1. Preheat the oven to 400°F and line a baking sheet with parchment paper.

2. Sift together the ingredients from flour through black pepper, into a large bowl.

3. Using a pastry cutter (or two knives held together), cut in the shortening until the mixture resembles lumpy bread crumbs. Stir in the frozen coconut oil flakes and cheese with a fork.

4. Add ½ cup of the milk and start to mix to form a loose dough. When ready, the dough will hold together when pressed; there will be some loose bits that you will need to press in. If too dry, add the rest of the milk 1 tablespoonful at a time, until it reaches a firmer consistency.

5. Gather the dough and press into a ball. Knead lightly to encourage it to hold together, then roll out the dough in a 7 by 10-inch rectangle about ⅜ inch thick.

6. Slice crosswise into long, thin strips about ¾ inch wide, so each straw is about 7 inches long. Holding one end of a strip, twist from the other end, for a decorative effect.

7. Place each twisted strip on the baking sheet and brush with soy milk, if desired.

8. Bake for 10 to 12 minutes, until golden.

9. Remove from the oven and let cool on the sheet for 5 minutes, then transfer to a wire rack and let cool completely. Serve hot or cold!

NOTE:

❖ To freeze coconut oil, place some coconut oil in the freezer in a plastic container for a few hours to freeze. Once frozen, remove from the container, and holding the oil with a paper towel (to avoid getting melting oil on your hands), quickly grate over a sheet of tinfoil, using the larger compartment on your box grater. Wrap in the tinfoil and return to the freezer until required. If you don't have the time to do the freezing and grating of the coconut oil, you can add room-temperature coconut oil to the mixture with the shortening and cut in. The results won't be as flaky, but are still pretty good!

Irish-Inspired Soda Bread

SERVES 8 TO 10

▶ **NO NUTS**

Now, if you're Irish, I'm sure you'll have an opinion as to the "correctness" of the way I've made my soda bread. It's more Irish-inspired than truly Irish, hence the name!

1 cup soy milk
1 teaspoon apple cider vinegar

2 cups all-purpose flour
½ cup whole-wheat pastry flour
1 teaspoon baking soda
1 teaspoon salt
1 teaspoon granulated sugar

½ teaspoon caraway seeds

Soy milk, for brushing (optional)

1. Preheat the oven to 400°F and line a baking sheet with parchment paper.

2. In a small bowl, combine the milk and vinegar, and set aside for 5 minutes to curdle.

3. Sift together the ingredients from flour through granulated sugar into a large bowl. Stir in the caraway seeds.

4. Make a well in the center of the dry ingredients and add the soy milk mixture.

5. Mix until just combined, then knead gently to ensure all the flour is incorporated.

6. Shape the dough into a 6-inch-diameter circle about 1 inch high and place on the prepared baking sheet. In the top of the bread, cut a cross that reaches three quarters of the way across. Brush with soy milk, if desired.

7. Bake the bread for 25 to 30 minutes, until browned and, when lifted off the sheet, it sounds hollow if the bottom is tapped.

8. Remove from the oven. For hard-crusted bread, let cool for 5 minutes on the sheet, then transfer to a wire rack and let cool completely. For softer-crusted bread, wrap in a clean tea towel straight out of the oven and let cool on the wire rack while wrapped.

9. Let cool completely before slicing.

Variations

Seeded Soda Bread

Omit the caraway seeds and add 2 tablespoons of your favorite seeds—poppy, sesame, sunflower, or pumpkin, or a mixture—for a textured, seeded loaf.

Herbed Soda Bread

Omit the caraway seeds and add an equal amount of dried thyme or rosemary (or up to 1 tablespoon of finely chopped, fresh) for a herb-infused loaf.

Mini Cheese and Onion Pasties

MAKES 8 PASTIES

▶ **NO NUTS • NO SUGAR**

A bakery chain in the United Kingdom that has a store on pretty much every High Street makes wonderful cheese and onion pasties. I craved them while (vegetarian and) pregnant. This isn't quite the same. For a start, I've made them smaller and more pasty shaped, not like the huge square things this chain made. There's no cheese in them, either, unless you add some (vegan, of course).

You can use homemade Plain Pie Crust (page 169), but that just doesn't replicate closely enough the ones in my memory.

1 tablespoon vegan margarine
1 medium onion, chopped finely (about 1 cup)
2 garlic cloves, minced

1 teaspoon salt
½ teaspoon mustard powder
¼ teaspoon onion powder
¼ teaspoon paprika
Freshly ground black pepper

1 cup cold mashed potatoes
2, 3, or 4 tablespoons nutritional yeast (see Notes)
3 tablespoons soy milk

¼ cup grated vegan cheese (optional)

One 16-ounce (400 g) package vegan puff pastry, thawed if frozen

Soy milk, for brushing

1. In a medium skillet, sauté the onion and garlic in the margarine over medium heat for about 10 minutes, until the onion is very soft, golden, and just starting to brown.

2. Add the ingredients from salt through black pepper and sauté for 1 minute more.

3. Add the cold mashed potatoes, nutritional yeast, and soy milk. Stir well to combine and continue to sauté for another 2 minutes.

4. Remove from the heat and stir in the vegan cheese, if using. Allow to cool to room temperature.

5. While the filling is cooling, preheat the oven to 400°F and line a baking sheet with parchment paper.

6. Roll the pastry to about ⅜-inch thick and cut out eight 6-inch-diameter circles (a

small pan lid or side plate is often this size, to use as a template).

7. Place 2 tablespoons of the filling in the center of each pastry circle, and ensure it is evenly distributed. With slightly dampened hands, bring up the opposite sides of the pastry to meet and form a half-moon shape. Starting at one end, crimp the edge of the half-moon with your thumb and first two fingers to form a seal and a pretty wavy edge, as best you can, otherwise the pastry will split in the oven. Stand the pasties 1 inch apart on the prepared sheet with the sealed edge uppermost.

8. Prick each side of the pasty with a fork and brush with soy milk.

9. Bake for 15 to 20 minutes, until golden brown.

10. Remove from the oven. Let cool for 5 minutes on the sheet, then let cool completely on a wire rack if planning to serve cold. Serve hot or cold, but they are better hot.

NOTES:

❖ I have left the amount of nutritional yeast to use up to you. How much you use will depend on how much you (and whoever else is eating the pasties) like it and whether you are adding any vegan cheese. I recommend adding 2 or 3 tablespoons, where directed, and then after you add the cheese, if you use it, taste and see if you'd like to add a little more.

❖ These reheat well. Heat the oven to 350°F, place on a parchment-lined pan, cover with tinfoil, and bake for 10 to 15 minutes, until warmed through. You can also microwave them (uncovered—tinfoil should not be microwaved!), but the pastry tends to get soggy.

Mini Sausage Rolls

MAKES 24 SAUSAGE ROLLS

▶ **NO NUTS • NO SUGAR**

Every single bakery (I may be exaggerating, but only slightly) in New Zealand, Australia, and the United Kingdom sells these, but not the vegan variety. It's not so much a North American thing, but why not? Great as a snack, for lunch with salad, dipped in ketchup, as a finger-food appetizer, as breakfast . . . (maybe I'm exaggerating again, but you get the idea).

The sausages can be made in advance and stored in the fridge or freezer until required. Just bring to room temperature before wrapping and baking. For larger, more meal-size rolls, shape into twelve larger sausages before wrapping in tinfoil, and bake for about 25 minutes.

If you've never made seitan before, please don't feel overwhelmed. It looks like a lot of work but it is basically mix dry ingredients, mix wet ingredients, mix together, knead, and then shape. My testers also want you to know that the effort is worth it, and I quote Kate: "I didn't like them, I loved them!"

One 16-ounce (400 g) package vegan puff pastry, thawed if frozen

½ cup (5 ounces) tofu, firm silken (vacuum-packed)

¼ cup vegan vegetable stock

1 clove garlic, chopped roughly

1 tablespoon soy sauce

1½ teaspoons blackstrap molasses

1½ teaspoons tomato paste

1 teaspoon freshly squeezed lemon juice (½ medium lemon)

½ teaspoon Dijon mustard

½ teaspoon liquid smoke (see Notes)

½ teaspoon Marmite (optional) (see Notes)

¾ cup vital wheat gluten
¼ cup nutritional yeast
¼ cup fine bread crumbs
½ teaspoon salt
½ teaspoon onion powder
½ teaspoon garlic powder
¼ teaspoon thyme
¼ teaspoon paprika
⅛ teaspoon ground cumin
⅛ teaspoon sage
Freshly ground black pepper

Soy milk, for brushing (optional)

1. Ensure the puff pastry is fully thawed and waiting in the fridge while you make the sausages.

2. Preheat the oven to 375°F and have a baking sheet handy, as well as tinfoil that has been cut into twenty-four 5-inch squares.

3. In your blender or food processor, blend together the ingredients from tofu through Marmite (if using), until smooth and lump free. Scrape down the bowl as required.

4. In a large bowl, whisk together the ingredients from wheat gluten through black pepper.

5. Add the blended mixture to the dry ingredients and mix well.

6. On a clean work surface, knead the filling mixture for 4 minutes or so to get the gluten activated. The mixture will be very firm. It should feel like firm play dough, no longer wet. If it is still wet, add more wheat gluten by the tablespoonful, kneading after each addition.

7. Shape into twenty-four 2½- to 3-inch logs (around a pinkie-finger length), and wrap each firmly in a square of tinfoil. Place on the prepared pan. (See Notes.)

8. Bake for 12 to 15 minutes, until aromatic and, when poked with a fingertip, feels firm but gives slightly.

9. Remove from the oven and let cool on the sheet in the tinfoil until easily handled, about 10 minutes. Remove the tinfoil and continue to let cool until required.

10. When ready to bake the sausage rolls, preheat the oven to 400°F and line a baking sheet with parchment paper.

11. Once the sausages are cool, roll out the puff pastry until ¼ inch thick, and cut the pastry into rectangles about 3 by 3½ inches. (The size of your pastry rectangles will depend on the size of your sausages. Make the shorter side slightly longer than the sausages, and the longer side ½ to 1 inch longer than that.) Doing a trial roll-up, using a rectangle of parchment cut so size, instead of the pastry, is a good way to get the sizing right.

12. Place the sausage along a shorter edge of the pastry and roll up to encase it. Seal the edge with a little soy milk, or pinch to seal, and place at least 2 inches apart on the prepared sheet, with the seal on the bottom. Score the top of each roll diagonally a few times, and brush with a little soy milk, if desired.

13. Bake for 20 to 25 minutes, until the pastry is well risen and golden.

14. Transfer to a wire rack and let cool completely if serving cold. Serve hot or cold.

NOTES:
- ❖ Liquid smoke is in most supermarkets, in the section with barbecue sauces. The most common flavors are hickory and mesquite. Both are good; use your preference.
- ❖ I couldn't imagine not adding the Marmite, for its yeasty savory flavor, but I appreciate that this condiment isn't easy for everyone to find, and some people don't even like it. Go figure. Anyway, if you fall into either of these categories you can leave it out, or substitute Vegemite or similar; the sausages will still work fine.

❖ One of my recipe testers rolled her sausages as follows: "To make the rolling out easier, I divided the dough in half, then rolled out each half as one long sausage to the same thickness, then scored each sausage into twelve sections. Easy to rectify if I hadn't guessed the lengths properly as well—just rescore and Bob's yer uncle." Thanks for the alternative, Jeni!

Oven Potato Farls

MAKES 8 FARLS

▶ **NO NUTS • NO SUGAR**

Not quite like you'd get in Ireland, but similar! One day, I made up this recipe when I had left-over mashed potatoes in the fridge but didn't want to make fried potato cakes.

Great with a bowl of soup, or a salad, or just by themselves, these are hearty, moist, and filling but have a delicate flavor from the chives.

1¼ cups grated raw potato, about one medium potato (7 ounces)

⅓ cup olive oil

¼ cup + 2 tablespoons plain soy milk

3 tablespoons chopped chives; fresh is best, but freeze dried is okay, too

1 cup cold mashed potatoes

1 cup all-purpose flour

½ cup whole-wheat pastry flour

3½ teaspoons baking powder

1 teaspoon salt

½ teaspoon freshly ground black pepper

1. Preheat the oven to 350°F and line a baking sheet with parchment paper.

2. With your hands, squeeze as much of the liquid out of the raw potato as you can. You should end up with 1 cup of squeezed-out potato. Combine in a small bowl with the oil, soy milk, and chives.

3. In a large bowl, mash together the mashed potatoes, flour, baking powder, salt, and pepper with a fork until it looks crumbly.

4. Add the raw potato mixture to the mashed mixture and combine to make a moist dough.

5. Form the dough into an 8-inch-diameter circle about ½-inch thick on the prepared pan. Slice into eight wedges like pizza slices, but don't separate them until after they are baked.

6. Bake for 40 to 45 minutes, until they are lightly browned and firm to the touch, and the shreds of potato look cooked.

7. Remove from the oven and let cool on the sheet for 5 minutes, then transfer to a wire rack and let cool completely if serving cold. Serve hot or cold.

Pea, Tarragon, and Cream Cheese Tart

SERVES 6 TO 8

▶ **NO NUTS • NO SUGAR • NO WHEAT**
excluding crust

Tarragon is a very herby herb—you could say a little grassy, even—and it goes really well with the delicate taste of young peas and smooth, creamy cheese. Great for dinner, warm with vegetables, or cold with a salad, this tart could well become a favorite in your house, as it has in mine. It may well end up being the best thing you've ever put in your mouth!

You need a gentle hand after you've added the cream cheese, as you want it to stay as lumpy as possible—for nice surprises as you eat the tart. However, I think you'll want to avoid tasting the filling mixture before it is baked; the chickpea flour really is *not* pleasant raw, so lick the mixing spoon at your own peril!

If you don't have an 11-inch loose-bottomed tart pan, a 9-inch pie plate is fine.

2 teaspoons olive oil

½ cup finely chopped onion (about ½ medium onion)

2 garlic cloves, minced

One 12-ounce package tofu, extra-firm regular (water-packed)

2 tablespoons fresh tarragon, chopped finely, or 2 teaspoons dried

2 tablespoons chickpea flour

2 tablespoons soy creamer or soy milk (see page 16)

1 tablespoon tapioca starch

1 tablespoon nutritional yeast

1 teaspoon salt

¼ teaspoon mustard powder

Freshly ground black pepper

1 cup thawed, drained frozen "petits pois" peas

¼ cup vegan cream cheese, broken into ½-teaspoon pieces

1 prebaked pie crust, such as Plain Pie Crust (page 169) or Savory Cornmeal Pie Crust (page 170), made in an 11-inch loose-bottomed tart pan if possible

1. Preheat the oven to 375°F.
2. In a medium skillet over medium heat, sauté the onions for about 8 minutes, until very soft and translucent. Add the garlic and sauté for 2 minutes more. Remove from the heat, and transfer to a large bowl.
3. In a blender or food processor, blend the ingredients from tofu through pepper until very smooth. Scrape down the sides as required.
4. Transfer to the mixing bowl and gently stir in the peas and onion mixture. Add the cream cheese chunks and fold in as gently as possible to avoid breaking them up. I find the easiest way to add the cream cheese is to use a spoon to drop the chunks randomly spaced into the filling mixture and then fold to just incorporate them.
5. Scrape the filling into the prepared crust, smooth until even, and bake for 35 to 40 minutes, until the filling is firm and golden. If using a pie plate instead of the larger tart pan, use the longer time, even adding another 5 minutes if necessary, because the filling will be deeper if the outside circumference is smaller.
6. Remove from the oven and let cool in the pan for 15 to 20 minutes prior to serving, if serving warm.

Pesto Muffins

MAKES 12 MUFFINS

▶ NO SOY • NO SUGAR

I say "I love . . ." too often, but here's another one. In summer, when there is an abundance of basil, I love making pesto! I also love muffins, in case you hadn't noticed, so here's a way to combine both these loves.

These are great as a snack, and also with salad at lunchtime or alongside pasta at dinnertime.

1¼ cups whole-wheat pastry flour

1 cup all-purpose flour

2 tablespoons nutritional yeast

2½ teaspoons baking powder

1 teaspoon baking soda

1 teaspoon salt

½ teaspoon freshly ground black pepper

1 cup Basic Basil Pesto (recipe follows)

1⅓ cups rice milk

1. Preheat the oven to 375°F and prepare twelve cups of a muffin pan by spraying with nonstick cooking spray.

2. In a large bowl, whisk together the ingredients from flour through pepper, then make a well and add the pesto and rice milk. Stir to just combine.

3. Spoon the mixture into the muffin pan. The cups will be full. Be sure to fill any unused cups with water, so the pan won't warp.

4. Bake for 20 to 22 minutes, until a toothpick comes out clean.

5. Remove from the oven and let cool in pan for 5 minutes, then transfer to a wire rack and let cool completely.

★ Basic Basil Pesto

MAKES 1½ CUPS PESTO

▶ NO SOY • NO SUGAR • NO WHEAT

This is my go-to pesto recipe, which I have also incorporated into recipe for Savory Pinwheels (page 212). The pesto recipe makes more than is needed for either recipe, so keep the rest in the fridge covered with a thin layer of olive oil to prevent discoloration, and use within 5 days on pasta, pizza, toast . . . wherever you'd like extra pesto yummyness.

4 cups fresh basil leaves (1 to 2 bunches)

4 garlic cloves, chopped roughly

1 cup pine nuts (see Note)

⅓ cup nutritional yeast

¼ cup olive oil

2 tablespoons water

½ teaspoon salt

1. Combine all the ingredients in a blender or food processor and blend until very smooth. You'll need to scrape down the sides a few times to ensure it's well mixed.

NOTE:

❖ Substitute walnuts or almonds for the pine nuts, if you'd prefer.

Variation

Basil and Cilantro Pesto
Replace up to 2 cups of the basil with fresh cilantro.

Roasted Garlic and Peppercorn Crackers 📷

MAKES ABOUT 36 CRACKERS

▶ NO NUTS • NO SUGAR

This is my husband's favorite flavor combination for bread bought fresh from the store. While I do bake bread with these flavors at home, I was curious to see how they would work as a cracker. I tried it and, wow, they are good. The garlic isn't too overpowering, and the peppercorns give them a nice little bite!

1¼ cups + 2 tablespoons all-purpose flour

1 teaspoon baking powder

1 teaspoon salt

½ teaspoon black peppercorns, partially crushed (see Notes)

1 head garlic, roasted and squeezed out (see Notes)

¼ cup vegan margarine

2 tablespoons vegan shortening

4 to 5 tablespoons soy milk

1. Preheat the oven to 400°F and line two baking sheets with parchment paper.

2. Sift together the ingredients from flour through salt into a large bowl. Stir in the crushed peppercorns.

3. Using a pastry cutter (or two knives held together), cut in the margarine, shortening, and roasted garlic until the mixture resembles coarse bread crumbs.

4. Make a well in the center and add 4 tablespoons of the milk. Mix to form stiff dough. If more liquid is required, add more milk by the teaspoonful until the dough holds together when pressed.

5. Press the dough into a ball and, on a lightly floured board, roll out to ⅛-inch thick or less. Using a 2-inch-diameter cookie cutter, cut out the crackers and place 1 inch apart on the prepared pan. Reroll and cut the scraps for more crackers.

6. Prick the crackers with a fork and bake for 8 to 10 minutes, until golden brown.

7. Remove from the oven and let cool on the baking sheet for 5 minutes, then let cool completely on a wire rack.

8. Once completely cool, store in a covered container.

NOTES:

❖ To partially crush the peppercorns, I place them in a small plastic bag and crush with my rolling pin.

❖ To roast the garlic, preheat the oven to 400°F. Remove the loose papery skin from the outside

of the garlic head, and slice off the top ¼ inch of the head, removing the tops of most of the cloves. Place the trimmed garlic on a square of tinfoil and drizzle a little olive oil over it. Wrap the garlic in the foil and place in the oven for 20 to 25 minutes, until soft to the touch. Let cool to make handling easier, then peel, reserving the roasted cloves.

Variations

"Cheesy" Garlic and Peppercorn Crackers

Sprinkle each cracker with a little finely grated vegan cheese before baking.

Healthier Garlic and Peppercorn Crackers

Use half all-purpose flour and half whole-wheat pastry flour.

Roasted Garlic and Fennel Crackers

Replace the crushed peppercorns with crushed fennel seeds, for a variation suggested by my tester Liz.

Savory "Cheesy" Biscuits

MAKES ABOUT 15 BISCUITS

▶ NO SUGAR • PEANUT ALERT!

At school in New Zealand, we had to take what used to be called Home Economics. One of the very first recipes we made was cheese scones. I used to love those things. Although these are not quite the same, when I get a craving for them, I go for these.

The vegan cheese is a nice addition and makes them extra tasty, but they're just as good without it.

1 cup plain soy milk

1 teaspoon apple cider vinegar

2¼ cups all-purpose flour

3 tablespoons nutritional yeast

2½ teaspoons baking powder

1 teaspoon salt

½ teaspoon dry mustard

Pinch of freshly ground black pepper

¼ cup vegan margarine

3 tablespoons smooth natural peanut butter

¼ cup grated vegan cheese (optional)

3 tablespoons crushed peanuts (see Notes)

Vegan cheese, for sprinkling (optional)

1. Preheat the oven to 400°F and line a baking sheet with parchment paper.

2. In a small bowl, mix together the soy milk and vinegar, and set aside for 5 minutes to curdle.

3. Sift together the dry ingredients (from flour through black pepper), into a large bowl.

4. Using a pastry cutter (or two knives held together), cut the margarine into the flour mixture until the mixture resembles pebbly sand. (See Notes.)

5. Whisk the peanut butter into the milk until smooth.

6. Lightly stir the soy milk mixture, peanuts, and cheese (if using) into the dry ingredients.

7. Turn onto a lightly floured board and knead once or twice. Pat into a rectangular shape about 1 inch thick. Cut into 2-inch squares and place on the prepared sheet. Sprinkle the tops with a little cheese, if desired.

8. Bake for 12 to 15 minutes, until risen and lightly browned. The bottoms will be a slightly darker but still lightly browned.

9. Remove from the oven and let cool on the sheet for 5 minutes, then transfer to a wire rack and let cool completely.

NOTES:

❖ To crush such a small amount of nuts, I either use a spice grinder or place them in a small resealable plastic bag and pass my rolling pin over them a few times.

❖ If you would prefer to use a fork for the cutting in the fat and mixing in the peanut butter, go right ahead. One of my testers found this to be the easiest way.

Savory Herbed Crackers

MAKES ABOUT 36 CRACKERS

▶ **NO NUTS • NO SUGAR**

I debated whether to call these crackers or savory cookies. I went with crackers, even though they aren't as thin or crispy as crackers you buy in the store. The cayenne provides just a little bite at the end; if you like your crackers spicier, use more! These are great with a little vegan cheese or a slice of tomato, or just as they are, for when you don't want a sweet snack.

A great project for rainy days with children (sans cayenne); use whatever shapes or sizes you want for the cutters. Just keep an eye on the time so they don't burn!

1 cup all-purpose flour

1 teaspoon baking powder

¾ teaspoon salt

½ teaspoon dried oregano

½ teaspoon dried marjoram

¼ teaspoon dried basil

¼ teaspoon freshly ground black pepper
⅛ teaspoon cayenne, or to taste

¼ cup vegan margarine
2 tablespoons vegan shortening

5 to 6 tablespoons soy milk
1 teaspoon agave nectar

1. Preheat the oven to 400°F and line two baking sheets with parchment paper.

2. Sift together the ingredients from flour through cayenne, into a large bowl.

3. Using a pastry cutter (or two knives held together), cut in the margarine and shortening until the mixture resembles coarse bread crumbs.

4. Make a well in the center and add the agave nectar and five tablespoons of milk. Mix to form a stiff dough. If more liquid is required, add more milk by the teaspoonful until the dough holds together when pressed.

5. Press the dough into a ball. Then, on a lightly floured board, roll to ⅛-inch thick or less. Using a 2-inch-diameter cookie cutter, cut out the crackers and place 1 inch apart on the prepared sheet. Reroll and cut the scraps for more crackers.

6. Prick the crackers with a fork and bake for 8 to 10 minutes, until golden brown.

7. Remove from the oven and let cool on sheet for 5 minutes, then transfer to a wire rack and let cool completely.

8. Once completely cool, store in a covered container.

Variations

"Cheesy" Herbed Crackers
Sprinkle the top of each cracker with a little finely grated vegan cheese prior to baking.

Seeded Herbed Crackers
Add up to 2 tablespoons of small seeds (hemp, chia, sesame, and/or poppy) with the dry ingredients, for a seeded cracker.

Healthier Herbed Crackers
Use half all-purpose and half whole-wheat pastry flour, for a healthier cracker.

Spanikopita Loaf

MAKES ONE 9-INCH LOAF

▶ NO SUGAR

Inspired by that quintessential Greek dish of the same name, and containing spinach and walnuts for your tasting delight, a slice of this is perfect for snacktime.

The loaf is moist and a little delicate, perfect for eating on its own. It is not so great for sandwiches, though if you toast it first, it holds together better. The crust is nice and crisp, and the insides delectably soft.

1¼ cups soy milk
½ cup tofu, firm silken (vacuum-packed, one third of a 12-ounce package)
¼ cup olive oil
2 tablespoons freshly squeezed lemon juice (1 medium lemon)

1½ cups whole-wheat pastry flour
1 cup all-purpose flour
2½ teaspoons baking powder
1¼ teaspoons salt
1 teaspoon dried oregano
¾ teaspoon baking soda
½ teaspoon dried marjoram
¼ teaspoon ground nutmeg

One 10-ounce package frozen chopped spinach, thawed and squeezed to remove liquid (about ⅔ cup after squeezing) (see Notes)

½ cup finely chopped walnuts (see Notes)

2 spring onions (scallions), chopped finely (about ¼ cup)

1. Preheat the oven to 350°F and line a 9-inch loaf pan with parchment paper.

2. Using your blender or food processor, blend together the tofu, lemon juice, soy milk, and oil until smooth and creamy.

3. Sift together the ingredients from flour through nutmeg into a large bowl. Using your fingers, toss in the spinach, walnuts, and onion, breaking up any clusters of spinach you come across.

4. Make a well in the center of the dry ingredients and add the tofu mixture. Stir to just combine, then spoon the mixture into the prepared pan.

5. Bake for 42 to 47 minutes, until a toothpick comes out clean.

6. Remove from the oven and let cool in the pan for 10 minutes, then transfer to a wire rack and let cool completely.

NOTES:

❖ If you want to use fresh spinach, start with about 4 cups, then wilt in a pan over medium heat with a splash of water, let cool, and squeeze out any liquid.

❖ If you don't want to get out your food processor for such a small amount, place the whole nuts in a resealable plastic bag and use your rolling pin to crush by rolling back and forth.

Spicy Corn Biscotti

MAKES ABOUT 16 BISCOTTI

▶ NO NUTS

These aren't as super crunchy crisp as commercially made biscotti. I blame it on the moisture from the corn, but they are very tasty. Perfect as an anytime snack, but I really think they come into their own served alongside a bowl of chili, for dunking, or with a thick bean soup.

2¼ cups all-purpose flour

½ cup cornmeal (see page 15)

2 tablespoons cornstarch

1 tablespoon granulated sugar

1¼ teaspoons salt

¾ teaspoon baking soda

½ teaspoon ancho chile powder

½ teaspoon dried oregano

¼ teaspoon ground cumin

¼ teaspoon garlic powder

⅛ to ¼ teaspoon chile flakes, or to taste

½ cup corn kernels (if from a can, well drained)

¾ cup + 2 tablespoons soy milk

¾ cup vegan vegetable stock

¼ cup (2½ ounces) tofu, firm silken (vacuum-packed)

1. Preheat the oven to 350°F and line a large baking sheet with parchment paper.

2. Sift together the dry ingredients (from flour through chile flakes), into a large bowl. Stir in the corn kernels.

3. Using a blender or food processor, blend the soy milk, stock, and tofu until smooth.

4. Add the wet ingredients to the dry and mix to just combine. The dough will be quite wet yet firm.

5. Using dampened hands and a rubber spatula, shape the dough into a 13 by 4-inch wide log, about 1½ inches high, on the baking sheet.

6. Bake for 30 minutes, until lightly browned and firm to the touch.

7. Remove from the oven and let cool on the sheet for about 1 hour, until completely cool (a longer cooling time is better for ease of slicing). Turn off the heat if not using the oven in the meantime, then reheat to 350°F when needed.

8. Transfer the cooled log to a cutting board and slice, on a long diagonal, into strips ½ to no more than ¾ inch thick (closer to ½ inch is better, otherwise the center will stay too moist).

9. Place the slices back on the baking sheet, standing on their short edge, if possible, and bake for a further 30 minutes, until very firm and crisp looking. (See Note.)

10. Turn off the heat, open the oven door slightly, and let the biscotti cool in the oven for 30 minutes before removing.

11. Remove from the oven, let cool on the sheet for 5 minutes, then transfer to a wire rack and let cool completely.

12. Store in a covered container.

NOTE:

❖ If you can't stand all the slices on the baking sheet (or they fall), put them cut side down. Flip halfway through the second baking, to ensure even browning.

Spicy Spinach and Cream Cheese Muffins

MAKES 12 MUFFINS

▶ **NO NUTS • NO SUGAR**

My sister Fiona works in Wellington, New Zealand, which, from what I hear, is surprisingly vegan friendly. The (nonvegan) original of these muffins was available at a place down the road from her work; she was upset when they were no longer on the menu. When I asked people to suggest flavor combinations for me to make, she immediately requested these!

One 10-ounce package frozen spinach, thawed (see Notes)

1¼ cups all-purpose flour

1 cup whole-wheat pastry flour

2½ teaspoons baking powder

1¼ teaspoons salt

¾ teaspoon paprika

½ teaspoon baking soda

½ teaspoon garlic powder

¼ teaspoon ground cumin

¼ teaspoon freshly ground black pepper

¼ to ½ teaspoon chile flakes, or to taste

2 cups soy milk

¼ cup canola oil

1½ tablespoons freshly squeezed lemon juice (1 medium lemon)

½ cup vegan cream cheese (about 4½ ounces)

1. Preheat the oven to 375°F and spray a twelve-cup muffin pan with nonstick spray.

2. Squeeze your thawed frozen spinach to remove as much water as possible. Then

squeeze again; you want all the liquid out of there. You'll end up with about ⅔ cup of spinach.

3. Sift together the dry ingredients (from flour through chile flakes), into a large bowl.

4. In another bowl, combine the soy milk, lemon juice, oil, and spinach. Mix well.

5. Using clean fingers, break off ½-inch bits of the cream cheese, and add to the dry ingredients. Toss very gently to coat with the flour.

6. Add the liquid ingredients and fold the mixture, but do not break up the cream cheese too much.

7. Carefully spoon into the prepared pans. The cups will be full. Fill any unused cups with water, to prevent the pan from warping.

8. Bake for 22 to 27 minutes, until a toothpick comes out clean. Be aware when testing that the cream cheese will not get firmer; if you test in a spot with cream cheese, there will be soft cheese on your toothpick. Retest where there is more likely to be baked dough. When lightly pressed, the tops of the muffins should bounce back.

9. Remove from the oven and let cool in the pan for 5 minutes. Transfer to a wire rack, and let cool completely.

NOTES:

❖ The standard size of a package of frozen chopped leaf spinach where I live is about 10 ounces (300 g). Use the closest you can find.

❖ If you want to use fresh spinach, start with about 4 cups, then wilt in a pan over medium heat with a splash of water, let cool, and squeeze out any liquid.

Sun-Dried Tomato, Olive, and Sausage Pie

SERVES 6 TO 8

▶ **NO NUTS • NO SOY • NO SUGAR**

This is a lovely savory pie, hearty enough to be dinner with a side of vegetables. One of my testers, Liz, assures me that kale is the perfect side for this. (Take it up with her, if you disagree!) It is also good for lunch, with a salad. The pie is good hot or cold and reheats well if wrapped in tinfoil and warmed in a 350°F oven for 15 or 20 minutes.

2 recipes Plain Pie Crust dough, savory variation (page 170), or enough store-bought pastry for a two-crust pie

¼ cup sun-dried tomatoes
½ cup boiling water

1 tablespoon olive oil
1 medium onion, chopped finely (about 1 cup)

½ recipe mini sausages from Sausage Rolls (page 232), made as 4 larger sausages, chopped into ½-inch pieces, or a store-bought equivalent (about 1¼ cups)

2 garlic cloves, minced

½ cup black olives, chopped roughly

½ cup + 2 tablespoons vegan vegetable stock
2 tablespoons tapioca starch or cornstarch
1 tablespoon tomato paste
1 teaspoon salt
½ teaspoon dried marjoram
¼ teaspoon ground fennel seeds

¼ teaspoon paprika

⅛ to ½ teaspoon chile flakes, or to taste (optional)

Freshly ground black pepper

Soy milk, for brushing

1. Prepare and prebake the bottom crust of the pie in a 9-inch pie plate, per instructions in the crust recipe (page 169). Keep the top crust dough wrapped in the fridge until required.

2. Preheat the oven to 375°F.

3. Combine sun-dried tomatoes and boiling water in a small bowl, cover, and soak for 15 minutes.

4. Sauté the onion in the oil for 5 minutes, add the sausages, and sauté for 5 minutes more, until the onion is soft. Add the garlic, sauté for a further 2 minutes, then remove from heat and add the olives.

5. In a blender or food processor, blend the soaked sun-dried tomatoes and their soaking water, the stock, starch, tomato paste, salt, and spices until very smooth. Scrape down the sides as required.

6. Add the blended mixture to the sausage mixture.

7. Scrape the filling into the prepared bottom crust. On a lightly floured board, roll out the top crust to a circle at least 1 inch wider all around than the pie plate, about ¼ inch thick. With a floured rolling pin, roll up the pastry from the board and transfer to top the filled pie. Crimp the edges to seal, using your thumb and first two fingers. With a knife, trim away any excess pastry and slit three vents in the top crust.

8. Decorate the top of the crust with shapes cut out of the excess pastry, if desired, and brush with a little soy milk.

9. Bake for 35 to 40 minutes, until the top crust is golden and the filling hot.

10. Remove from the oven and let cool in the pie plate for 15 to 20 minutes prior to serving. Serve hot or cold.

NOTE:

❖ A handy hint: Place the pie plate in the oven on a baking sheet, in case of any spills.

Tomato and Herb Biscotti

MAKES ABOUT 16 BISCOTTI

▶ **NO NUTS • NO SUGAR**

I made this one over and over and got incredibly frustrated, but finally I have it. These are lovely, richly tomato-flavored biscotti, a little delicate but perfect with soup, salad, pasta, chili, and as a savory snack.

1 cup all-purpose flour

1 cup whole-wheat pastry flour

½ cup cornmeal (see page 15)

2 tablespoons cornstarch

1 tablespoon fresh thyme, chopped finely (see Notes)

1 tablespoon fresh rosemary, chopped finely (see Notes)

1¼ teaspoons salt

¾ teaspoon baking soda

½ teaspoon dried marjoram

¼ teaspoon garlic powder

¼ teaspoon freshly ground black pepper

2 tablespoons finely chopped sun-dried tomatoes

1 cup vegan vegetable stock

¾ cup canned, crushed tomatoes

¼ cup (2½ ounces) tofu, firm silken (vacuum-packed)

2 teaspoons freshly squeezed lemon juice (½ medium lemon)

1. Preheat the oven to 350°F and line a large baking sheet with parchment paper.

2. Sift together the dry ingredients (from flour through black pepper), into a large bowl. Stir in the sun-dried tomatoes.

3. Using a blender or food processor, blend the stock, tomatoes, tofu, and lemon juice together until smooth and creamy.

4. Add the wet ingredients to the dry and mix to just combine. The dough will be quite wet yet firm.

5. Using dampened hands and a rubber spatula, shape the dough into a 12 by 4-inch log about 1½ inches high, on the baking sheet.

6. Bake for 30 minutes until lightly browned and firm to the touch.

7. Remove from the oven and let on the sheet for at least 1 hour until completely cool (a longer standing time is better, for ease of slicing). Turn off the heat if not using the oven in the meantime, then reheat to 350°F when needed.

8. Transfer the cooled log to a cutting board and slice, on a diagonal, into strips ½ to ¾ inch thick (no more than ¾ inch, otherwise the center will stay too moist).

9. Place the slices back on the baking sheet, standing on their short edge, if possible, and bake for a further 35 to 40 minutes, until very firm and crisp looking. (See Notes.)

10. Turn off the heat, and let the biscotti cool in the oven with its door shut for 20 minutes. Then let cool inside the oven, with the door open, for a further 30 minutes, until the oven is cool.

11. Store in a covered container.

NOTES:

❖ Although fresh is best, it works perfectly well to substitute 1 teaspoon of dried herbs for the tablespoon of fresh.

❖ If you can't stand all the slices on the baking sheet (or they fall), put them cut side down. Flip halfway through the second baking, to ensure even browning.

Upside-Down Olive, Sun-Dried Tomato, and Roasted Red Pepper "Cake"

SERVES 6 TO 8

▶ **NO NUTS • NO SUGAR**

A slice of this is perfect for lunch on a summer day with a nice salad on the side and a long cool drink at your elbow. Good hot and cold.

½ cup sun-dried tomatoes

1 roasted red pepper, sliced into thin strips (see Notes)
½ cup black olives, sliced

1¼ cups soy milk
1 tablespoon freshly squeezed lemon juice (½ medium lemon)

1 cup whole-wheat pastry flour
1 cup all-purpose flour
2 teaspoons baking powder
½ teaspoon salt (see Notes)
½ teaspoon baking soda
½ teaspoon garlic powder
¼ teaspoon dried sage
¼ teaspoon dried thyme

¼ cup olive oil

3 tablespoons finely chopped red onion

1. Preheat the oven to 400°F and grease an 8-inch springform cake pan with olive oil or spray it with nonstick spray.

2. Soak the sun-dried tomatoes in boiling water for 10 minutes, until softened. Slice into thin slices.

3. Arrange the sun-dried tomato slices, sliced black olives, and red pepper slices in an attractive pattern on the bottom of the cake pan. Finely chop any unused toppings and place in a bowl for later.

4. In a small bowl, combine the soy milk and lemon juice, and set aside for 5 minutes to curdle.

5. Sift together the ingredients from flour through thyme into a large bowl. Make a well and add the soy milk mixture, onion, oil, and finely chopped reserved toppings. Mix to just combine.

6. Transfer the dough into your prepared pan, taking care not to disturb your pretty arrangement. The dough will be quite thick and wet.

7. Bake for 30 to 35 minutes, or until a toothpick comes out clean.

8. Remove from the oven and let cool in the pan for 5 minutes before removing the collar and inverting onto a wire rack to cool further.

9. Allow to cool for at least 15 minutes if serving warm, for ease of slicing. Serve warm or cold.

NOTES:

❖ If you buy roasted pepper packed in oil, skip the roasting part.

❖ To roast a red pepper, if doing it yourself, slice in half and remove the seeds and membranes. Heat your grill (broiler) and place the pepper cut side down on a tinfoil-lined baking sheet. Place under the grill and roast until the skin of the pepper gets blackened. Remove from the heat, then using the tinfoil lining, wrap up your pepper completely and leave for 5 minutes or so; this will make it sweat, and the skin will be easier to remove. Once you can handle your pepper without burning your hands, peel off and discard the skin and slice as required.

❖ There isn't a lot of extra salt in this one, as the olives are quite salty. If you are a salt fiend, you can increase the salt in the recipe to 1 teaspoon.

Variation

Use your favorite vegetables as a topping on the bottom of this "cake." Other topping suggestions:

✳ Sliced tomato

✳ Lightly cooked asparagus

✳ Sliced red onion

✳ Sliced zucchini

✳ Leftover roasted or grilled vegetables

✳ Corn kernels

✳ Crushed chile flakes or finely chopped chile peppers

✳ Whatever you fancy, really

Sauces, Icings, and Toppings

Buttercream, More or Less

Crazy Whip Topping

Date Paste

Drizzle Icing

Ganache-Style Chocolate

Sugar Glaze

THESE ARE THE recipes that are used throughout the book to elevate your baking from great to sublime! They don't "belong" to any one recipe, as such (a sauce, icing, or topping that is for use with a specific recipe can be found with that recipe), so they need their own section. They are used with a variety of goodies from the other sections. Consider them the mix-and-match accompaniments of the baking world, and use at your discretion.

Most of these store well in the fridge, though many do get firmer the longer they are stored. If this happens, they all can be heated in the microwave to restore them to a soft and usable texture. Please, try to stop eating any leftovers straight from the container in the fridge!

Buttercream, More or Less

MAKES ABOUT 3 CUPS BUTTERCREAM

▶ **NO NUTS • NO WHEAT**

I love the rich, creamy taste of this buttercream. This is helped by having shortening and margarine in it, and the resulting flavor and fluff. The "More or Less" refers to the firmness of the icing, and is up to you. If you want a firmer buttercream, use the coconut oil as stated; this is my preference. As coconut oil is solid at room temperature, by refrigerating the cream, it becomes harder and holds its shape. By using no coconut oil, you get a softer, creamier buttercream. If you choose not to use the coconut oil, increase the amount of shortening by 1 tablespoon. My children, who despise coconut, gobble this up, so there is no taste or flavor issue.

This recipe lends itself well to flavoring and coloring to suit all your frosting needs! As written, there is enough for spreading on a batch of cupcakes or a single layer cake, if you don't go "over the top." If you want to be fancy and pipe the frosting, or be super-duper generous with it, double the recipe. You can always keep some in the fridge for another day.

And, speaking of fridges, if you refrigerate coconut oil (including any frosting leftovers), you'll notice that it gets very hard. To use, allow to come to room temperature, which will take a while, or microwave briefly on high (in 5- or 10-second bursts), until soft enough to spread.

1 tablespoon coconut oil (see above)

¼ cup vegan margarine
2 tablespoons vegan shortening

½ teaspoon vanilla extract

¼ teaspoon other extract to match your recipe, or more vanilla (see Note)

2 cups confectioners' sugar, sifted if lumpy

3 to 5 teaspoons soy milk or soy creamer (see page 16)

1. If your coconut oil is very hard (this will depend on the temperature in your kitchen), microwave on high in 5-second bursts until soft but not melted. Add the shortening and margarine; cream until well combined and fluffy, with no lumps. If creaming by hand, a whisk does this part of the job best.

2. Add the extracts and mix well.

3. Add the confectioners' sugar and mix well, until quite crumbly looking. If mixing by hand, a wooden spoon is your best bet here.

4. Add the soy milk a teaspoonful at a time, so you can judge the consistency. Mix until well combined and at the level of fluffiness you desire.

NOTE:
❖ Instead of using the extracts you can add espresso, spices, or anything you can think of for flavoring, and even create an adults-only buttercream by adding an alcohol flavoring.

Crazy Whip Topping

MAKES LOTS, ABOUT 3 CUPS TOPPING

▶ **NO NUTS • NO WHEAT**

A spoonable vegan cream like the dairy topping you store in the freezer? Who would have thought?

While I was growing up in rural New Zealand in the late '70s/early '80s, there wasn't a commercial version of this in the stores, and, even if there were, I doubt very much that Mum (or Dad) would have allowed it in the house. You know what product I'm talking about, right? According to my testers, this is somewhat similar, but not so similar that you'd mistake it for the "real thing."

Use as you would cream or ice cream; for adding a topping to sweet biscuits, scones, or pies; or anywhere you'd like a little cool, sweet yummyness.

6 ounces tofu, firm silken (vacuum-packed, half of a 12-ounce package)

2 cups confectioners' sugar

1 cup canola oil

⅔ cup soy milk

1 tablespoon freshly squeezed lemon juice (½ medium lemon)

1 teaspoon vanilla extract

1. Place all the ingredients in a blender. Start slowly, then increase the speed to blend until completely smooth and thick. Scrape down the sides as required.

2. Place in a sealable container and store in your freezer. The longer you leave it, the harder it will get; it will still be scoopable, but more like ice cream. If you are storing for longer than a couple of weeks, place some in the fridge for a few hours prior to serving (it will melt a little at room temperature) to get a more scoopable texture.

Variations

The permutations are endless, so think up some of your own. Here are a few of mine:

Lemon Topping

Replace ½ teaspoon of the vanilla extract with lemon extract and add 1 teaspoon lemon zest.

Lime Topping

Use lime juice instead of lemon juice and add 1 teaspoon of lime zest.

Orange Topping

You guessed it. Orange juice instead of lemon juice, ½ teaspoon of orange extract instead of the vanilla and add 1 teaspoon of orange zest.

Berry Topping

Fold ½ cup of Strawberry Sauce (page 94) or Blueberry Sauce (page 109) into the topping just prior to serving.

Pineapple Topping

Fold ½ cup of drained, crushed, canned pineapple into the topping just prior to serving.

Nutty Topping

Fold ½ cup of your favorite toasted and chopped nut into the topping just prior to serving.

Date Paste

MAKES 1 CUP DATE PASTE

▶ NO NUTS • NO SOY • NO SUGAR • NO WHEAT

This is used in a number of recipes, including but not limited to Date Pinwheels (page 200), Sticky Toffee Pudding Cake (page 111), Spiced Raisin Breakfast Cake (page 110), and Date and Pecan Cookies (page 132). I thought it would be handy for it to have a reference page all of its own. The amounts can be varied to suit the recipe, just ensure you have equal amounts of dates and water, which equal the amount of paste you need, to start with.

It is easy to make in advance and store in the fridge for up to a week in a covered container.

1 cup whole dried dates

1 cup water

1. In a small pan, soak the dates in the water for 1 hour.
2. Bring to a boil over high heat, lower the heat to medium, and boil for 10 minutes, adding water by the tablespoonful, if required, to prevent the mixture from sticking.
3. Remove from the heat and let cool for 10 minutes.
4. Mash with a fork, or use an immersion blender, to a thick paste.
5. Keep at room temperature until required if using right away; otherwise, store in the fridge and bring to room temperature prior to using.
6. If you have less than 1 cup of paste after cooking as directed, add unsweetened applesauce to make up to the required quantity.

Drizzle Icing

THE YIELD DEPENDS ON THE THICKNESS OF THE ICING

▶ **NO NUTS · NO WHEAT**

You can use this for anything, depending on how thick you make it. From piping designs on cakes to giving your loaf a Jackson Pollock makeover, this is a great icing to know. It also lends itself to the addition of both flavor extracts and colors. Brilliant!

If you have leftovers and are storing them in the fridge, allow the icing to come to room temperature, then stir well prior to using.

1 tablespoon vegan margarine

1 drop of vegan food coloring of choice (optional)

¼ teaspoon flavored extract (vanilla if no other flavor is desired)

¾ cup confectioners' sugar

Water (amount details follow)

1. In a small bowl, cream the margarine. You want it quite fluffy. Add the food coloring (if using) and flavoring. Mix well to incorporate.
2. Add the confectioners' sugar and mix well. You'll end up with what looks like a crumbly powder.
3. Add water by the ¼ teaspoon, for consistency control, to obtain your desired thickness. I've found:
   - 2½ teaspoons of water gives a consistency for piping.
   - 1 tablespoon of water gives a spreadable consistency.
   - 3½ teaspoons of water gives a thick drizzle.
   - 4 teaspoons of water gives a thinner drizzling consistency.
4. Use as desired or directed.

NOTE:

❖ For an adult taste, substitute a liqueur for the extracts!

Ganache-Style Chocolate

MAKES A LITTLE MORE THAN ½ CUP GANACHE

▶ **NO NUTS • NO WHEAT**

Do you need instructions on where to use this? Everywhere!

Using the smaller amount of creamer makes quite a thick ganache. If you want it a little thinner, maybe for drizzling and not spreading, use the larger amount. You can always add more later if you're not sure, so start with the lesser amount.

½ cup good-quality vegan chocolate chips, or a vegan bar chocolate cut into small pieces

1 tablespoon brown rice syrup

1½ to 2 tablespoons soy creamer (see page 16)

1. Melt the chocolate chips, either in the microwave on high in 15-second bursts, stirring after each heating, or over a double boiler, stirring frequently.

2. Add the other ingredients and stir until well mixed and starting to thicken.

3. Let cool for 10 minutes prior to using, stirring every now and then.

4. Store leftovers (ha!) in the fridge and heat gently (as you did to melt the chocolate) prior to using.

Sugar Glaze

MAKES ABOUT ¼ CUP GLAZE

▶ **NO NUTS • NO SOY • NO WHEAT**

An all-purpose, change-to-suit-your-recipe, icing-type glaze that can be poured either over warm baking for a thin, crustlike glaze, or over a cold baked item for a thicker, more icinglike glaze.

½ cup confectioners' sugar, sifted if lumpy

1 tablespoon water

¼ teaspoon flavoring (see Variations)

1. In a small bowl, combine all the ingredients and mix until smooth.

2. Pour over the baked item and spread with the back of a spoon as required.

3. Sprinkle the glaze with an appropriate garnish while still wet, if desired.

Variations

Vanilla Glaze
Add ¼ teaspoon of vanilla extract.

Lemon Glaze
Add ¼ teaspoon of lemon extract, and garnish with lemon zest.

Orange Glaze
Add ¼ teaspoon of orange extract, and garnish with orange zest.

Almond Glaze
Add ¼ teaspoon of almond extract, and garnish with finely chopped almonds.

Cinnamon Glaze
Add ¼ teaspoon of ground cinnamon.

Ginger Glaze
Add ¼ teaspoon of ground ginger, and garnish with chopped crystallized ginger.

Allergy and Suitability Information

Because they are vegan, *all* the recipes in this book are dairy and egg free.

The following recipes as written are free of other common allergens.

WHEAT-FREE RECIPES (MANY STILL CONTAIN GLUTEN)

Bars, Slices, and Squares

Agave Crackle Cups (page 53)
Chocolate Crackle Cups (page 56)
Reindeer Squares (page 66)
Rich Brownies (page 68)

Biscuits, Scones, and Loaves

Spelt Coconut Chip Biscuits (page 85)
Straight-Up Spelt Banana Bread (page 87)

Cookies

Spelt Carob Cookies (page 138)
Spelt Jam Thumbprint Cookies (page 138)

Muffins

Apricot and Cranberry Muffins (page 145)
Beet Chocolate Muffins (page 147)
Caribbean-Inspired Muffins (page 150)
Zucchini and Currant Muffins (page 162)

Pies, Tarts, and Handheld Pastries

Savory Cornmeal Pie Crust (page 170)
Sweet Cornmeal Pie Crust (page 171)
(You'll Never Guess What's in This) Chocolate Pie (page 174)
Bakewell Tart (page 174)
Buttery Tarts (page 175)
Coconut and Pecan Chocolate Pie (page 176)
Creamy Dreamy Lemon Mousse Pie (page 177)
Lime Coconut Tart (page 181)
Sticky Nut Pie (page 184)
Sweet Potato Pie (page 185)
White Balsamic Fruit Tarts with Jam Glaze (page 187)

Savory Goodies

Arugula and Pine Nut Muffins (page 225)
Arugula Tart (page 225)
Asparagus, Pine Nut, and Roasted Garlic Quiche (page 226)
Pea, Tarragon, and Cream Cheese Tart (page 234)

Sauces, Icing, and Toppings

Buttercream, More or Less (page 249)
Crazy Whip Topping (page 249)
Date Paste (page 250)

NUT-FREE RECIPES

Bars, Slices, and Squares

Agave Crackle Cups (page 53)
Banana and Chocolate Chip Biscotti (page 53)
Chocolate Cereal Squares (page 56)
Chocolate Crackle Cups (page 56)
Currant Squares (page 57)
Ginger Crunch (page 59)
Lemon Bars (page 60)
Mini Lavender Bites with Sour Cream Icing (page 61)
Nanaimo Bars (page 63)
Rhubarb Squares (page 67)
Shortbread (page 70)
Two-Bite Chocolate Chunk Brownies (page 72)

Biscuits, Scones, and Loaves

Apple Tea Loaf (page 75)
British Scones (page 76)
Carrot and Pineapple Scones (page 77)
Chai Chocolate Mini Loaves (page 78)
Cranberry Scones (page 78)
Date Biscuits (page 79)
Gingerbread (page 81)
Jaffa (Chocolate and Orange Marble) Loaf (page 81)
Lemon and Blueberry Biscuits (page 83)
Lime and Poppy Seed Loaf (page 84)
Spelt Coconut Chip Biscuits (page 85)
Spiced Raisin Whole-Wheat Scones (page 86)
Straight-Up Spelt Banana Bread (page 87)
Sunny Sunflower Tea Loaf (page 88)

Cakes and Cupcakes

Balsamic Berry Bundt Cake (page 93)
Berry-Infused Cupcakes (page 94)
Citrus Bundt Cake (page 95)
Coffee and Caramel Cupcakes (page 96)
Cola Chocolate Cupcakes (page 97)
Espresso Chocolate-Chip Coffee Cake (page 98)
Lamingtons (page 102)
Secret-Ingredient Chocolate Cake with Blueberry Cream (page 108)
Sticky Toffee Pudding Cake (page 111)
Tropical Pineapple Cake with Coconut Ice Icing (page 112)
Vanilla Bean Cupcakes (page 114)
Zebra Cake (page 115)

Cookies

Car Tire Cookies (page 119)
Cocoa Oatmeal Cookies with Cocoa Nibs (page 120)
Coconut Cookies (page 121)
Coconut and Oatmeal Cookies (page 122)
Gingered Chocolate Chip Cookies (page 124)
Green Tea Latte Cookies (page 124)
No-Bake Apricot Cookies (page 126)
No-Bake Chocolate Truffle–Inspired Cookies (page 128)
Oatmeal Raisin Cookies (page 129)
Orange Chocolate-Chip Cookies (page 130)
Pinkalicious Cookies (page 132)
Plain Cookies (page 133)
Princess Cookies (page 136)
Seed Cookies (page 137)
Spelt Carob Cookies (page 138)
Spelt Jam Thumbprint Cookies (page 138)
White Cookies (page 139)
Whole-Wheat Rum Raisin Cookies (page 140)

Muffins

Apricot and Cranberry Muffins (page 145)
Beet Chocolate Muffins (page 147)
Blackberry and Apple Crumble Muffins (page 148)

REFINED SUGAR–FREE RECIPES

While it is not an allergen, you may appreciate knowing these recipes are free of refined sugar.

Bars, Slices, and Squares
Agave Crackle Cups (page 53)

Biscuits, Scones, and Loaves
Date Biscuits (page 79)

Cakes and Cupcakes
Spiced Raisin Breakfast Cake (page 110)

Cookies
Cocoa Oatmeal Cookies with Cocoa Nibs (page 120)
Maple Crosshatch Cookies (page 126)
Whole-Wheat Rum Raisin Cookies (page 140)

Muffins
Apricot and Cranberry Muffins (page 145)
Corny Corn Bread Muffins (page 152)

Pies, Tarts, and Handheld Pastries
Savory Cornmeal Pie Crust (page 170)
(You'll Never Guess What's in This) Chocolate Pie (page 174)
Vanilla Crème Puffs (page 186)

Yeasted Treats
Canadian Anniversary Bread (page 196)
Date Pinwheels (page 200)
Walnut and Banana Cinnamon Rolls (page 220)

Savory Goodies
Arugula and Pine Nut Muffins (page 225)
Arugula Tart (page 225)
Asparagus, Pine Nut, and Roasted Garlic Quiche (page 226)
Chile and Cilantro Corn Bread (page 227)
Mini Cheese and Onion Pasties (page 231)
Mini Sausage Rolls (page 232)
Oven Potato Farls (page 234)
Pea, Tarragon, and Cream Cheese Tart (page 234)
Pesto Muffins (page 235)
Roasted Garlic and Peppercorn Crackers (page 236)
Savory "Cheesy" Biscuits (page 237)
Savory Herbed Crackers (page 238)
Spanikopita Loaf (page 239)
Spicy Spinach and Cream Cheese Muffins (page 241)
Sun-Dried Tomato, Olive, and Sausage Pie (page 242)
Tomato and Herb Biscotti (page 243)
Upside-Down Olive, Sun-Dried Tomato, and Red Pepper "Cake" (page 244)

Sauces, Icing, and Toppings
Date Paste (page 250)

PEANUT ALERT!

Be aware that the following recipes contain peanuts, so do not make them if you are unsure of the allergy status of the person who will be eating the baked good, if sharing in any situation. If selling at a bake sale, ensure the ingredients list is prominently displayed.

Bars, Slices, and Squares
Elvis Blondies (page 58)
Rocky Road Brownies (page 69)

Cakes and Cupcakes
PB&J Marble Cupcakes (page 106)
Peanut Buttercream (page 107)

CHILD-FRIENDLY RECIPES

While all of the recipes are suitable for everyone, the following are more geared to pleasing a child's taste (or at least my children and the children of my testers). It depends on the child, of course, I don't want to make any assumptions here!

Acknowledgments

Lots of people to thank. Bear with me.

I mentioned my wonderful family in the dedication, but can't let this opportunity pass to say a big "Thanks!" to them again.

Thanks to Mum for teaching me how to bake and cook and for having the rule that we make it ourselves! And to Dad for being so very pedantic that he makes the perfect proof-reader (and other things, too, you know that). To all my siblings, thanks for being such very good sisters and brother, and aunts and uncle, too! Thanks to my sisters Fiona Wellgreen and Linda Findon, for even testing recipes for me! Then to my sister Sonia Swan, and my brother Iain Wells, who didn't test for me; I know you wanted to, really, and were with me in spirit, so thanks for good wishes and support sent over the miles and over Facebook.

I must thank my wonderful recipe testers who, from all points on the globe, signed up to be part of this adventure with me. They bought ingredients they'd never bought before, made things for the first time, and discovered that they liked things they never thought they would. Thank you to them and their families, house mates, neighbors, work mates and friends for baking up a storm, eating loads, and giving great feedback. In random order, thanks to:

In Europe
Lane Wiseman, Grafenwoehr, Germany
Shirley Saliniemi, Finland
Liz Wyman, England
Jennifer Talbot, Spain

In Australasia
Fiona W., Wellington, New Zealand
Penny Tayler, Melbourne, VIC, Australia

In the Caribbean
Ann, Bermuda

In Canada
Charlene Vikse, Coquitlam, BC
Robynn Dicks, Edmonton, AB
Tanya Roberts, Calgary, AB

In the United States
Jocelyn, Portland, OR
John Plummer, Nashville, TN
Caitlin, IA
Elizabeth, Knoxville, TN
Courtney Blair, MN
Melissa Cormier, Philadelphia, PA
Meilani Clay, Washington, DC
Radioactivevegan, Knoxville, TN
Kim Lahn (a.k.a. Veg-in-Training), AZ
Debyi Kucera, Prescott, AZ
Jamie Neary, Conshohocken, PA

Celia Ozereko, VA
Nicole Carnes, Portland, OR
Laura Poe, Kansas City, MO
Kate Lawson, MA
Kendy Paxia, Modesto, CA

Thanks, too, to my taste-testers who happily and with very few complaints ate everything I made and put in front of them. These fine folks and their families, clients, work mates, and neighbors all helped immensely with their feedback, and getting all the baking out of my house! So, to Karen Jackson, Andrea Dawson, Palo Koorjee, Ruby Li, Denise Gsponer, Starla Beselt, Shannon Brisson, Nancy MacDonald, my parents-in-law Joe and Frances Kelly, everyone at the Mary M. Manifold School of Highland Dance, and finally to assorted staff and parents from Lyndhurst Preschool and Stoney Creek Community School (especially Laurie Schweers, the best kindergarten teacher in the world) all in Burnaby, British Columbia, Canada, a BIG thank-you for getting fat with me!

Just in case you wonder about such things, I took a poll of my tasters and testers at the end of testing for them to choose their favorite recipes. Their top 10 favorites, not mine, in no particular order of preference, are:

Orange and Almond Biscotti (page 65)
Reindeer Squares (page 66)
Chai Chocolate Mini Loaves (page 78)
Lemon and Blueberry Biscuits (page 83)
Coffee and Caramel Cupcakes (page 96)
Zebra Cake (page 115)
No-Bake Apricot Cookies (page 126)
(You Won't Believe What's in This) Chocolate Pie (page 174)
Mini Sausage Rolls (page 232)
Pea, Tarragon, and Cream Cheese Tart (page 234)

A shout-out to the readers of my blog at http://veganyear.blogspot.com, who over the years have made suggestions for things for me to make (some of which even made it into this book), commented on my posts, cheered me on, and inspired me to just keep blogging.

Thanks to the individuals and organizations who kindly gave permission to have links to their websites or books included in this book, notably Isa Chandra Moskowitz, Alicia C. Simpson, and Worldwide Vegan Bake Sale.

The testing process was made much easier by my having been a tester for some great authors beforehand. Thanks to Isa Chandra Moskowitz and Terry Hope Romero, who collectively and separately showed me the testing ropes without even knowing it!

Last, and by no means least, there would be no book without Matthew Lore of The Experiment, who over the Christmas/New Year week of 2009/2010 took a chance on an aspiring cookbook author with an idea. Gratitude forever.

Index

About the Author

Carla Kelly, the eldest of five siblings, has been baking treats for her family since before she was ten. A vegan for over five years and a vegetarian for fifteen more before that, she has a knack for concocting and sharing tasty recipes—to the delight of her neighbors and friends, and especially her husband and their two daughters. She writes the popular blog The Year of the Vegan and lives in British Columbia.

Visit Carla at:

VeganYear.blogspot.com